FOR THE SHABBAT TABLE

Rabbi Chaim Wilschanski

FOR THE SHABBAT TABLE

Rabbi Chaim Wilschanski

gefen
publishing house   בית הוצאה לאור

JERUSALEM ◆ NEW YORK

Typesetting: Marzel A.S. – Jerusalem
Cover Design: Studio Paz, Jerusalem
Cover Illustration: Judith Crown

Edition 9 8 7 6 5 4 3 2 1

Gefen Publishing House
POB 36004
Jerusalem 91360, Israel
972-2-538-0247
isragefen@netmedia.net.il

Gefen Books
12 New Street
Hewlett, NY 11557, USA
516-295-2805
gefenbooks@compuserve.com

Printed in Israel

Send for our free catalogue

Library of Congress Cataloging-in-Publication Data
Wilschanski, Chaim.
For the Shabbat table / Chaim Wilschanski
     p.   cm.
ISBN: 965 229 200 1
1. Bible. O.T. pentateuch—Sermons. 2. Jews—Anecdotes. I. Title.
BS1225.4.W55 1999
296.4'7—dc21
                                                                          98-45885
                                                                          CIP
                                                                          R98

תפארת בנים אבותם

This ספר is lovingly dedicated
to the memory
of our dear parents ז"ל

הרב משה בן חנוך הלוי ז"ל
ורעיתו מרים Hoffman ע"ה

רב פסח בן יהושע הלוי ז"ל
ורעיתו מרים ביילע Wilschanski ע"ה

Their lives and homes were permeated with
תורה עבודה וגמילות חסדים

גם לזכר נשמות משפחתינו

האדמור ר' מרדכי יוסף בן אדמור ר' ירחם מרדזין ז"ל
הרבנית מרת שושנה בת הרב משה הלוי ע"ה

Dedicated by their children
the Radziner Rebbe Rabbi Jacob Lainer
Rabbi Moshe Lainer
and Rebbezin Rivka Feinstein

May this ספר also be a Memorial
לעלוי נשמות of all members of our family ז"ל
who died על קדוש השם in Auschwitz and elsewhere.

The author and his rebbezin

Dedicated to the memory of

Ruza and Sidney Last ז״ל

who were devoted members of the

Garden Suburb Beth Hamedrash

for many years

Dedicated in memory of

ברוך בן דוד הלוי ז"ל

Mr. Berthold Mosheim

רחל בת מרדכי ע"ה

Rosel Mosheim

פייגא בת אברהם חיים הלוי ע"ה

ע"ה Flossie Zelko

and our many relatives

who died in the Holocaust

Carol and Frank Mosheim

Dedicated לעלוי נשמת
Reb Efroim Sukmanski ז״ל

A תלמיד חכם of renown and an esteemed member of the
Garden Suburb Beth Hamedrash, London

His שעורי גמרא and דברי תורה, distinguished
by their vigour and insight, elicited
the highest regard.

◆ ◆ ◆

לעלוי נשמת מו״ה יוסף בן יהודה דב
Wineman ז״ל

Dedicated by
The Wineman Family

Rabbonim he esteemed highly with the utmost humility
And treated them constantly with the greatest respect.
From his lips exuded wisdom with the utmost civility
As friends it was Torah students he chose to select.
Expert himself in Torah absorbed with the utmost assiduity
Learning both oral and written in their every aspect.

Dealing and conduct in business with the utmost honesty
Acting kind deeds in a manner most circumspect.
Vigorously helping the downtrodden with utmost secrecy
Investing in charity a *mitzvah* he was able to perfect.
Devoted to his parents he honoured with utmost dignity.

Zecher Rav Tuvo in family unity as a main object.
Tzadik he leaves behind worthy offspring of utmost integrity
Livrocho their aspirations to keep the banner of Torah erect.

♦ ♦ ♦

In memory of our beloved
wife and mother Irène Lass
מרת יוטא רחל בת ר׳ מרדכי בצלאל ע״ה

We are happy and privileged to sponsor
Rabbi Wilschanski in
publishing this wonderful work,
full of warmth and humour.

Leonard Lass and Family

◆ ◆ ◆

In loving memory of

ר׳ אשר בן אברהם דוד Loftus ז״ל

Dedicated in loving memory of
David and Rachel Newman and Jack Kaufman
of blessed memory
May the wit and wisdom of Rabbi Wilschanski's
inspired work educate and delight future generations

Ted (Theodore) and Gillian Newman

◆ ◆ ◆

In loving memory of
Sidney Grose

ר' שמואל בן יצחק ז"ל
1914-1998

◆ ◆ ◆

In loving memory of my dear mother
גיטל בת יעקב
Geralde Green ע"ה

Forever in my thoughts
Michael Spencer

◆ ◆ ◆

לזכר נשמת ר' יעקב צבי בן הרב ישראל יוסף לעוו Lew ז"ל

ACKNOWLEDGMENTS

First and foremost I thank Hashem for inspiring me to spread the wonderful treasures of his holy Torah.

I also wish to express my sincere thanks to my dear wife Eva for the wonderful help and support she gave me to produce this work as well as for her constant encouragement and aid in all my activities.

My gratitude goes out to my children. Rachelle, for proofreading, Naomi for word processing, Judith, David and Michael for encouraging me, and to my grandaughter Zippora for her cover idea.

In addition, my hearty יישר כח to all sponsors of this book.

Last, but definitely not least, I thank my loyal *Baale Batim* of our *Beth Hamedrash* for being such a stimulating audience.

For the Shabbat Table perfectly exemplifies the genius of this outstanding and beloved rabbi, whose extraordinary *ahavas yisroel*, learning, and humour totally energized all those who heard him speak. It is a marvelous thing that his weekly texts can now become available to a wider audience.

The essays possess a good structure; short, even pithy, with a clear-cut theme or set of well-formulated points or questions, with the solutions often summarized at the end. This means that they are both memorable and accessible to people who want to read something quickly, but also profound and stimulating. Rabbi Wilschanski's style is highly personal and includes a liberal sprinkling of well-chosen, sparkling anecdotes, witticisms, and unexpected modern metaphors, thereby enabling his message to penetrate effortlessly in an ethos of *darchei no'am*. His is a remarkable genre, seamlessly combining the gravitas of Torah with humourous, often pungent comment on the absurdity of much in the contemporary world — deep Torah thoughts, in today's language and today's issues.

It is this fundamental accessibility which marks him out as a first-class communicator, with both the young and the *baale batim*. Part of this success undoubtedly lies in his constant effort, through a wide range of sources, to offer explanations for ideas or for specific *pesukim*, and to demonstrate the underlying interconnectedness of Torah. Another reason is surely the *ahavas yisroel* that constantly shows through his style of exposition; there is an unashamed pleasure, a fulsome excitedness in the way in which he reveals solutions to questions about the *peshat* — as if the process of discovering the eternal wisdom of Torah is in itself a gripping story which he wants to share with his readers and, thereby, plead with them to go out themselves and soak up the *simcha shel mitzvah*. The style is thus not at all forced; on the contrary, his text (like the person himself, in the full flow of speaking in his *Beth Hamedrash*) reads beautifully and convincingly, and one comes away feeling that one has been privileged to peep into the mind of a true *ma'ayon hamisgabber*, overflowing with *brochos* for his fellow Jews because of his own *lev tov*.

This is a memorable *sefer*, and I wish it every possible success.

Dr. Jonathan Webber
Oxford University
A freaquent visitor to the Beth Hamidrash

As a friend and colleague of Rabbi Wilschanski for many years standing, I have had many occasions to listen to his output of homiletical material. His presentations are always full of charm and wit, based on a wide range of classical sources and present-day allusions. It is pleasing that these excursions into Rabbinic lore and homiletics will now be made more widely and more permanently available in this collection of his writings.

For many readers, particularly of the younger generation, the author's light touch and his often humourous interpretations will be appealing. Amusing anecdotes mix happily with more profound reflections on the rich tapestry which readers will find both instructive and entertaining.

A particularly felicitous feature are the anecdotes relieving the heaviness of the subjects and renewing the constant interest of the readers. Indeed, Rabbi Wilschanski displays some of the special skills of the classical Maggid who could keep his audience spellbound, sometimes for hours at a stretch.

I hope this volume will be widely welcome as an effort to revive a very special flavour of Jewish homiletics and moralist writing. I wish the distinguished author every success.

The Right Hon. The Lord Jakobovits
Emeritus Chief Rabbi, London

Contents

BERESHIT

PHYSICAL AND
SPIRITUAL CREATION

בראשית

"בראשית ברא אלקים את השמים ואת הארץ"

"In the beginning Hashem created Heaven and Earth..." Rashi explains that the Universe was brought into being by G-d because of the Torah which is called *beginning* (Prov. 8:22), and because of Israel, who are called *beginning*."

(Jeremiah 2:3)

"ה' הנני ראשית דרכו קדם מפעליו מאז"

"The Lord made me at the beginning of His way, the first of His works of old."

(Proverbs 8:22)

"מביט בתורה ובורא את העולם"

"Hashem looks into the Torah and creates the world."

(Midrash Bereshit Rabba 1:2)

The divine Torah is the master plan for the creation and makes our lives meaningful and full of spiritual warmth.

This reminds me of the following remarkable anecdote:

Many hold that the miracle of the Israeli victory of the Yom Kippur war surpasses even that of the Six Day war. People asked General Sharon, who was in charge of the division that pursued and surrounded the Egyptian army across the Suez Canal, "Tell us, how did this extraordinary event come about?" He replied: "Our army is not a professional but a civilian army. The division which defeated the Egyptians consisted of doctors, lawyers, accountants, surveyors, dentists and other professional people. *They know how to charge.*"

During my many visits to non-Jewish Schools in London to address Jewish assemblies I remarked: "I want to know how to charge the spiritual batteries of our young people." I told them: "I have good news to convey to you: Amongst the many thousands of Jewish students with whom I share words of Torah I did not discover a single flat battery. Even those students who, unfortunately, have strayed very far from our Holy Torah possess a spark of Judaism. One only needs to recharge their batteries. That applies of course to all of us. Which is the best battery? A Long Life one! There is no better one than the Torah which has a "Long life on its Right" "and is a Tree of Life" (Prov. 3:16,18).

Let us commence this pleasant task of generating spiritual warmth by delving into many topics contained in the Sidrot of our Holy Torah. The first subject is the connection between the physical creation and the spiritual one – Torah.

We live in an age of fantastic scientific discoveries: Space, atoms, microchips and computers, etc. The comprehension of nature and Torah go hand in hand. Just as the knowledge of nature and technology makes such great progress, so does knowledge of Torah. Torah contains innumerable secrets. "Gematria," the study of the numbers contained in Hebrew letters, has been with us for a long time and has revealed many secrets. There is in fact nothing that is not hinted at in the Torah. Rabbi Akiva even explained the dots and crowns on the letters of the Torah.

Let me give one example of "gematria" – how the Torah and the creation of the world are intertwined.

The numerical value of בראשית ברא אלקים is 1202; the same number as תנ"ך – Torah, Nevi'im and Ketuvim! – Torah is the blueprint of the creation as well as the spiritual motor that drives the world.

One of the innumerable machines man has invented is the computer. Many things in nature are computerised in a most sophisticated manner, e.g. DNA – in each of our millions of cells is a computer program of a person's genetic makeup. It would require a thousand volume encyclopaedia to write down the DNA program in just one of the millions of cells. Therefore, why should we not make use of man-made computers to discover more secrets of our Torah? This is being done at the Centre for Jewish Studies in Jerusalem and other towns in Israel. A divine coding system has been unravelled. A new dimension! The computer illuminates and presents a fascinating new angle on what was already known. It is just mind-boggling! This also confirms that Torah and creation go hand in hand. All 125,000 letters of the Torah text were put in a computer. There are of course billions of possible combinations. To find a unifying combination would take hundreds of years. What was found by the computer, amongst many other things, was that the number 7 is such a very prevalent combination. However, it is not only the number 7, but also multiples of 7 such as 5x7 or 9x7, etc. Why? Obviously 7 combines earthliness, namely the six days of creation, and Ruchniut, Shabbat spirituality. Again a confirmation of the connection between nature and spirit.

Literally more than 100 Mitzvot (commandments) and minhagim (customs) are based on that number.

> E.g. 7 days of the week;
> 7 weeks of the Omer;
> 7 years of the Shmitah;
> 7x7 is the Yovel;
> 7 people are called up on Shabbat to the Torah;
> 7 days of Shivah;
> 7 (Shevah) Brachot;
> 7 clean days after impurity;
> Tishrei, the 7th month, which contains so many great days, etc., etc.

Look at the first verse in Bereshit: It contains 7 words, 28 letters which is a multiple of 7. Count the number of times Elokim is mentioned in the story of the Creation, and you will find that it is 35, not 34 and not 36. Count the number of words in the story of the Creation: 434; add the 179 words in the 10 Commandments and it comes to 613 – 613 Mitzvot. Because of the Torah, which is called Reshit – the world was created. They belong together. Look at the 6th day of the Creation – "Yom Hashishi – vayechulu hashamayim veha'aretz." (The sixth day – and the heavens and the earth were finished.) Count from the Yud at the end of Yom Hashishi 7 letters and further 7 letters you will find the word "Yisrael." This is a clear hint that the Heaven and the Earth were created bishvil Yisrael shenikra Reshit – For the sake of Yisrael which is called Reshit, Beginning.

In many episodes in the Torah the principal object is repeated seven times. In the binding of Isaac, for example, Hashem spoke to Avraham seven times. It consisted of seven acts. "They came, He built, He arranged, He bound, He put him, He stretched out, He took" (Gen. 22:9-10).

The midwives in Egypt are mentioned seven times (Exod. 1:15-20).

The Tablets which Moses broke are mentioned seven times, both in the Sidra Ki Tisa (Exod. 31:18-32:19) and in the Sidra Ekev (Deut. 9:9-17). Leprosy is mentioned 21 times in the Sidrot Tasria and Metzora. The Cohen dealing with it is mentioned 56 times, not 57 or 55, but a multiple of seven.

At the story of Pinchas in Numbers 25:1, Vayeshev Yisrael, the name of Eliyahu is quoted at intervals of 63, a multiple of 7, starting from the Aleph of Yisrael, hinting at what our Rabbis say, that "Pinchas is Eliyahu" (Midrash Yalkut Shimoni, Pinchas 2). But why here an interval of 63? Because the numerical value of "Navi"[1] is 63. It is uncanny that this is a code on two levels! However, note that Eliyahu is without a "Yud" as in the Haftarah of Shabbat Hagadol (Mal. 3:23).

This brings us to the final example par excellence: In the Midrash, Rabbi Yitzchak started his lectures with the verse of Tehillim 119:130; "Pesach Devorecha Yoir – The beginning of your word give light" (Midrash Bereshit Rabba 3:1). The Vilna Gaon says that the first verses of the Five Books are constructed to hint at the Menorah; after all, Torah is light.

The first verse in   Bereshit has 7 words – 7 branches of the Menorah;
Shemot has 11 words – 11 knobs;
Vayikra has 9 words – 9 flowers;
Bamidbar has 17 words – the Menorah was 17 cubits
high (according to one opinion);
Devarim has 22 words – 22 cups.

Now we understand clearly why a Sefer Torah which has even one letter missing is passul.[2] Since the Torah is a most complex coding system it cannot tolerate even one missing letter. It is just like a computer program which would go completely haywire if only one letter or number was lacking.

The Talmud (Eruvin 13a) tells us the story about Rabbi Yishmael who cautioned his son, a scribe: "My son! Be careful in your work, for your work is heavenly. If you delete or add one letter, you may destroy the whole world." It is

---

1. Prophet.
2. Disqualified.

the master plan of the creation. The codes which have been discovered are so complex that they defy the possibility of human authorship. After all, the letters of the Torah and the many sevens must fit in with the text. They also put to shame those *apikorsim*[1] who claim different authors for various parts. This coding system is everywhere in the Torah. "Torat Hashem Temimah".[2] We only know a little now, but what about what we do not know?

May this Shabbat Bereshit be the beginning of a further recharging of our batteries and deeper study of our Torah, so that many more wonderful secrets will see the light of day.

---

1. Freethinkers.
2. The Torah is perfect.

TWO WORLD REBELLIONS

נח

דור המבול – The Generation of the Flood and
דור הפלגה – The Generation of the Dispersion.

Two explorers went on safari in Africa. Suddenly a lion jumped out of the bush. One said to the other: "Did you not read in a book that in a situation such as this, one should stand perfectly still and look the lion straight in the eye? Then the lion will slink away." The other one replied: "You have read the book, I have read the book, but DID THE LION READ THE BOOK?"...

We Jewish people were called גור אריה יהודה (Gen. 49:9), "a lion cub is Judah," by our Forefather Jacob when he blessed his sons. We are also called "The People of the Book," namely the book par excellence, *our Holy Torah*, which we are required to read, enjoy and observe its mitzvot – thus we are lions who *DO READ* the Book. Just a few days ago on Simchat Torah,[1] we finished reading the Torah and started it again. Let us today read from the second portion, Noach.

It contains the narratives of two rebellions. The first one, when the people of the world became corrupt physically and morally and G-d decided to wipe them out by a flood – all except Noach, who was saved with his family and animals in an ark. Afterwards, G-d made a rainbow as a pledge not to bring a flood of a calamitous nature again.

The second rebellion took place later, when the people built the Tower of Babel in order to worship their technology rather than worship G-d. Punished by G-d with not being able to understand one another's language, they could not continue this revolution and were dispersed all over the world.

---

1. The festival of rejoicing in our Torah.

Let us discuss the following points today:

(a) Why did G-d handle the two rebellions differently? The first he punished with water and not with other means of destruction and the second with dispersion.

(b) What is the deeper significance of the rainbow?

(c) What can we learn from these stories?

To answer these questions I would like to begin with the following striking anecdote:

A king had a son who was colour-blind, yet wanted to be an artist. A teacher was found who brought him to such a high level that he could paint in front of audiences. However, one day his exhibition fell flat. He only managed blotches of various coloured paints. What was the reason? His teacher made very faint boundaries on the canvas which the audience could not see and the prince painted by numbers, filling them in. The results were exquisite and admired by all. However, one day the pupil decided to rebel and become independent, and to paint by himself. The result: just irregular splashes of paint, a real shambles!

This leads us to answer the first question. The people of that generation over-stepped the boundaries of civilized order, so G-d made the seas as well as the clouds break through their barriers and cover the dry land. *Middah keneged middah*.[1] Furthermore, G-d decided to put the clock back and to turn the earth back to its original state as it was at the Creation, when water covered everything. Noach and the animals in the ark had to begin anew. Finally, the impure earth had to be purified by a huge מקוה.[2]

Incidentally, מקוה for Jewish ladies is a fundamental part of Jewish practice. The woman dips under natural water and emerges newly created, symbolically, just as the dry land emerged from under the waters at the creation of the world.

Whilst before the Flood people had no unity, they were robbing and murdering indiscriminately, during the 12 months in the ark there was perfect peace. This was continued by the next generation, as it is stated in the Torah שפה אחת ודברים אחדים (Gen. 11:1). The Earth was of one language and of one speech, namely Hebrew (Rashi).

So it appeared that the fault of the generation of the Flood was rectified.

---

1. Measure for measure.
2. A ritual bath.

However, this unity was *misused* by building the Tower of Babel to revolt against G-d and to worship their own scientific skills. Therefore, G-d destroyed this *wrong kind of unity* – mixed up their languages and scattered them all over the world. Now it is clear why G-d acted differently to suppress the two rebellions.

This leads us to answer the second question. The rainbow is a *symbol of peace*. A bow directed to shoot imaginary arrows *away* from the world – it connects heaven to earth and encompasses the whole horizon, symbolically the whole world. It consists of many colours which blend into one another, symbolizing the many colours of mankind, meaning the many talents and achievements co-operating in one huge arc of peace. That is how *real* unity should be. *Unity but not uniformity!* It is interesting to note that if one rotates the colours of the rainbow quickly they all appear white, a symbol of purity.

In contemporary times there are many who revolt against the boundaries of proper civilization, particularly the moral dividing lines and barriers. They call it MODERNITY. But in fact they are doing nothing more than reinstating the corrupt society as practised by the ancient generation which suffered the Flood. ואין כל חדש תחת השמש,[1] says King Solomon (Eccl. 1:9). And there are also many today who worship science and technology rather than G-d. This also is not new. It dates back to the generation of the Tower of Babel. Amongst the Jewish people there are those who use so-called MODERNITY to revolt and break away from the 613 Divine guidelines, the commandments of the Torah. That will make their spiritual lives a hodge-podge of unrelated colours. Eventually they will be drawn into the raging waters of assimilation, never to be heard of again.

But we who are called גור אריה יהודה[2] read in our portion today that revolution against G-d cannot succeed. Rather, let us paint our lives with the wonderful colours of the 613 מצות,[3] *within* the Divine boundaries of our Holy Torah. Then our life's portrait will be beautiful and exquisite. Let us cooperate in this endeavour with our fellow Jews in unity but not uniformity. Let each and every one of us contribute his or her exquisite colours to make a rainbow of peace connecting heaven to earth, encompassing the Jewish world as well as the world at large.

---

1. "There is nothing new under the sun."
2. Lions.
3. Commandments.

AVRAHAM AND LOT

לך לך

"הלא כל הארץ לפניך הפרד נא מעלי
אם השמאל ואימנה ואם הימין ואשמאילה"

"...Is not the whole land before you? Separate yourself from me,
(Abraham said). If you (Lot) go to the left, I will go to the right, and
if you go to the right, I will go to the left...."   *(Bereshit 13:9)*

Comparing the מדרגה[1] of Abraham with that of Lot, his nephew, reminds me of the following charming anecdote:

A friend asked a new bride, "Has your husband lived up to all the nice things he said to you before you were married?" "No," she replied, "only one." "Which one?"

"I am not good enough for you!"

Lot, although he had good traits, was not good enough in comparison with Abraham, as we shall see:

There is a famous story mentioned in the "Ethics of the Fathers," Chapter 6, Mishna 9. It is about Rabbi Joseph, the son of Kisme, who lived in a town of sages. He was offered a million golden dinars and precious stones and pearls if he would come to live in a town where there was no Torah. He replied: "Even if you gave me all the precious stones in the world, I would not live in a place without Torah!" The question arises: Where is the source for his decision? Why did Rabbi Joseph not go to live there and use the money to establish Jewish schools, yeshivot and synagogues and *make* it into a town of Torah?

In order to answer this, we would like to solve the following *Chakirah*.[2]

Which lifestyle is to be recommended if one wants to influence others:

    (a) to go to them

    (b) to invite them to come to us

---

1. Standard.
2. Investigation.

We can find the answer by studying the different personalities of Abraham and Lot.

In our Sidra it says, "When Abraham left his birth place, Lot went with him" (Gen. 12:4). This was ostensibly to proclaim the name of G-d, but the Torah says straight after that in the same verse... "Abraham was 75 years of age..." Why? Lot calculated: "How can I let my old uncle, who has no children and is very wealthy, go abroad alone?"

The Torah says that there was a quarrel between the shepherds of Abraham and Lot (Gen. 13:7). The midrash elaborates on this (Bereshit Rabba 41:5). The shepherds of Lot let their sheep graze in the fields which belonged to farmers. When reproached by the shepherds of Abraham, they said, "The land will belong to Lot eventually in any case, as Abraham has no children."

But what a fallacy this is! They could not inherit before the death of Abraham, and even after his death, they would have to buy the land, just like Abraham bought the *Kever*[1] of Machpelah. What about G-d's promise? He will fulfill that in His own time. That was not the only thing they did wrong. They turned the tables round. They said YOU are robbers for muzzling OUR sheep and not feeding them well. So Lot whitewashed his actions. He went where the money was, namely to the wealthy city of Sdom. People must have admired him then. What a smart operator! What a realist, in contrast to the fanatic Abraham. Lot went there ostensibly to make them better citizens, but was he successful? *Not one* was saved from the city apart from Lot and his family.

Sdom was the first city that had immigration controls. Why did they award Lot an entry permit? Only because he looked like Abraham – as the Torah says – "We are brothers..." comments Rashi (Gen. 13:8) – "We look alike..." therefore, they admitted him to be used as a *Kosher stamp*. The presence of Lot, a look-alike of Abraham, who was well known and was highly regarded as a Prince of G-d (Gen. 23:6), would make their city into a respected place. His hospitality, when he invited the two angels to his house, he learned from Abraham, but due to the bad influence of the wicked city of Sdom he was prepared to hand his daughters to the mob surrounding his house, rather than his guests. After the destruction of Sdom, the daughters committed incest with their father. Again, they had a good cover up by saying that there was no-one else living.

---

1. Grave.

Therefore, they had to "save the world". One could call this "a froomer[1] Yetzer Horah."[2]

In the end, where did this mixed up conduct of Lot lead? He had to be rescued *twice* by his "fanatical" uncle. When Abraham rescued him the first time at great risk to his life by defeating the four kings, he gave him back his wealth. But when he was rescued for the second time from Sdom, he lost all in the destruction of this city, as well as his wife and his sons-in-law. Furthermore, his descendants, Amon and Moav, were not allowed to marry Jews (Deut. 23:4).

On the other hand, however, let us now consider what happened to the fanatic "right-winger" Abraham. He practised a different way of life, namely the second option of our Chakirah. He had a straightforward, clear-cut, *pure* life-style. His house was open on all four sides for people *to come to him*. His hospitality was of a standard of the most modern five star plus hotel, but he took no payment. When travelers or visitors thanked him he would say, "Do not thank me, thank Hashem." When he was asked, "Who is that?" he would attempt to persuade his guests to drop their idols and worship G-d (Midrash Bereshit Rabba 49:1). He did not aspire to the wealth of Sdom, though it was his right as a victor, yet he was wealthy. Eventually he went to Yerushalayim, the Holy city, as the Torah says, "He met Malki Zedek, Melech Shalem, the king of Yerushalayim" (Gen. 14:18). He became known as "the Prince of G-d," (Gen. 23:6) and was given the title by G-d "Father of a multitude of Nations" (Gen. 17:4). Avraham, our Father, taught us how to harness one's contradictory qualities of character to one's supreme goal: *Avodat Hashem*.[3]

He was a peaceful person: "If you go left, I go right..." (Gen. 13:9) yet he became a military man to save Lot. He was wealthy, yet he had contempt for money which originated from impurity – Sdom – "...not even a shoelace..." (Gen. 14:23). He would not allow a Canaanite wife for his son, yet he prayed for their worst town – Sdom (18:23-33). He prayed for Yishmael, his son by Hagar, "I wish Yishmael should live before you (G-d)" (Gen. 17:18). Yet he expelled him when G-d told him he should listen to Sarah (Gen. 21:12). He was a very kind and hospitable person, yet he was ready to practise the greatest cruelty on Yitzhak when he was commanded (Gen. 22:10). And finally, he passed 10 tests

---

1. Pious.
2. Evil inclination.
3. Service to G-d.

given to him by G-d (Avot 5:3). He had to make many delicate and difficult decisions in his life.

Now we have the answer to our first question: Where was the source in the Torah not to live in a town where there is no Torah, even if one wants to improve its standard? We see now, *from Avraham our Father*. We also have the clear distinction between Lot and Avraham. Whilst Lot chose comfort, material security and success, middle of the road situation, white-wash, froom yetzer horah yet he lost his high standards, as well as all his possessions and his wife; Avraham chose *pure* ideals of Yiddishkeit and was very successful in every way: "*Habitu el Avraham Avichem...*"[1] (Isa. 51:2). We also have now the solution to our chakirah. To influence others, one must not go and live in their surroundings – as Lot did – but invite them to one's own circle – as Abraham taught us. If we harness all our various and sometimes contradictory talents and character traits towards spreading the ideals of Torah, in the correct manner, then we can hope and pray that Hashem will bless us also with success in every sphere as He blessed Avraham Avinu.

---

1. "Look up to Avraham your Father."

TRUE HOSPITALITY

וירא

"וישא עיניו וירא והנה שלשה אנשים נצבים עליו
וירא וירץ לקראתם מפתח האהל וישתחו ארצה"

"...And he lifted up his eyes and looked, and behold three men stood near him, and when he saw them he ran to meet them and he bowed down to the ground...."

(Bereshit 18:2)

Today's subject is "Hospitality." The hospitality of Avraham was of a very high standard indeed. But there are a few questions posed by the Lutzker Rav, Rabbi Sorotzkin ז״ל.

1. Why did Avraham order יקח נא מעט מים[1] for the guests to wash their feet? Why save on water?
2. Why was the wife of Lot, who also offered hospitality to the two angels who visited Sodom, turned into a pillar of salt? Why salt in particular and not something else?
3. Here Avraham saw three *men*; there Lot saw two *angels* (Gen. 19:1). In fact the three men were angels. The Midrash says that Avraham was great and he saw men, but Lot, who was not so great, saw angels (Bereshit Rabba 50:3). This seems to be very strange. It appears that Avraham made a mistake and Lot did not. Is this the case?

To answer these problems: Hospitality is practised in modern society to a very sophisticated degree. The reference is to modern hotels. All conceivable services are laid on, all possible devices employed to make the stay even more than "a home away from home." The politeness, the readiness to serve at the drop of a hat, etc. However, one is reminded of the following: one goes to a hotel for a

---

1. A little water.

change and a rest. The change goes to the waiters and the rest goes to the proprietor.... Furthermore, after paying the rest to the proprietor one finds at the reception desk the following notice: "Have you left anything!" It should have read: "Have you anything left?"...

Avraham was ill. It was the third day after his Brit Milah and he was sighing. Was it about the state of his health, was it about livelihood or taxes? No! It was because of lack of guests! That would be understandable if he were a hotel proprietor. But again no. Although he did provide an equally good service in his days, but it was all for free.

And when his guests thanked him, he would say, "Do not thank me, thank G-d" (Midrash Bereshit Rabba 49:7). This led to a discussion about G-d, which eventually meant that Avraham made men *gerim*[1] and Sara influenced the women – as our Rabbis say (Bereshit Rabba 39:21). So he extended the physical side of hospitality, which is an emulation of the quality of G-d, into a vehicle for propagating G-d in the wider world, a spiritual means.

Like the best hotels, he did this in an exquisite manner. First of all, he called the leader of the strangers *"Adoni,"*[2] and this was straight after the Brit Milah when he was entitled to be set apart from the rest of the world. He had not a trace of feeling of superiority!

"....Then he ran to meet them...." In accordance with the Gemara, Tractate Shabbat (104a), where the Gemara explains the Aleph Beth; "אלף בינה" – learn understanding – Torah. Gimmel Daled "גמל דלים" be kind to poor people. Why is the leg of the Gimmel directed towards the Daled, the poor? Because the benefactor should "run" after the poor. Furthermore, Avraham left G-d who had come to visit him – because he was sick (Avraham). Again in accordance with the Gemara Shabbat (127a) hospitality is greater than receiving the Divine presence. What is the reason? The guests need you, but the Divine Presence does not. After all, hospitality is about emulating G-d: as He is merciful, so should you be as well.

Furthermore, he said, "I will give you some bread" (Gen. 18:5). He gave them three tongues of calves which he served with mustard, for their enjoyment. "Zadikim say little, but *do* a lot" (Gemara Bava Metzia 87a).

The great Chofetz Chaim, when he invited guests on Friday night, first made

1. Proselytes.
2. My master.

Kiddush and had part of the meal with his guests, only then did he sing שלום עליכם.[1] Why? Because guests are hungry, but angels can wait....

The wonderful reception produced a MODEL AFTER-DINNER speech by one of the guests. He (one angel) said, "I shall return to you next year, and Sarah your wife will have a son." It was *short, pregnant* with meaning and caused *laughter....* ותצחק שרה....[2]

This leads us to answer the problems we set out at the beginning. Why only a little water? Rabbi Sorotzkin ז״ל, answers as follows: Our Rabbis say: כבדהו – You should honour a stranger (Kalla Rabbati 9), but also suspect him – וחשדהו. Concerning honouring, Avraham gave of the best. But in those days some people would bow down to the dust of their feet to worship their own efforts. To remove that idol worship one only needs a *little* water.

We asked why did the wife of Lot become a pillar of salt? The answer is: Lot's wife did not add salt to her meals. Why? In Sodom hospitality was forbidden, but she could not bear to see a person go hungry. So she broke their laws and gave food to hungry persons but not to the extent that they should *enjoy* the food as well by adding salt to make it tasty. That far, her kindness did not reach. To have pity, yes, but to give pleasure, no.

Did Lot recognise them as angels better than Avraham? Surely Avraham was greater? We give the answer by means of the following anecdote. Rabbi Zushe and Rabbi Elimelech of Lizhensk once stopped during their travels at Lodmir in Poland. They were invited by a poor tailor for Shabbat, but by no one else. Years later when they became famous they came to Lodmir in a coach pulled by horses. This time a reception committee of the town greeted them and the president of the congregation invited them, but they did not accept the invitation. They said: "Why did you not invite us when we came here the first time, but you do invite us now? What is the difference? It is the horses! You look after them please and we stay for Shabbat with the tailor." Avraham would entertain even *ordinary* people, but Lot only *angels* – great personalities. So the standard of Avraham was much higher after all.

If we compare the hospitality of Lot with that of Avraham, we find that Lot's reception of the angels was instrumental is saving his life and that of his daughters. As written in Tanach (Prov. 10:2,11:4), "Charity saves from death"

---

1. Peace be upon you Angels.
2. And Sara laughed.

but it had no further consequences. His descendants Ammon and Moav were not allowed to marry Jewish people.

However, the higher degree of kindness of Avraham not only made great spiritual impact on the wider world but also caused the crucial short after-dinner speech, resulting in the birth of Yitzchak and the establishment of the Jewish people.

In contemporary times many people practise הכנסת אורחים[1] on a grand scale; but who are the guests? Only "angels" who have plenty of food in their freezer at home, not poor people. These hosts are disciples of Lot.

"הביטו אל אברהם אביכם"[2] (Isa. 51:2) – and invite to our homes ordinary poor people as well, and so fulfill this great Mitzvah on a high level. Let us also emulate his example by spreading knowledge of the message of Hashem and His Torah far and wide.

---

1. Hospitality.
2. Let us look to our father Avraham.

ELIEZER, THE MASTER – MARRIAGE BROKER

חיי שרה

"ויאמר עבד אברהם אנכי"

"....And he said 'I am the servant of Avraham....'"   *(Bereshit 24:34)*

Today's Sidra consists of two parts – the burial of Sarah in the Cave of Machpelah, and the marriage of Yitzchak and Rivka, brought about by the *Shadchan*[1] Eliezer.

Let us concentrate on the happy part. Our Rabbis say that "the talk of the servants of our Fathers is more important than the Torah of the children (Bereshit Rabba 60:11). That is the reason why this story takes up such a lot of space – more than the creation of the world plus the Ten Commandments! It is clear that the Torah wants to teach us character improvement – *middot tovot* – by means of this episode.

The "Master Shadchan" Eliezer was a very modest person. He did not call himself Executive Director of the Household of Avraham, but a *servant* of Avraham. That reminds me of a new Rabbi who was introduced to his congregation. The chairman praised the Rabbi profusely at the meeting of the congregation: "How fortunate we are to have a Rabbi who is so learned that the greatest scholars turn to him, so compassionate that little children confide in him, so truthful that judges swear by him, he is indeed saturated with virtue." The Rabbi tugged at the chairman's sleeve, saying "....do not forget my modesty...."

Eliezer, however, besides being so modest, possessed many other qualities too. One of them was his truly impressive diplomacy in dealing with Rivka and her parents.

In *Chochmat Hamatzpun* by Rabbi Ibgui the following questions are raised:

---

1. Marriage broker.

a)   Why did he give the rings and bracelets to Rivka before he knew who she was?

b)   Why did he not eat before he gave his talk to the family of Rivka?

c)   Why did he insist on returning home immediately?

All these questions are solved with one answer, which is introduced with the following anecdote:

A miser always refrained from giving charity by saying, "I will only give a dowry to a poor maiden." In order to keep him to his promise the citizens of the town arranged a match between a homely maiden and an elderly tailor. A delegation came to see him to ask him for a dowry. He replied, "I do *not like* the match...."

Eliezer also did not like that match. He said אֻלַי, perhaps the woman may not go with me. The word אולי, "perhaps," is written אֵלַי, "to me" (Gen. 24:39) – without a "vav". He wanted his own daughter to be the bride of Yitzchak. She was beautiful and kind and was fit to play that role in every way. Therefore, he could have performed his mission with only little enthusiasm, so as to make it fail. There are always plenty of excuses available, but he did not make use of any of them. He was called המושל בכל אשר לו – in charge of all Abraham's household (Gen. 24:2). But our Rabbis explain this literally – he ruled over himself, over his own inclination; therefore, he went to the other extreme to put aside his own desires. As the Gemara says in Sanhedrin (25b): How can a person who broke the law by lending money for interest do repentance? By not lending for interest to a gentile, too, which is permitted. In this way, he breaks his bad habit by going to the other extreme. For this reason Eliezer gave the bracelet and ring to the girl who fetched water for him and who watered his ten camels without asking her who she was first. He decided that, in order to speed things up so that his own innermost desire should not influence him, it was worth the risk. That is why he did not eat before he spoke to the family and insisted on returning immediately with Rivka. Furthermore, when a מצוה[1] is due, one must not eat before performing it, just as in the case of morning prayers. Eliezer had a מצוה to discharge.

Abarbanel enumerates ten changes in Eliezer's story to the family as compared to the actual words which Avraham had spoken to him. All were designed to diplomatically sway her family. For example, Avraham said, "go to

---

1. Commandment.

my birthplace" (Gen. 24:4). He told them, "Go to my family" (Gen. 24:40) to give them more importance. He omitted the words "Do not take my son there...." (Gen. 24:6) in order not to insult them. He did not tell them that he gave the girl the presents *before* asking who she was (Gen. 24:22), but he told them that he questioned her first (Gen. 24:47). He also did not reveal his anxiety as to whether his assignment would be successful, but played it cool (Gen. 24:21). He did not tell the family that he had made a character test on Rivka by asking for water, but he did tell them that immediately after he prayed to G-d to send the right girl, Rivka appeared and was very hospitable to him (Gen. 24:45). That, he explained to them, was an omen, a Divine sign, (Gen. 24:48) and they exclaimed, "You are right. מהשם יצא הדבר – This matter has come from G-d" (24:50).

He certainly went beyond the call of duty. He used speed to overcome his personal interest and achieved tremendous success due to his great diplomatic skill.

One has to make many decisions during one's life. We can learn a number of things from this episode of Eliezer: In the first place, even one graced by high titles should realize that he is really only a servant of Hashem. Secondly, one must use speed to overcome one's own interest, such as laziness, lust and other bad habits, if one wants to be successful in His service. When one is asked to do a mitzvah in the service of G-d, does one hear the word אֵלִי, perhaps it is a good idea, or אֵלַי, "to me"? I am too busy, it is the wrong time, the wrong place, etc. Let us follow the example of Eliezer. Then our lives will become fuller and richer, and we will be successful in our mission and will often be able to exclaim, like the family of Rivka, this is indeed from G-d. מהשם יצא הדבר.

THE ROLE OF YITZCHAK?

תולדת

"ואלה תולדת יצחק בן אברהם"

"....And these are the generations of Yitzchak the son of Avraham."

(Bereshit 25:19)

Compared to the other two forefathers, Yitzchak seems to be the least prominent, yet there is a great deal to say about him.

Let me begin with the anecdote of two Russian workers who were offered jobs in Siberia some years ago (good wages and conditions, etc.). One took up this offer and promised to write to the other one: "If the letter is written in blue ink it will be true, but if in red take it with a pinch of salt." After some time a letter arrived in blue ink. It contained many praises, "The pay is very good and the conditions are excellent. There is only one shortage, namely red ink!" I am afraid I had to use quite a lot of red ink to shorten this article.

Whilst Avraham was a pioneer and Yaakov a fighter, Yitzchak seems to have been passive. At the *Akedah*,[1] the verse states: "G-d tested Avraham" and not Yitzchak (Gen. 22). His name was not changed like those of the other two forefathers. As regards his work, we are told that he dug up the wells of his father and he even required the service of Eliezer, the marriage broker!

Yet his role was equally important in a number of ways. Let me illustrate this with the following anecdote: A student applied for a place at the university. The father had to fill in an application form. One of the questions was: Is your son a leader? The father replied, "I am not sure of that, but he is an excellent follower." In a letter of acceptance the Dean made the following remark:

"As our freshman group will consist of several hundred leaders, we congratulate ourselves that your son will also be a member of the college. We shall thus be assured of one good follower!"....

---

1. The binding of Yitzchak.

Yitzchak was a good follower of Avraham. A chain is only as good as the weakest link. His contribution to the tripod of our *Avot*[1] was *gevurah* – strong commitment to the service of G-d – up to the very limit of being prepared to surrender his life.

However, his contribution was much greater than that. Avraham's special distinction was *chesed*[2] but *chesed* needs *gevurah* to control it. For example: A government introduces a welfare state, but the hand-outs need a firm control, otherwise it would just make life easy for the layabouts and not really help the needy: *chesed* without *gevurah* leads to softness and trouble.

"ואלה תולדת יצחק בן אברהם"

"….and these are the generations of Yitzchak the son of Avraham."

Yitzchak consolidates the work of Avraham.

There is still much more we can learn from Yitzchak's personality. The Torah gives a lot of space to the story of the three wells which Yitzchak dug (Gen. 26:18-22). One teaching is that we must persevere; if at first we do not succeed, we have to try again and again. The first two wells were disputed and became objects of strife. Only the third one remained in the possession of Yitzchak.

Once a young man told his Rabbi, "My *yetzer harah*[3] keeps bothering me. What shall I do?" The Rabbi answered: "When you ride an untrained horse, what do you do? You try and try again until you subdue it. So you should deal with your *yetzer harah*." So even if Yitzchak was unsuccessful the first two times, he dug another well and succeeded. Secondly, we can learn that it is a greater mitzvah to do things personally than to do things through someone else. The first two wells were dug by Yitzchak's servants, and they were disputed; but the third one, ויחפור – he dug it himself – and he was successful.

However, a question presents itself: Why did the Philistines close the wells of Avraham up with earth? Was it not a case of cutting the nose to spite the face? After all, water is a very precious commodity in those parts of the world. They should just have taken the wells for themselves. But the famous commentator Rabbi Jacob Mecklenburg ז"ל, in his book הכתב והקבלה, gives a convincing answer: Avraham called these wells, which were public meeting places, by

---

1. Forefathers.
2. Lovingkindness.
3. Evil inclination.

religious names, e.g. באר לחי ראי (Gen. 25:11) – The well of the living (G-d) who sees. That is why the Philistines filled them up, to erase any trace of religion.

At first the Philistines were jealous of Yitzchak and said, "Go away because you've become strong through us" (Gen. 26:16). But now Avimelech – their king – regretted having expelled him and he said "ראינו כי היה ה' עמך" – "We have seen that G-d was with you" (Gen. 26:28). Yitzchak overcame all difficulties and achieved a spectacular קדוש השם.[1] How often do we find in history that nations who expelled us realized the benefit of having us amongst them? When we now look at Yitzchak's achievements, we find they were enormous – to say that he was a passive onlooker or a weak link is wide off the mark. He uncovered the wells of Torah which his father dug and gave them the name of godliness which his father gave them, and thus he kept the chain of Torah alive בגבורה.[2] Obstacles are there to be overcome. It is true we need leaders, but followers are equally important.

In our lives, let us be followers and remove the earthliness covering the *Mayim Chayim* – of the wells of the Torah – and never give up digging these wells until we succeed. Then as Ramban points out, the two wells, which are a prediction of the two Temples, will unfortunately be destroyed and filled with earth, but the third one – may it be built soon – will be forevermore, so that all nations will exclaim – "We have seen that G-d was with you!"

"ראה ראינו כי היה ה' עמך"

---

1. Sanctification of G-d's name.
2. With strength.

THE STATUS OF A PERSON ויצא

"ויצא יעקב מבאר שבע וילך חרנה"

"....And Jacob went out of Beer Sheva and he went to Choron."

(Bereshit 28:10)

This subject is a vast one. However, I am reminded of the following anecdote:

A certain Rabbi was once extolling in his sermon the wonderful miracles of G-d's creation, the immense intricate marvels of Hashem's nature. He proceeded to exclaim with great enthusiasm, "Every blade of grass is a sermon!" During the following week, one of his congregants observed the Rabbi mowing his lawn. "That is right, Rabbi" – he remarked – **"Cut your sermons short!"** That is exactly what I intend to do....

Jacob had to flee from the wrath of his brother Esau. When he reached the place where the future Temple would be built, he lay down to sleep and surrounded his head with stones – to protect himself from wild animals (Rashi). He *dreamed* about a ladder going up to heaven and angels ascending and descending it. G-d promised to guard him and to give the Land of Israel to his descendants.

After more than 20 years Jacob spent working for Laban, he decided to return to Israel. There he *met* angels (Gen. 32:2).

The following questions arise:

1) Why did Jacob see angels in a *dream* inside Israel, but *meet* them when he was outside Israel? After all, Eretz Yisrael is on a higher level!

2) Rashi explains that the angels of Israel went up, and the angels from outside Israel went down to accompany Jacob. That is why in the dream they ascended first and then descended. Surely, this

"changing of the guards" should have taken place at the *borders*, not in Jerusalem?

3) What was the point in protecting his head from wild animals if the rest of his body was unprotected?

To introduce the answer to all these questions, I wish to share with you the following anecdote:

In Poland, a Rabbi walked over to one of his congregants after the *Amidah* prayer and gave him a hearty *"Shalom Aleichem."* The person concerned was very surprised. "Rabbi, I have not been away. Why 'Shalom Aleichem'?" The Rabbi replied: "I could not help noticing that during the *"Amidah"* your mind was far away in the market place of Warsaw. Now that you have returned...Shalom Aleichem!"

The Lutzker Rav, Rabbi Zalman Sorotzkin ז"ל, said: One's personality and status is not where one finds oneself *physically*, but where one's *thoughts* are.

This answers all our questions. At the beginning of the *Sidra*, Jacob was *leaving* Israel, therefore his spiritual status was lower, and he could only see angels in a dream. But at the end of the *Sidra*, he was about to *return* to Israel. At this point he reached a higher standard and he *met* the angels. There it says he called the name of the place MACHANAYIM – two camps (Gen. 32:3). The "changing of shifts" of the different angels (those who were outside Israel and those from Israel who came to meet him) occurred there (Rashi).

That answers question number two. The angels changed already in Jerusalem and not at the border, because that is where he determined to *leave* Israel; therefore, there the angels of Israel ascended and the angels from outside descended.

The third problem is also answered. Jacob had just left the Yeshivah of Shem and Ever, where he studied for forteen years (Bereshit Rabba 68:5) and entered the hustle and bustle of the outside world with its polluted spiritual atmosphere. His task was now to protect his *head*, the seat of his mind and of his thoughts. That is the deeper meaning of the stones round his head. However, the protection of his body he left to Hashem. As our rabbis say: Everything is in the hands of G-d except the fear of G-d הכל בידי שמים חוץ מיראת שמים (Berachot 33B).

The Savraner Rebbe used to say: The command in the Torah: "you shall make a fence round your roof" (Deut. 22:8) includes also the protection of one's head, to keep out evil thoughts, as the Gemara in Yoma (29a) says: הרהורי עבירה קשים מעבירה – *The thoughts of sin are worse than sin itself....*

This leads us to another explanation of why the angels were going up first and then coming down. Jacob had a high standard of spirituality when he was resting there, despite the fact that he wanted to leave Israel. He had just left Yeshivah, therefore, angels came *up* to him from heaven. In spiritual matters there is no earthly pull of gravity. However, after working for Laban for 20 years, Jacob dreamed of speckled and streaked goats (Gen. 31:11), so the angel told him that it is high time to return home. Now his standards had dropped, because his head was full of goats. Before he dreamed about a ladder going up to heaven – a dream of spirituality – a symbol of high standard.

Finally, we can also resolve the following problem: The Midrash says that Moshe Rabbenu discovered a secret from the angels, namely ברוך שם כבוד מלכותו לעולם ועד. *Blessed be His name, whose Glorious Kingdom is for ever and ever....*

He divulged this to the Jewish people with the proviso to say it quietly, because it is secret. However, on Yom Kippur when we *ourselves* are like angels – we do not eat or drink and daven all day – we say it aloud. If so, the question arises why do we say it aloud on Kol Nidre night, just after having had a Mitzvah meal, but quietly at Maariv[1] after Neila when Yom Kippur is over? Surely we have fasted and prayed all day. In the light of the above, the answer is very convincing: At Kol Nidre our heads, our minds and our thoughts are directed to higher spiritual matters connected with the Great Day. At that time we are like angels. But after the Neila prayer our thoughts are directed to "Food, Glorious Food" – so we are not angels any more and we cannot say the secret verse aloud any more (Rabbi Z. Sorotzkin ז״ל).

In contemporary times, many give priority to enhancing their bodily pleasures but neglect their heads and minds. The message of our Sidra is loud and clear: Our task is to read, to learn, to observe and to enjoy our holy Torah, to protect our heads from the pollution of materialism and to occupy our minds with higher spiritual matters. We should also turn our thoughts to our Holy Land and give it our support, and by doing so raise our standards as true Torah committed Jews.

---

1. The evening prayer.

THE BATTLE WITH ESAU　　　וישלח

"וישלח יעקב מלאכים"

"....And Jacob sent messengers...."　　　　　　　*(Bereshit 32:4)*

Rashi comments that the messengers were angels, those whom he met at the end of last week's *Sidra*. Jacob sent them to make peace with his brother Esau, who hated him...because Jacob had taken the blessings from their father Yitzchak. There is such a wealth of Torah in this *Sidra* and such a lot to discuss, but I am reminded of the following anecdote:

A *non-Jewish* lecturer once delivered a long and boring after-dinner speech. (Let us not make a mistake, there are many *Jewish* orators who also deliver long and boring after-dinner speeches, but in this case it just happened to be a non-Jewish one.) The host noticed that he had a plaster on his cheek and asked him, "What happened?" The reply was: "Before I came here, I shaved with a razor" (incidently, this is something which is not permitted for Jews) – "and I was concentrating so hard on my speech that I cut myself." "Next time," said the host, "concentrate on your shaving and cut your speech!" That is what I propose to do. Cut my speech....

The following questions require explanations:

1. What was the underlying cause of Esau's hatred for Jacob?
2. Why was Jacob afraid? Surely G-d promised him (Gen. 31:3) "Return to the Land of your Fathers and I shall be with you?"
3. How did Jacob prepare himself to confront Esau?
4. Before meeting Esau, Jacob had to fight the guardian angel of his brother – the Satan – an encounter from which he emerged with great credit. However, the question arises, why did the Satan not attack Abraham or Isaac?

I wish to introduce the answers with the following story. Rabbi Shneur Zalman of Liadi once had a bitter dispute with Rabbi Baruch, so he sent messengers to resolve the matter, but Rabbi Baruch replied "I cannot accept messengers, look what happened to Jacob. Even angels are not good enough to promote peace. *Personal* contact is paramount!" In the end, Jacob had to meet Esau personally.

The whole trouble started because Rivka, the wife of Yitzchak, was under a misapprehension. She thought that her husband wanted to bestow the *spiritual* successorship to Esau. This she was determined to prevent by all means, even by deceit, because she rightly saw that Esau was not at all fit for this exalted position.

The truth of the matter was, however, that Yitzchak only wanted to create a "Yisachar – Zevulun" relationship between the two brothers. Jacob – the scholar – like Yisachar, and Esau – the provider – like Zevulun. We see clearly that before Jacob left to travel to Laban, his father gave *him* the blessing of Avraham – successorship and the Land of Israel (Gen. 28:4).

Rivka's well-meant but mistaken decision to deprive Esau of the blessing by deception was the cause of many troubles. Her order to commit trickery was later repaid by the fact that Jacob was given Leah instead of Rachel, and he was cheated with goat's blood by his children, because he misled Yitzchak his father with goat-skin. Above all, this was the cause of hatred against Jacob throughout history. Our Holy Torah, תורת אמת[1] requires truth and nothing but the truth. Now we understand the answer to question number two: Why was Jacob afraid to meet Esau? Rashi says, "Perhaps the sin might cause trouble." What is the meaning of this?

If we look at Chapter 27, verse 40, we find that Yitzchak blessed Esau as follows:

"ואת אחיך תעבד והיה כאשר תריד ופרקת עלו מעל צוארך"

"....You shall serve your brother and it shall come to pass when you shall
break loose and you shall shake his yoke from off your neck."

Rashi comments: If Jacob rejects the yoke of the Torah, then you shall be on top. The implication is: The original blessing was meant that there should be a *partnership* between Jacob and Esau, but since Jacob took away Esau's material blessings by deceit, Yitzchak had no choice but to revise his plan and substitute

---

1. Torah of Truth.

a different one. The new plan was that there should be a *rivalry* between the two, a pendulum that can swing either way. The blessing that Yitzchak gave to Jacob, "Be a lord over your brother" הוה גביר לאחיך (Gen. 27:29) will now be *conditional* on Jacob's conduct. Therefore, Jacob had no lack of trust in G-d's promises, but he was afraid that perhaps he would not *deserve* them. He was concerned with the state of the pendulum. Does his conduct measure up for him to be on top? That is what Rashi means: "Perhaps the sin might cause trouble." Jacob was afraid that perhaps Laban's influence might have caused him to sin unwittingly, in which case he would not deserve to be on top.

Now we understand Rashi (Gen. 32:5), "I lived with Laban and observed the 613 Mitzvot." Many commentators ask: Why did Jacob tell this to Esau? Is Esau interested to know that his brother kept the Mitzvot? However, according to the above, Jacob meant to reassure Esau that he has *no cause* for complaint. Unfortunately, this did not succeed, because Esau still organised an army of 400 soldiers against his brother, but they did make peace eventually. Incidentally, this state of the pendulum only exists between Jacob and Esau, but not between Yitzchak and Yishmael – the father of the Arabs. There it appears that *coexistence* is the ideal state of affairs. Since Jacob was not sure, he had to prepare to meet Esau and his 400 soldiers למלחמה.[1]

There is another question which requires a solution: Rashi says (Gen. 32:9) that the order of his preparations were: presents, prayer and war. However, the verses in the Torah (Gen. 32:8-22) give the opposite order: first, preparation for war by division of his camp into two parts, *then prayers*, and *then* presents. The answer is very convincing. When so many soldiers are marching against you, you have to make military dispositions *immediately*, and then proceed to the other two. That is the order in the Torah. But to *use* these means the pattern is reversed; at first one must try peaceful solutions such as presents, then prayers, and only if all else fails, war; that is the order that Rashi gives.

As the Ramban points out "what happened to our fathers is a sign for the children" (Gemara Sota 34a and Midrash Bereshit Rabba 70:6). In all our history, "if one camp is defeated the one which is left shall escape" (Gen. 32:9).

"והיה המחנה הנשאר לפליטה"

---

1. For war.

When we lost the Temple in Yerushalayim, those who survived went into exile, and if they had to leave one country they escaped to another. The great Chofetz Chaim was asked at the time when Hitler became powerful, "Where will it end?" He answered, "Look at Ovadiah 1:17. בהר ציון תהיה פליטה. Mount Zion will escape." Later in the war, Hitler's General Rommel attempted a pincer movement up to Iran from Africa, to capture Israel and Egypt as well. In Israel a fast day was already proclaimed, combined with special prayers. Hitler announced that in three days he would be at the Wall! However, General Rommel's plan was thwarted, with the help of Hashem and he had to retreat *before* he could reach Israel. That was one of the turning points of the Second World War combined with the defeat of the Nazi hordes on the Russian front at that time. What a fantastic prediction!

Although the brothers did not have to resort to war in the end, Jacob did have to fight the guardian angel of Esau – the Satan. This leads to the answer to the fourth question: Why did the Satan not nip the Jewish people in the bud immediately by attacking Abraham or Isaac? The famous Rabbi Elchanan Wasserman ז"ל resolved this problem in a convincing manner:

Avraham was the pillar of חסד.[1] His tent was open on all sides for guests.

Yitzchak was the pillar of עבודה,[2] even up to the point of sacrificing his life.

Jacob was the pillar of תורה.[3] He studied for 14 years at the Yeshivah of Shem and Ever (Bereshit Rabba 68:5).

The Satan does not believe in *skirmishes*. He knew that a nation is not founded by kindness or by prayer, but by education of the next generation. Therefore, he attacked Jacob, the pillar of Torah education. That is a *decisive* battle. Torah is the spiritual ammunition of our people. But he did not succeed and will never do so. How fitting is the גמטריא[4] of Yisrael, Jacob – 182, plus Satan – 359 equals Yisroel – 541. Jacob could overcome the Satan. Therefore he was called Yisrael! ("שרית" you prevailed over "קל" the divine, i.e. the angel – the Satan.)

Bilaam, the non-Jewish prophet, exclaimed:

---

1. Loving kindness.
2. Service to G-d.
3. Torah.
4. The numerical value.

"מה טובו אהליך <u>יעקב</u> משכנותיך <u>ישראל</u>"

"How goodly are your tents, Oh Jacob, your – spiritual – dwelling places,
Oh Israel (Num. 24:5).

The Gemara says (Sukkah 52b):

"אם פגע בך מנוול זה משכיהו לבית המדרש"

"If you happen to meet this 'ugly one' – the evil inclination – pull him into the
Beth Hamidrash. There you will defeat him. At home, one is only the level of
Jacob, but in the houses of study, one is *Yisrael*.

May our pendulum in the battle with Esau swing in our favour by
frequenting Batei Midrash[1] and studying and observing our Torah (and so
recharging our spiritual batteries to swing the pendulum in our favour). Then
the other verse in Ovadia (1:21) shall also be fulfilled soon in our days:

"ועלו מושיעים בהר ציון לשפט את הר עשו והיתה לה' המלוכה"

"The Saviours shall go up on Mount Zion to judge Mount Esau and the
kingdom shall be to G-d."

---

1. Houses of study.

YEHUDAH AND TAMAR

"וְהָיָה בָּעֵת הַהוּא וַיֵּרֶד יְהוּדָה מֵאֵת אֶחָיו"

"....And it came to pass that time that Yehudah went down from his
brothers...."   *(Bereshit 38:1)*

Once a rabbi was asked by one of his congregants: "What will be the
subject of your sermon?" The rabbi replied "I shall speak about "The milk
of human kindness and dignity." To this the congregant remarked:
"Condensed, I hope!" I shall speak today on this very subject in a condensed
manner.

In our Sidra, the story of Joseph and his brothers is interrupted by that of
Yehudah. Yehudah separated from his brothers, married and had three sons: Er,
Onan and Shelah. Er married Tamar, but he was "evil in the eyes of G-d" – he did
not consummate the marriage, in order to preserve the beauty of Tamar, and so
G-d killed him. Onan married the widow to perform the *Yibbum*.[1] However,
he also did not consummate the marriage because he did not want to give a
family – in a spiritual sense – to his late brother. Therefore, G-d killed him too.
Both committed great sins which are regarded as murder of any potential
offspring.

Tamar waited to be given Shelah as a husband, as Yehudah promised, but it
did not happen because she had an undeserved reputation of "Ishah katlanit" – a
wife whose various husbands died. Therefore, she had to think of something
else. She disguised herself as a harlot. Yehudah, who used her services, did not
recognise her and gave her a signet ring, a cord and a staff, as a pledge. When
Tamar was later found to be pregnant, she was reported to Yehudah, the head of
the family, who sentenced her to be burned to death. At her trial, she did not
accuse Yehudah, in order not to put him to shame in public, but merely pointed

---

1. Levirate marriage.

to the signet ring, the cord and the staff, and said: "Whose are these?" Yehudah admitted his ownership of these articles immediately and said: "She is right, I am to blame." Tamar went on to give birth to twins, Peretz and Zerach (Gen. 38:25, 26). Peretz (Gen. 38:29, 30) became part of the chain leading to the dynasty of King David and Moshiach.

Let us deal with the following problems:

1. Why did השם השגחת – the supervision of events by G-d – not allow Shelah to perform *Yibbum*, but did permit his father to do so?
2. The Gemara says (Sota 10b) that Yehudah married Tamar eventually. How could he marry his daughter-in-law?
3. Why is the story of Joseph and his brothers so suddenly interrupted by this episode?

To answer these questions:

Before the giving of the Torah, *Yibbum*[1] could be performed not only by a surviving brother but by any relative. Had Shelah performed *Yibbum*, he would only have rebuilt – so to speak – one family, but now when Yehudah, the father, performed *Yibbum*, being the father of both, he "rebuilt" both – the dead Er and Onan with Peretz and Zerach (Alshech Hakadosh). All this was in conformity with the law because he was in reality not the father-in-law of Tamar, since the marriages of Er and Onan were not consummated. Before the Torah was given, any non-consummated marriage was not valid.

Only Tamar knew these facts, but she did not divulge them. She did not disgrace her dead husbands. Rather, she suffered the reputation of אשה קטלנית.[2] She did not put Yehudah to shame in public either, but was prepared to be killed. On four occasions the Gemara teaches us that it is better to be thrown into a fiery furnace rather than put someone to shame in public (Berachot 43b, Bava Metzia 59a, Ketubot 67b, Sota 10b).

In this respect, Yehudah's conduct was also exemplary because he did not make a "cover up" when Tamar confronted him with the articles which he had given her as a pledge. On the contrary, he admitted his guilt in public immediately by exclaiming צדקה ממני "She is righteous FROM ME" (Rashi: she is pregnant from me).

---

1. Levirate marriage.
2. A wife whose husbands die early.

Now we understand the answer to the third question, too: Why is this episode in the middle of the story of Joseph and his brothers? The stories contain a number of similarities. Let us mention just one. Yehudah said to his father Jacob when he showed him Joseph's coat soaked in blood: "<u>Recognise please</u>, is this your son's coat or not...." (Gen. 37:32) that caused his father untold anguish.

Now Yehudah was told by Tamar "....<u>recognise please</u>.... to whom belongs the ring, the cord and the staff?...." (Gen. 38:25) that caused Yehudah deep shock. Measure for measure! However, above all, the deeper significance of this narrative is as follows:

At this <u>darkest</u> hour, when Jacob was grieving for the missing Joseph, and Yehudah was demoted from leadership by his brothers for his advice to sell Joseph and not to return him to his father, just then the beginning of <u>light</u> was created in the most mysterious circumstances! This light was brought about by Tamar's extraordinary regard for the dignity of her dead husbands and for Yehudah, by not disgracing them in public, and also by Yehudah's admission to the truth in his relationship with Tamar and not covering it over in public. Both are called גבורי רוח – "Heroes of the Spirit."

Eventually, both Yehudah and Tamar become ancestors of King David and Moshiach. Looking at this chain of ancestors, we will see that a number of its parts are very mysterious. For example: The daughters of Lot who committed incest with their father, because they thought that they were the only people left after the destruction of Sodom and Gemora, had two children, Amon and Moav, by this act of incest. Moav became the ancestor of Ruth, whose story is also full of mystery. Now Tamar and Yehudah are also part of this ancestry.

However, the answer to this problem is found in Job 14:3:

"מי יתן טהור מטמא"

"who can withdraw purity from impurity...."

The books of Kabbalah[1] explain this verse by saying, only Hashem can collect the sparks of goodness which are scattered throughout creation and use them for His Divine plan. All the personalities of this chain possessed extraordinary sparks of distinction and purity which made them worthy to be part of it. They truly displayed "milk of human kindness."

---

1. Mysticism.

In our contemporary society, one finds that generosity to other people, as well as consideration for their dignity, is often trampled on in order to reach success. We must realise that every person is made in the image of Hashem and deserves kindness and respect. This is the message of this obscure and perplexing episode of Yehudah and Tamar. May we all look forward to the high point of this chain – ביאת המשיח,[1] speedily in our days.

---

1. The coming of Mashiach.

DREAMS AND THEIR MEANING   מקץ

"ויהי מקץ שנתים ימים ופרעה חלם"

"....It came to pass at the end of two full years that Pharaoh dreamed...."

(Bereshit 41:1)

Three men were talking about the frailty of people. The conversation was lively. Each one gave his interpretation:

The first: The trouble with a lot of people is they eat too much.

The second: It is not how <u>much</u> one eats but <u>what</u> one eats that matters.

The third said: It is neither what you eat nor how much you eat, but what <u>eats you</u> that is the problem.

Our Sidra contains part of the fascinating narrative of Joseph and his brothers, one of the most beautiful stories in the world. It tells us what was eating the brothers – so to speak. It relates their hatred of Joseph, who was the favourite of Jacob their father. It describes the sale of Joseph to Egypt, where he became Viceroy and saved them and Egypt by using the stored up food from the good years for use during the bad ones. Strangely enough, it was a story built on dreams: Joseph's dreams of sheaves and stars, the butler's and the baker's, as well as Pharaoh's dreams of the fat and thin cows and ears of corn. It is truly a vast subject, but I am reminded of another story of a bitter quarrel – this time between husband and wife. The wife said angrily: "I will give you a piece of my mind...." The husband retorted "....only a <u>little</u> helping please!...." Let us today give a little helping of this vast subject.

My points today are:

1. What is the real meaning of dreams?
2. Why after the first dream of sheaves did the brothers <u>hate</u> him וישנאו אותו (Gen. 37:4), but after the second dream, the sun and moon and eleven stars (referring to his father, stepmother, mother

and eleven brothers bowing down to him) ויקנאו אותו they were envious of him (Gen. 37:11)? Furthermore, why did he tantalize them by telling them the second dream, since he realized that it may cause hatred?

3.   Why did Joseph give <u>advice</u> to Pharaoh to store up food for the lean years? He was only asked to interpret the dreams not to give advice. (Vilna גאון).

4.   In which way do the dreams of Pharaoh on the one hand, and Jacob and Joseph on the other, differ?

5.   How can we connect the *Sidra* with Chanukah, which we are just celebrating now?

The answer to the first question is given by Rabbi Shlomo Kluger ז"ל. Modern knowledge claims new discoveries regarding dreams, e.g., Freud, that dreams are revelations of sub-conscious desires. However, the Talmud in Berachot 55b, discusses dreams. It says that there are various categories of dreams. One type of dream is: What a person thinks during the day, he dreams about at night. Another type is prophecy.

In view of this, the brothers dismissed Joseph's first dream simply by interpreting that Joseph had ambitions to be their leader, encouraged by their father, who gave him a coat of many colours. They thought that Joseph was thinking all day long of ruling over them, and that was anathema to them since a king must be of the tribe of Judah. This is clearly demonstrated by the blessing of their father Jacob later on, who said:

"לא יסור שבט מיהודה"
"....the sceptre shall not depart from Yehudah...." (Gen. 49:10)

But the second dream could not be of the first type, because Joseph certainly never expected his father and stepmother – the sun and the moon – to bow down to him. So it must be <u>prophecy</u>. That made them envious. Therefore, he <u>had to tell</u> them the second dream, because as our rabbis say (Sanhedrin 89a): "One must not suppress prophecy." – Look what happened to Jonah! Therefore, his father kept this in mind.

That answers the third question too. Since Joseph realized now that his dreams were prophecy, strengthened by his correct interpretation of the baker's and butler's dreams, he regarded Pharaoh's dream as prophecy as well.

The interpretation depends on who the dreamer is. A king's dream must be of a <u>national</u> importance, therefore, the advice to store food was not an addition, but part of the dream. That explains why the Torah mentions ויקץ פרעה "and Pharaoh woke up...." to give a strong hint to him to <u>act</u> to save the country, as Joseph said.... "What He intends to do, He showed to Pharaoh...." (Gen. 41:28).

"אשר אלקים עושה הראה את פרעה."

This reasoning as to the crucial importance of <u>who</u> the dreamer is, gives us the lead to answer the fourth question too. Pharaoh's dreams went <u>downwards</u>, towards earthliness – first cows and then ears of corn – whilst Jacob's and Joseph's dreams went <u>upwards</u>: Jacob dreamed of a ladder from earth going up to heaven, and Joseph from sheaves to stars. One must go higher in one's life, not lower!

Life is a dream כחלום יעוף[1] as we say during the ימים נוראים,[2] at the end of the *Untane Tokef* prayer. But what kind of a dream? Some people regard life as a passing dream without any interpretation, without any sense or purpose, just to savour earthly pleasures. But this is הבל הבלים – vanity of vanities (Eccl. 1:1). The Torah attitude is: It is a wonderful dream, but one that requires elucidation, as Joseph said: הלא לאלקים פתרונם – "The interpretation belongs to Hashem" and His holy Torah. That is how we understand the purpose of our lives.

To dream of sheaves – material well being – is fine, as long as it is combined with sun, moon and stars, with a higher, heavenly outlook. As long as we use the sheaves for our elevation, to achieve Torah and Mitzvot. As long as we combine גשמיות עם רוחניות[3] that is the right interpretation of life.

In the days of the Hasmoneans, some 2,000 years ago, many people were dreaming the dreams of Hellenism, material life, assimilation, going downwards, until Mattathias and his sons rekindled the light of the Torah and gave them the right exposition and illumination (Tractate Shabbat 21b). We go upwards in holy matters, as Hillel teaches us. However, this interpretation must be combined with action, just as Joseph advised and performed actions, and the Hasmoneans <u>fought</u> successfully for that pure light of the Torah and its interpretation. They did not only dream!

---

1. Like a fleeting dream.
2. The Days of Awe.
3. Materialism with spirituality.

Our task in these spiritually dark days, permeated with wrongly interpreted dreams of assimilation, is to rekindle the light of the Torah with pure oil – so to speak – not contaminated with all kinds of so-called "pluralism". We must give the correct interpretation of our wonderful dream of life.

Let us always go up higher in holy matters and never downwards.

מעלין בקודש ואין מורידין (Tractate Shabbat 21b)

"ועתה אל תעצבו ואל יחר בעיניכם
כי מכרתם אותי הנה כי למחיה שלחני אלקים לפניכם."

"....And now be not grieved nor angry with yourselves that you sold
me here, because Hashem sent me before you to preserve life...."

(Bereshit 45:5)

A housewife once rebuked her maid in front of a visitor: "The house is not clean and dusted properly." However the visitor noticed that everything was perfect, turned to the lady and said "Madam, I think the dust you see is on your own glasses" – and so it was.

We have reached in our *Sidra* the final act of the captivating story of Joseph and his brothers, namely the reunion. However, looking at the surface of this whole narrative, it appears to contain a lot of "dust," so to speak. There are many problems which we shall try to solve with the help of our great rabbis, and in the course of it to reveal some of its exquisite and wonderful content, once the "dust" covering it is cleared.

There is an amazing amount of *mida keneged mida*[1] incorporated in this narrative.

Firstly, we will try to find some of these pieces, secondly we will show how the seemingly cruel actions of Joseph – such as his failure to let his father know that he was safe, his treatment of his brothers by accusing them of being spies and thieves, etc. – were in fact justified. Finally, what can we learn from this episode?

Before answering these questions, I would like to share with you a famous parable of the Dubno Maggid:

A king had a precious ring. One day he found a scratch on the diamond,

---

1. Measure for measure.

which was the centrepiece of the ring. No one could remove it. Finally, a jeweller from a far away country was summoned. He declared, "What a pity that such a fine ring should not be perfect!" The bystanders thought that he was referring to the ugly scratch. However, he continued: "There is something missing. Such a treasure should bear the coat of arms of its owner. This scratch is the perfect beginning of it." So the scratch was used to make the ring beautiful and complete. Thus says the Dubno Maggid: Adversity is often nothing but the scratch of the ring of life from which the triumph of perfection can and must be achieved. Such are the ways of Hashem.

It all started with evil tales told by Joseph to his father, e.g., that some of his brothers were calling the other brothers, those whose mothers were originally maid-servants, "slaves." For that, Joseph was sold as a slave. Also, they were suspected of immoral actions. For that, Joseph was made suspect by the wife of Potiphar. The reaction of his brothers was also *mida keneged mida*. They considered that Joseph was trying to destroy the family, so they tried to destroy him. Yehudah said, "Recognise the coat of your son." So did Tamar, his daughter-in-law, who was disguised as a harlot, say to Yehudah later, "Recognise, to whom does this ring belong?" They all caused Jacob to rend his garments when he was told that Joseph was missing. So they, later on, tore their garments after Benjamin was accused of theft. Menashe, the son of Joseph, who pursued them (according to Midrash Tanchuma 10), caused his uncles to tear their clothes. Therefore, the inheritance of the Tribe of Menashe was torn, half on one side and half on the other side of the River Jordan.

Their father Jacob also suffered – measure for measure:

He did not fulfill the mitzva of honouring his father and mother for 22 years – when he was away at Laban's house – so he lost his son Joseph for 22 years. (Joseph was 17 when he was sold (Gen. 37:2)). His father saw him again when he was 39 years of age. Joseph came to Egypt when he was 30 years of age (Gen. 41:46). 7 years of plenty, plus two years of famine makes Joseph 39 years old (Gen. 45:6). He cheated his father Yitzchak by covering himself with goat skin. So did his sons cheat him by dipping Joseph's coat into goat's blood.

After Joseph gained power, he dealt with his brother also in this way:

They had no mercy on him and he did not have mercy on them. They accused him of being a spy so he accused them as spies. They sold him for silver, so he accused them by means of a silver cup. Eventually, Joseph provided food for his father during his 17 years' stay in Egypt (Gen. 47:28), exactly the same number of years that Jacob provided for Joseph, who was sold when he was 17 years of age (Gen. 37:2). There are many more examples.

This brings us to the second question: Why was the apparent cruelty of Joseph justified? Since the Gemara says (Sanhedrin 89a) that anyone who suppresses prophesy deserves to die, therefore, he regarded it as a holy task that the dreams, which he rightly regarded as prophesies, should come true (Ramban). The dreams clearly hinted that he must *not make himself known* to his family, because if they knew that he was their brother, the act of bowing down would only be a lark and a game. He had to also contrive to bring Benjamin down to Egypt to make the dream of the 11 stars come true. Now we have another reason why he accused them of being spies. As the Klei Yakar explains: He had to prevent them from making enquiries about him, and the best way to achieve this, was by putting them under suspicion by the State that they were spies.

But now the question arises, why did Hashem give him the guidance not to disclose his identity?

The Rambam says in the Laws of Teshuvah[1] (2:1) that repentance is only real if it is done under similar circumstances as the sin. Therefore, had they known who he was and had they apologised to him, the repentance would not have been of any value, because they would have had no choice but to say "sorry." He was, after all, the Viceroy of Egypt. However, *not* knowing who he was, they did repent sincerely, because when there was no interpreter present, they said: "....but we are guilty of the treatment of our brother Joseph...." (Gen. 42:21). They could now show their perfect unity by not being jealous anymore when Benjamin received many more presents, by not abandoning him when he was taken back to Egypt; after all, he too was the son of Rachel, just like Joseph, and they did not need to sell him as a slave. It was all done for them...yet they all went back to Egypt with him. This was true repentance under similar circumstances as the sin.

Incidentally, Yehudah, who was very concerned for Benjamin, remained later in history his best friend; when the Kingdom was divided after King Solomon's death, Benjamin joined with Yehudah and not with the other ten tribes who

---

1. Repentance.

were lost. If not for that fact, Yehudah would have been isolated and lost too. So Yehudah saved us Jews – his descendants.

Joseph himself also did Teshuvah through the Divine guidance of the dreams. He was very impetuous, but now – guided by the dreams – he practised restraint and did not make himself known. This must have been agony for him. Often he had to weep. Only when he saw how unity was now re-established, by the brothers' great loyalty to Benjamin, and when he realised the great solidarity of Yehudah to his brother, he saw that the prophesy of the dreams had been achieved. It was at this point that Joseph could not restrain himself any longer and he showed his love to his brothers in an extraordinary degree. "Love destroys hatred" (Gemara Sanhedrin 105b) – that is the highest kind of "measure for measure" that a human being can achieve.

He told them to come to Egypt, despite the risks of resentment by the population. He did not take any revenge, on the contrary, he treated them very well.

He did not relate any more evil tales. His father never knew that the brothers had sold him. When Jacob gave his blessings and rebuked his children (Gen. 49:1-27), he did not admonish the brothers for selling Joseph. He was under the impression that Joseph had been kidnapped. Joseph showed that he was no traitor to his family, but on the contrary, he took his father for burial to Israel unconcerned with the display of open disloyalty to Egypt that this entailed.

Above all, he showed that, despite being in such a high position in Egypt, he remained true to Judaism by educating his children so well that we bless our sons "....May Hashem make you like Efraim and Menashe...."

Had Joseph revealed himself earlier, the repentance of his brothers, and indeed his own repentance, would not have been possible under circumstances similar to those when their sins were committed. The unity of the 12 tribes would not have been restored and Jacob would have gained one son and lost ten (Rabbi S.R. Hirsch ז״ל). In the end, the heavenly pattern consisting of so many pieces of *mida keneged mida* finally brought the puzzle to a grand solution. The ugly scratch in the life of Jacob's family was turned into part of the coat of arms of the Master Jeweller – Hashem. This has cleared a lot of the "dust" covering this narrative.

All this is very relevant to our times. We can learn from Joseph to be concerned and helpful to others so that Hashem will surely be merciful to us as well. Then Hashem will give us *mida keneged mida* a million-fold, as was the case when Miriam waited for her baby brother Moshe for one hour. When she became leprous, millions of people waited for her for seven days. That is about five hundred million times of *mida keneged mida!* (There were at least 3 million people waiting for her for 168 hours!)

Just as Joseph's brothers asked many questions, but in the end two words "ANI YOSEPH" – I AM JOSEPH – answered them all – so too all our many questions about many strange events in the world will be answered in the days of Mashiach with two words "ANI HASHEM" "I am the Lord" (Chofetz Chaim). May it be soon in our days.

BLESSINGS OF JACOB

ויחי

"ויקרא יעקב אל בניו ויאמר האספו ואגידה לכם
את אשר יקרא אתכם באחרית הימים"

"....And Jacob called his sons and said: 'Gather yourselves together
that I may tell you that which shall befall you at the end of
days'...."
                                                                (Bereshit 49:1)

A certain rabbi had a very knowledgeable member in his congregation. This person used to interrupt him: "This comes from this *Sefer*,[1] that from another, etc." until in exasperation the preacher exclaimed: "Please keep quiet!" "That is your own!" was the reply. I shall try to quote the authors of my sources – if they are known to me and add נופך משלי – a little coin of my own. After all, the Rabbis say (Avot 6:6):

"כל האומר דבר בשם אומרו מביא גאולה לעולם"

"Anyone who says something in the name of the one who says it, brings redemption to the world." – Surely a very worthwhile aim!....

Our subject today: The blessings of Jacob which he gave to his children before his death. Three questions arise in connection with this topic.

1. Isaac, his father, also gave blessings to his two sons before he died. He lived for 180 years (Gen. 35:28), but Yaakov only reached 147 years (Gen. 47:28). Why was Yaakov's life 33 years shorter?
2. On what foundation are the blessings built?
3. We find fundamental differences between the blessings of Yaakov, our father, and those of Moses, our teacher, at the end of the Torah. One of many examples: Here Benjamin is called "....a wolf that

---

1. Book.

catches prey...." (Gen. 49:27) whilst there he is referred to as: "....the beloved of the Lord...." (Deut. 33:12).

By way of introduction to the answers, I would like to relate the famous parable of a person who was taken on a tour of *Gehinnom*[1] and *Gan Eden*.[2] To his great surprise, he saw in Gehinnom a magnificent banqueting hall and tables laden with all kind of delicacies, but the "celebrants" were *starving*. What was the reason? They had very long knives and forks tied to their arms. Consequently, they could not bring the delicious food to their mouths. Soldiers were on guard to supervise the use of the cutlery provided.

When later he was taken to Gan Eden, the very same spectacle presented itself. However, there the celebrants *enjoyed* themselves thoroughly. What was the reason? They fed one another across the table!....

To look after *oneself* only is Gehinnom. To *share* with others is Gan Eden.

Now for our solutions: Two reasons were given why Jacob's life was shortened by 33 years. It is well known that Abraham's life was reduced by five years: he lived for 175 years (Gen. 25:7), whilst Yitzchak lived for 180 years, so as to be spared the aggravation of seeing his grandson Esau going astray (Rashi, Gen. 25:30). דעת זקנים מבעלי התוספות refer, in connection with Jacob's span of life, to Gen 47:8-9. There it says "....Pharaoh asked Jacob: "How old are you?" – because he saw that Jacob looked very old and sad. Jacob replied – "The years of my sojournings are 130 years. Few and evil have been the days of my life and they have not attained unto the days of the lives of my fathers in the days of their sojournings." He complained that his life was very troubled. It is true that he had very good reasons for that. However, all his many afflictions turned out well in the end. He escaped successfully from the clutches of Laban, he made peace with Esau, he regained his daughter Dinah who had been kidnapped, and was re-united with his long lost son Joseph. In view of his grumbling, Hashem decided to cut his life-span by 33 years – exactly the number of Hebrew words in these two verses.... There is another explanation given by the Baal Haturim: When his wife Rachel hid the idols of her father Laban, Jacob, who did not know that Rachel had them, exclaimed: "He who has the idols shall not live לא יחיה" (Gen. 31:32). The numerical value of יחיה[3] is 33. And it says in Proverbs 26:2,

---

1. Hell.
2. Paradise.

"The curse of a wise man comes true." Therefore, he lost 33 years of his life. In addition Rachel lost her life when giving birth to Benjamin (Midrash Bereshit Rabba 74:3).

How true is the saying: "The word is like a diamond – it should be rare, it should be valuable and carefully handled. It is a good instrument, but remember: it may cut!"

Now that we have discovered some of the reasons why Jacob's life was shortened, we can move on and elucidate the foundation of his blessings. He certainly wanted the fragile beginnings of our nation to lead to its *everlasting* life. This is clearly demonstrated in the verse with which we began: "Gather together...." *Unity!* A lifespan of an individual is limited and varied but that of a nation should be a בנין עדי עד.[1] A precondition of this is that the people must be united. Now that the bitter quarrel between Joseph and his brothers has been resolved, unity had been achieved in his family. Therefore the foundations of the everlasting Jewish people were in place. That is why the blessings are preceded with האספו – "Gather together!" That is what Jacob cautions his 12 sons: *Consolidate* this partnership and harmony as a nation. Do not just feed yourselves but help one another across the tables – so to speak. Remember: Man is not an island. Work together and then, with the help of Hashem, you will succeed to make the Jewish nation into an eternal structure. Incidentally, that is why public prayer with a Minyan is so important. We always daven in the plural. We pray for the *whole* Jewish people and often for the *whole* of mankind. The Minyan is representative of the *whole* people.

This leads us to answer the question of Rabbi Akiva Eger: "Why did Jacob bless them altogether: surely the danger of jealousy, which was the source of all the trouble so far could arise again?" However, they all realized now that every individual must contribute his or her unique abilities to the *Klal Yisrael*, to serve Hashem and the people in unity. This can be compared to the spokes of a wheel. Although the spokes point in different directions, they are all part of the same wheel and are essential to its function.

We have now reached the final problem: Why are the blessings of Jacob and Moshe Rabbenu so different? The eminent Abarbanel gives a most convincing answer. He says that the central theme of Jacob's blessing is to demonstrate to

3. To live.
1. A permanent building.

his children who will be kings in the distant future. It cannot be Reuven and his tribe because he is "unstable as water" and cannot rule over his brothers. It cannot be Shimon and Levi and their tribes because they are too violent – they destroyed Shechem and its inhabitants to rescue Dinah. However, Judah and his tribe shall be kings.

"לא יסיר שבט מיהודה"
The sceptre shall not depart from Yehudah....
(Gen. 49:10).

Abarbanel continues: "Judah possesses all the relevant qualities for this high station. He is acknowledged as leader by his brothers. He is fit to be victorious in war. He is not unstable or violent. The other brothers and tribes have many qualities but are not eligible to become kings." Now we understand why Jacob calls Benjamin "a wolf, who catches and eats prey...." He meant to point out that he is not fit to be king.

Moshe Rabbenu, however, gives his blessings to the tribes according to their portions in Israel. He blesses Benjamin, in whose territory the Temple will be built, and calls him "ידיד השם"[1] (Deut. 33:12). He (Hashem and His Temple) dwells between 'his shoulders' ובין כתיפיו שכן. The reason why Benjamin was so distinguished is because he was the only one born in Eretz Israel and the only one who never bowed to Esau (because he was not born yet at the time). He also was the only one who had nothing to do with the sale of Joseph.

What can we learn from all this?

We must be grateful to Hashem for the wonderful gifts that He bestows upon us, to be שמחים בחלקינו.[2] A discontented murmurer shortens his life. Furthermore, we must be very prudent and not be careless with the use of our words. Finally, it is of the utmost importance to work for unity among ourselves. After all, most of us are descendants of Judah and should take the lead in this very important matter. We should feed one another both physically and spiritually "across the table." The rewards for this will be endless and boundless, particularly for our generation, which lacks this fundamental ingredient of a blessed life. Then the words of Jacob our Father will be fulfilled:

---

1. Beloved of Hashem.
2. Happy with our portion and not to grumble.

את אשר <u>יקרא</u> אתכם באחרית הימים. *Suddenly*, totally unexpectedly – יקרא – Moshiach will come באחרית הימים,[1] and everyone will be caught by surprise (Baal Shem Tov). May it be soon in our days.

---

1. At the end of the days.

SHEMOT

SERPENTS

שמות

O ur *Sidra Shemot*, which is the beginning of the second book of the Torah, deals with the terrible tribulations which the Bnei Yisrael suffered in Egypt. It contains a veritable feast of material requiring a lot of explanation. However, I am reminded of a story of a husband who said to his wife as she was going to the shopping centre: "Please get some anti-freeze." When she returned she was wearing a brand new mink coat! Next day the husband confided to one of his friends: "My wife had plastic surgery." Upon hearing this news, the friend expressed his regret and wished the wife a speedy recovery. However, the husband replied: "It was not a serious operation, I merely cut her plastic credit card in half." Torah is אש דת – "the fire of the Law." It gives us spiritual warmth, particularly now in the freezing winter weather, but I have to cut my words of Torah. Space permits me to choose only one of the many subjects contained in our *Sidra*.

One of the stories mentioned is very mysterious (Exod. 4: 2-4). Hashem commanded Moshe Rabbenu to take his rod and cast it onto the ground in front of the Jewish People. It turned into a serpent. Then he was told to take it by its tail and it became a staff again. Later, (Exod. 7:9-12) he and Aharon did the same in front of Pharaoh. Surprisingly, when Pharaoh's magicians repeated the act, their rods also became snakes. After Aharon's serpent turned back into a staff, it swallowed their rods.

We find more serpents in the Torah: When the Jewish people became dissatisfied with the heavenly Manna food, they were punished by snakes which killed many people; but when Bnei Yisrael repented and said "we have sinned," Moshe Rabbenu was told to make a brass serpent and to set it upon a pole. Then "if the snake had bitten anyone, when he looked up at the brass snake, he would live" (Num. 21:4-9). Three questions present themselves:

1. Why did the staff turn into a snake and not into something else?

2. Why did the grumblers get their punishment via serpents and not by other means?

3. Torah is for all time, what can we learn from these stories for our times? Thank G-d we do not encounter any snakes in our streets.

To introduce the answer I would like to share with you the following charming anecdote: Having joined the National Trust in England, a mother decided to make the most of the school holidays by taking her little daughter to many stately homes belonging to the National Trust. But her feeling of cultural achievement was rudely shattered when the daughter brought home her school project book at the beginning of the next term. There she saw the following entry: "This holiday was different; Mother spent all our time taking us round Public Houses (Pubs, English Drinking Places)...."

I shall endeavour to enhance our cultural achievements in Torah thought and philosophy by exploring the Torah's great Divine Treasure House, so that we shall discover truly amazing answers to our questions.

I feel sure that these narratives of snakes are based on the following:

If we cast our minds back to the very first serpent in human history (Gen. 3:1) we will find that the snake made Adam and Eve dissatisfied with the wonderful generosity of Hashem, who had placed them in the Garden of Eden and provided them with all their needs. "Eat from the fruit of the forbidden tree and you will become like Hashem yourselves" (Gen. 3:5). What was the consequence? They had to leave Paradise and look after themselves (Gen. 3:19).

"בזעת אפיך תאכל לחם"

"....with the sweat of your brow shall you eat bread...."

That is the answer to the first question. A staff gives support to a person, a staff of G-d implies that Hashem gives you His support. If you throw that staff to the ground, that will lead you to the deadly serpent, the slanderer and the tempter. No! Take it by its tail and it turns back to the staff of Hashem! If you do that, the divine rod will swallow Pharaoh's staff and will overcome all obstacles and dangers. This was a clear hint that the Egyptians will be drowned. Pharaoh is called by the prophet Ezekiel (29:3)

"פרעה ....התנים הגדול"

"Pharaoh... the great dragon that lies in the midst of his rivers."

What is needed is to place your staff into the hands of Hashem and not be deceived by the false promises of the serpent. Then the "Dragon of Egypt" will be swallowed by the heavenly rod.

In the light of this, everything falls into place: The same kind of dissatisfaction overcame our people in the desert, who were given everything they needed by Hashem, namely food, water, and clothing like in Gan Eden,[1] but the new generation that about to enter Israel, wanted to be independent, just like Adam and Eve. Therefore, they were made to suffer from snakes to remind them that their ingratitude was symbolically נחש הקדמון – the original snake of Adam and Eve. Up to now, they were protected by the pillar of cloud from those poisonous snakes that abound in the desert. However, once they expressed their discontent by grumbling about the exquisite Manna food, G-d took His protection away and they were attacked by these snakes. Similarly, Adam and Eve were expelled from Paradise and left to their own devices.

The Mishna says in Talmud Rosh Hashana (29a), "Does a copper snake kill or revive? But when people looked up to the heaven they lived, if not, they perished." The question arises, why did they need a brass snake to look up to heaven? Is it an aerial to bring down the Divine Presence? The answer is two-fold:

A) To make them realise that they were exposed to snakes all the time and only G-d protected them.

B) The Gemara Berachot (33a) narrates: There was a snake in the neighbourhood of Rabbi Chanina ben Dosa which killed many people, but when it attacked him, the <u>snake died</u>. When he was questioned about this he made the famous statement:

"לא ערוד ממית אלא החטא ממית"
"It is not the snake that kills but the sin"....

Here they were shown the truth of this statement in a symbolic manner. A snake cannot kill if one is grateful to Hashem and if one looks up to Him, but on the contrary, it heals. The Talmud tells us that Rabbi Chaninah was very modest in his life-style. He lived on carobs from one Shabbat to the next. Therefore, the snake, a symbol of dissatisfaction, had no effect on him. Incidentally, the symbol of the medical profession is a serpent: Even the doctors realise that one must always look up and pray to Hashem to heal the patient.

---

1. Paradise.

"כי אני השם רפאך"
"For I am the L-rd who heals you".... (Exod. 15:26).

This leads us to the final problem. Surely we are not attacked by snakes! Furthermore, the copper snake has long been destroyed, so what has it all got to do with us? The fact is, however, that we are being attacked by snake-like creatures, not just by one or two but by untold millions every day and night, namely by bacteria and viruses. One can see them under a powerful microscope; some look like snakes and some of them are deadly, but Hashem has given us His divine staff and support to defend our bodies against all assault, by means of a complex immune system. A famous doctor once remarked that it is not sickness but health that is the greatest of medical mysteries. We know only too well what happens if this system is damaged. We need only to think of the plague of AIDS.

But it is not only our bodies, but also our spiritual and moral life-style which is protected by the divine immune system of our Torah, by the 613 Mitzvot.

King Solomon says (Eccl. 10:8):

"He who makes a breach in the fence (of the Torah) will be bitten by a snake" (which hides in hedges – Rashi).

A person who does not observe the boundaries which our Creator has given to us exposes himself to these deadly snakes. Similarly, the so called "Moderns," who try to breach this spiritual immune system by abolishing this and that law of our Torah in the name of 'Modernity' do the work of the tempter and slanderer, נחש הקדמון.[1] We know what the consequences are. Many are lost without trace in the furnace of the permissive society.

Is not our Torah an exquisite Treasure House? Even narratives of snakes contain important teachings for all time. Our task is to look up to Hashem and give Him our most sincere thanks for נסיך שבכל יום עמנו "miracles which He gives us every day...." as we say in our *Amida* prayer.

We must support ourselves on the staff of Hashem, and this staff will swallow up all obstacles we encounter in our lives. Our lives will then be safe and happy and will blossom and bear fruit just like the staff of Aharon did in the Tabernacle in the desert.

---

1. The original serpent.

THE TEN PLAGUES

רבי יהודה היה נותן בהם סמנים דצ"ך עד"ש באח"ב

Rabbi Yehudah used to refer to the plagues by means of a mnemonic
device (by taking the initial letter of each plague).   *(Pesach Hagadah)*

A Chassidic Rebbe once remarked: There are two kinds of readers of
serious books – some treat books as if they were squeezing grapes with
their finger-tips and only watery juice which does not ferment will be the result.
Thus, if they just glance hurriedly over the pages, they complain that there is no
merit in the book. The other group squeeze the full juice of the grapes. This juice
does ferment and turns into pleasing wine. They do find delight in the reading of
the book.

Let us try to penetrate a little more deeply into the greatest Book, the divine
Torah, and we will be surprised how חז"ל[1] read this chapter of the plagues.

There are a number of questions which require solutions.

1. We find often that Hashem hardened Pharaoh's heart (Exod. 9:12,
    10:20, 10:27). If that is so, what about בחירה?[2]
2. What is the significance of Rabbi Yehudah putting the initial letters
    together – any child could do it?
3. Why were just these chosen when Hashem has unlimited ways and
    means?
4. Finally, what is the significance of the number 10?

Permit me to introduce the answers with the following anecdote:

Some years ago, in Russia, a Jewish man was sentenced to ten lashes. He
knew that the lashes would be applied with great force. A friend advised him to

---

1. Our great Rabbis.
2. Freedom of choice.

bribe the Russian policeman so that he should mete out the punishment in a bearable manner. The first, second and third, right up to the ninth stroke proved to be tolerable but the tenth one was so severe that he feared all his bones would be broken. After he recovered from the beating he took the policeman to task and said to him: "What about our agreement? Why were you so harsh with me at the tenth stroke?" The policeman replied: "I wanted to show you what a bargain you got for your money"....

Pharaoh could bear the first nine plagues because they were not meant to be indiscriminate punishment for his ill-treatment of the Jewish People, but a means by which his people, our people, and the rest of the world would be educated to realise that Hashem is the Creator and Master of the world. However, the tenth plague was designed to force him to let us leave Egypt.

Let us try to answer the questions in order:

First, Rambam explains: If we look carefully at the first five plagues we find that Pharaoh *himself* hardened his heart (Exod. 7:22, 8:11, 8:15, 8:28, 9:7) so Pharaoh *did* have בחירה.[1]

A point was reached when he deserved more severe punishment. This can consist of ill health or death, etc. However, here Hashem *punished* him with "hardening of the heart" in order to give him the other five plagues. The question arises why would Pharaoh have succumbed just after the fifth plague had not Hashem hardened his heart? The answer is very convincing: Up to the plague of *boils* the magicians who were his ministers stayed with the King and encouraged him in his refusal to let us go. At the plague of *boils*, however, the magicians could not stand before the King and Moshe because they themselves were afflicted (Exod. 9:11), so Pharaoh was left "holding the baby" by himself and he would have given in had not Hashem hardened his heart (Exod. 9:12).

Another answer: Generally the question is asked, why should the son of a thief be expected to observe Mitzvot in the same manner as the son of a famous Rabbi? Where is justice? Rabbi Dessler ז"ל solved this problem as follows:

We must realise that every person has his own point of בחירה.[2] The point of בחירה for the son of the thief is very low indeed – should he steal or not? If he does succeed *Yetzer Horah*[3] – to steal, he will gradually rise to better

---

1. Freedom of choice.
2. Freedom of choice.
3. Evil inclination.

surroundings. If he succeeds in this matter of raising his standards, his reward will be just as great as that of the son of the Rabbi whose point of בחירה was whether he should study Gemara for six or seven hours a day.

"לפום צערא אגרא" – "the reward will be according to the effort" (Ethics of the Fathers 5:26). Therefore, if Pharaoh's heart would not have been hardened by Hashem, his point of בחירה would have tilted towards the good side against his will by witnessing the miraculous plagues. Thus he needed "the hardening of his heart" to keep his freedom of choice.

Now that we have discovered the fairness of the plagues let us move on to explain the underlying idea of Rabbi Yehudah's statement. According to the famous Maharal Mi Prague, Rabbi Yehudah divides the ten plagues into three groups: The power of Hashem is everywhere:

> **Below the ground** – blood, frogs, water and lice (dust)
> **On the ground** – animals and human beings (wild animals, pestilence and boils)
> **Above the ground** – hail, locusts and darkness of the sky followed by the "killing of the firstborn"

Pharaoh was duly warned twice in each group. Two warnings are sufficient according to Halacha. The first warning was a private one – by the river – and the second was a public one – in his palace.

The plagues became progessively worse in each group. In the first group the Egyptians could protect themselves from the first two, they could buy water from the Jewish people and could barricade themselves against frogs but could do nothing against the third – lice, which were on their bodies.

In the second group they could protect themselves against wild animals, but not against boils.

In the third group they could protect themselves against hailstones and were even told to do so, so much so that Pharaoh exclaimed, "Hashem is the righteous one and I and my people are wicked," but they could not protect themselves against darkness and certainly not against the killing of the firstborn.

The teaching that the power of Hashem extends everywhere below the ground, on the ground and above the ground was brought home to Pharaoh and the whole of Egypt in ever increasing measure.

Now we understand that before the first plague it says (Exod. 7:17):

"בזאת תדע כי אני השם"

"With this you shall know that I am the L-rd."

Before the second group starting with wild animals it says:

"למען תדע כי אני השם בקרב הארץ"

"In order that you shall know that I am the L-rd in the midst of the land" (Exod. 8:18).

Hashem does not abandon his creation to its fate but directs it. Before the final group, starting with hailstones it says (Exod. 9:14):

"בפעם הזאת אני שלח את כל מגפתי...בעבור תדע כי אין כמני בכל הארץ"

This time I am sending ALL my plagues... so that you shall know that there is NO ONE like me in the whole world (even above the ground).

Now we understand why it says, "I am going to send all my plagues" before the plague of hailstones, because this is the beginning of the final group. We see the most amazing system of education in these plagues proving that Hashem is powerful everywhere. Most of them were brought about after due warnings and were stopped by prayers on the part of Moshe Rabbenu. As we said before, the tenth plague was of a different category. G-d did not say that He would kill the firstborn during the approaching middle of the night only, but in the middle of the night generally. After the killing of the first-born the first night, the next oldest would be slain the following night, and so on till the end. Rashi says in Exodus 12:30 that the eldest of the house is called the firstborn, as it says in Psalms 89:28:

"אף אני בכור אתנהו"

"Also I (King David) was made the firstborn."

We know that David was not the firstborn, but it is implied, as Rashi says there, "a great person." That is why the Egyptian people urged that we should be sent out quickly because they said, "We are all dying" (Exod. 12:33).

There are many more teachings contained in these plagues. One of them is מדה כנגד מדה.[1] The Egyptians made us feel like strangers so they themselves were

---

1. Measure for measure.

made to feel like strangers in their own land. They were not even safe in their own homes, because of the frogs, wild animals, and darkness, etc. (Rabbi S. R. Hirsch).

Furthermore, who made Egypt safe from complete destruction by starvation and made them very wealthy? Joseph. Therefore, all that wealth had to be destroyed or taken out of Egypt by us because the Egyptians ill-treated the Jewish People. There are still many more explanations contained in these plagues. This answers question No. 3, namely why were just these chosen?

We have now reached the final problem, i.e., what is the significance of the number ten? The Mishna says in Ethics of the Fathers 5:1:

"בעשרה מאמרות נברא העולם"
"The world was created with ten words."

For example, Hashem said "let there be light", "let there be animals." He could have created it just as well with only one word. However, this is intended to teach us that every detail was created separately and is being supervised by Hashem continually. The world is not one big creation that looks after itself. We say in the morning davening every day (after ברכו):

"מחדש בטובו בכל יום תמיד מעשה בראשית"
"Hashem in His goodness renews His work of the creation every day."

Pharaoh believed that nature is running itself and, therefore, he worshipped the Nile and sheep. Hashem taught him decisively that nature without Divine guidance turns into תוהו ובוהו – void and disaster.

Life-giving water turns into blood. There is no balance of nature – no predators to prevent the appearence of large numbers of frogs, lice, and wild animals. There is no protection against germs, no immune system; pestilence and boils plagued them. Fire and water exist side by side in the hailstones. Beneficial winds brought locusts, light is turned into darkness and the very life of people is in jeopardy. Without השגחה פרטית,[1] everything in nature goes haywire.

Now we understand that Pharaoh received ten plagues for not recognising the fact of creation by ten words.

We, in turn, received **Ten Commandments** which are the headlines of the

---

1. Special supervision from Hashem.

613 *Mitzvot* (Bamidbar Rabba 13:15, quoted by Rashi Exod. 24:12) in order to maintain the world which was created with ten words. May the great and wonderful teachings contained in the ten plagues help us to fulfill the **Ten Commandments** and all the 613 mitzvot connected with them – with all our hearts and souls.

TEFILLIN

אב

"וְהָיָה לְךָ לְאוֹת עַל יָדְךָ וּלְזִכָּרוֹן בֵּין עֵינֶיךָ לְמַעַן תִּהְיֶה תּוֹרַת ה' בְּפִיךָ"

"And it shall be a sign on your hand and a memorial between your eyes – The Torah of Hashem shall be in your mouth for with a strong hand Hashem brought you out of Egypt." *(Shemot 13:9)*

The *Sidra* contains the last three of the ten plagues, the laws of Pesach, and the exodus from Egypt. It concludes with two of the four paragraphs which are written inside the Tefillin. They are *Kadesh* and *Vehaya Ki Yeviyacha* (Exod. 13:1-16). The other two are *Shema* (Deut. 6:4-9) and *Vehaya Im Shamoa* (Deut. 11:13-21).

The subject of this talk is **Tefillin**. Their significance is indeed of the highest order, so much so that the mitzvah of Tefillin equals that of Shabbat, as it is stated in the Gemara Menachot (36b).

"One does not wear Tefillin on Shabbat because they are 'a sign on your hand' and Shabbat is also a sign 'between Me and you" (Exod. 31:13).

Furthermore, by donning Tefillin nearly every day, we relive the exodus from Egypt (it is inscribed in the Tefillin). They truly are portable monuments of our victory over oppression, with the help of Hashem. There are many more teachings contained in this mitzvah. The question arises: Why can't we absorb any lessons which Tefillin teach us simply by study, thus keeping them constantly in our minds? I shall try to give the answer with an anecdote.

A Rabbi's neighbour happened to be a Vicar. One day, the Vicar observed the Rabbi leaving his house in a great hurry. Asked for the reason, the Rabbi replied that he had to catch a train for an important appointment. The Vicar consulted his gold watch and told him: "Plenty of time Rabbi! No need to rush!" They strolled to the station together discussing various problems. However, when they arrived at the station, the train had just left. The Vicar apologised profusely: "I had such faith in my watch." The Rabbi retorted: **"Faith must go hand in**

hand with good works!...." *Similarly, spiritual guidelines must be converted into* practical *Mitzvot if they are to be enduring.* That is how human nature works. Without practical application of these teachings they do not endure.

However, some questions need to be answered:

1. In which way do Tefillin and Shabbat compare?
2. The Torah says that you should put the Tefillin on the head – between the eyes. Our Rabbis teach us, however, that this is not meant on top of the nose but in the middle of the forehead, above the beginning of the hairline. Why just there?
3. Why must the Tefillin of the hand be put on before the Tefillin of the head, but the Tefillin of the head must be taken off before the Tefillin of the hand?

By way of introduction to the answers, let us share the following anecdote:

During the last century, Kaiser Franz Josef once visited the main Synagogue in Budapest. In the Synagogue Hall was a portrait of the Kaiser. However, an anti-Semite removed it just before the visit. The Kaiser was told about it. When he met the Rabbi, who was not aware of this matter, he angrily confronted him with the accusation: "You are not loyal citizens – my portrait has been removed from your Synagogue Hall!" The Rabbi, who was very sharp, answered in a flash: "Your Majesty! We Jewish people don Tefillin every day but not on Shabbat. The reason is Tefillin is our sign of service to our G-d. Shabbat is a similar sign. Therefore, on Shabbat we do not lay Tefillin. When Your Majesty is not here, we require your portrait. However, now that we have the great honour to be able to welcome your Majesty in person, your portrait is not needed." So he got himself and his congregation out of trouble....

The connection between the sign of Tefillin, "And it shall be for you a sign on your arm" (Exod. 13:9) and that of Shabbat... "Between Me and the Children of Israel it shall be a sign forever," (Exod. 31:17) seems clear. The sign of Shabbat is two-fold. Twice the Torah mentions the Ten Commandments and for each time a different reason is given for Shabbat. In *Yitro* the Torah says:

"זכור את יום השבת לקדשו... כי ששת ימים עשה ה' את השמים ואת הארץ
וינח ביום השביעי"

"Remember the Sabbath Day to keep it holy,
because in six days Hashem made the Heaven and Earth and He
rested on the seventh day" (Exod. 20:8 and 20:11).

However, in the Sidra of Vo'etchanan it says,

"וזכרת כי עבד היית בארץ מצרים ויצאך ה' אלקיך משם ביד חזקה

ובזרע הנטויה על כן צוך ה' אלקיך לעשות את יום השבת"

"Remember that you were a slave in the land of Egypt and Hashem
brought you out from there with a strong Hand and an outstretched
Arm, that is why Hashem commanded you to keep the Shabbat day"
(Deut. 5:15).

Shabbat stands for two fundamental principles of Judaism.

a) That Hashem is the Creator of the world;
b) That Hashem has not abandoned the world to its own devices and
   let it run by itself, but He supervises it constantly and is involved in
   its progress. As the book of Kabbalah[1] puts it "לית אתר פנוי מיניה" –
   "There is no place where He is not found."

This is illustrated by the fact that Hashem took us out from Egypt. We, being
Hashem's servants, acknowledge both these facts by ceasing work on Shabbat at
his command.

These very principles are found inside the Tefillin. In *Shema* and *Vehaya Im
Shomoa*:[2] Hashem is the only one (Creator) and He has given us מצות.[3] In *Kadesh*
and *Vehaya Ki Yeviyacha*:[4] Hashem brought us out of Egypt. He is the Master of
History.

This leads us to answer the second question: Why do we put Tefillin above
the hairline and between the eyes?

Modern science has mapped out the functions of many areas of the brain
which consists of millions of cross-linked neural connections. It is a fantastic
computer. Scientists say: If one wanted to make a computer with many – not all –
of the functions of the brain it would have to be the size of this planet!

---

1. Mysticism.
2. 2 of the 4 paragraphs written inside the tefilin.
3. Commandments.
4. The other 2 paragraphs in the tefilin.

"מה גדלו מעשיך ה'"

"How great are the works of Hashem" (Psa. 92:6).

The site of the higher mental and ethical functions, as well as that of foresight and planning, is exactly above the hairline of the front part of the head; that is where we place our Tefillin. People who by accident have lost this part of the brain have no foresight, moral or ethical values. They are like animals. The Tefillin bind us to use this planning centre according to the guide-lines of the Torah, to dedicate the intellect to the service of Hashem and his Torah.

"למען תהיה תורת ה' בפיך"

"In order that the Torah of Hashem be in your mouth...." (Exod. 13:9).

However, this gift, the mind, bestowed to mankind, could be misused as an ominous threat to the existence of the world. Just think of the weapons of mass destruction.

Tefillin concentrates the mind into a force of noble living. Chazal[1] put this teaching in these words:

"שלשה סרסורי עברה הן עין ראה הלב חומד וכלי מעשה גומרים"

"There are three agents of sin: The eye sees, the heart desires, and the vessel of action (hands) finish off" (Rashi, Num. 15:39).

Therefore, the Tefillin are put on these very places as guardians. They guard the intellect, the heart and the arm. Not only the brain needs to be watched, but also the heart (the Tefillin of the hand are placed opposite the heart), because envy and greed are the cause of so much trouble. The hands need to be tied too. They lose freedom of movement for theft or violence, which, unfortunately, is so prevalent in our times, but they should be tied to the service of Hashem. Furthermore, they bind all Jews together.

This reminds me of a story of a refugee who emigrated to the United States. When he was standing near the Statue of Liberty, he waved his hands with great enthusiasm, "Now I am free, thanks to Hashem." However, his arm hit a bystander on the nose. The latter rebuked him saying: "Why did you hit me?" The immigrant replied:

"This is a free country, and I can clap my hands," but the bystander retorted: "Yes, it is a free country, but your freedom ends where my nose begins...."

---

1. Our Rabbis.

The Gemara in Menachot (43b) says the following:

"חביבין ישראל שסבבן הקב״ה במצות תפילין בראשיהן ותפילין
בזרועותיהן ציצית בבגדיהן ומזוזה לפתחיהן"

"Yisrael is beloved that Hashem has surrounded them with Mitzvot;
Tefillin on their heads, Tefillin on their arms and Tzitzit on their clothing
and Mezuzah on their houses...."

Tefillin protect our intellect, our hearts, and our arms. Tzitzit are a constant reminder of our duties as soldiers in the army of Hashem. They are our uniform.

"למען תזכרו ועשיתם את כל מצותי"

"So that you may remember and perform all my commandments"
(Num. 15:40).

And Mezuzot elevate our homes into little sanctuaries. They are our heavenly guards.

The Gemara in Brachot (6a) tells us that Hashem also wears Tefillin but they contain the inscription:

"Who is like Your people Israel...."

This means, of course, if one may say so, He is tied to us, if we deserve it.

Finally, to answer the third question: Tefillin of the hand must be put on before those of the head to teach us that *Naaseh*, we shall do, is the first priority before *Nishmah*, we shall listen, as we said on Mount Sinai (Exod. 24:7).

Consequently, the Tefillin of the head must be removed first so that they should never be worn without נעשה, we shall do. Thus, we are receiving the Torah afresh practically every day. Furthermore: "Faith must go hand in hand with good works!"

Let us conclude with a famous parable of the Dubno Maggid: *Emet*[1] complained to *Mashal*[2] that none wanted to admit it to his home because of its old age. Parable, which was adorned in fashionable, attractive clothes replied: "I am also old but people enjoy my company. They are partial to anything which is decorative and a little disguised. I will loan you my clothes and everyone will love you." Since that day, *Emet* and *Mashal* go hand in hand and are very much liked and welcomed....

---

1. Truth.
2. Parable.

Tefillin are called טטפות (Deut. 6:8) which means adornments. They adorn the truth. – What a wealth of truth is contained in the Tefillin! They are equal in importance to Shabbat. They are a sign of acknowledgment to Hashem as creator of the Universe as well as Master of History. They make us relive the Exodus from Egypt frequently. They are portable monuments of our victory over Egypt. They guard the planning centre in our brains so that we may live each day according to the guidelines of our Torah. They guard our eyes and our hearts and bind our hands to the service of Hashem. They tie all Jews together in unity. They make us confirm that "we shall do" before "we shall listen." May Hashem accept this symbol of practical service to Him and bind Himself to us with His Tefillin.

TRUST IN HASHEM

בשלח

"ויושע ה' ביום ההוא את ישראל מיד מצרם... ויאמינו בה'
ובמשה עבדו"

"On that day Hashem saved the Jewish people from the hands of
the Egyptians... and they believed in Hashem and Moshe His
servant...."   *(Shemot 14:30 31)*

This week's *Sidrah* deals with the aftermath of our exodus from Egypt, the pursuit of Pharaoh, the splitting of the Red Sea, the Song of Moshe Rabbenu – that is why this Shabbat is called the Shabbat Shira,[1] the Manna, the water from the rock, and the war against Amalek.

We trusted in Hashem and He gave us this wonderful help to leave Egypt and all it stood for, behind us. This brings to mind the story of an Israeli grocery shop which had the following notice above the cash desk:

"We trust in Hashem, but everyone else must pay cash."

There are various questions: The *Sidra* begins with the statement that Hashem did not lead the people by way of the land of the Philistines because it was near.

1. What is the meaning of these words – **because it was near**?
2. Why did Moshe Rabbenu only ask for three days leave, surely we wanted to leave for good?
3. Why did the Torah emphasise that we left armed – – ?
4. Why were we told to turn back towards Egypt at one stage?
5. Why did Hashem request that we should take gold and silver out of Egypt? If He wanted us to have worldly treasures there are unlimited means open to Him.

---

1. Shabbat of Song.

To introduce the answers, I wish to share with you the following anecdote. A woman visited the Belzer Rebbe and asked him to pray for her so that Hashem should help her overcome a serious problem. He replied: "Have *Emunah*."[1] However she remonstrated "when I daven in the mornings I find in my siddur:

"ויושע ה' ... ויאמינו בה'"
"And Hashem saved... and they believed in Hashem."

If Hashem helps me then I will have faith." Said the Rebbe "No one ever got the better of me except this woman...."

There is a phenomenon in לשון הקדש,[2] which fascinates the students:

A word may mean both itself and its opposite: חסד for instance, means "Loving kindness and generosity," but it also means "depravity" a shameful thing, e.g., "The man shall take his sister חסד היא" (Lev. 20:17). קדש means "holy" but also defiled (Deut. 23:18) "there shall be no קדשה (harlot) of the daughters of Israel."

"והוצאתי אתכם מתחת סבלת מצרים"
"I shall take you out from under the burdens of the Egyptians" (Exod. 6:7).

סבלות means "oppressive burdens," yet the same word means "patience," the ability to **bear an oppressive burden**, סבלנות. In fact, this phenomenon occurs in English too. The expression "to suffer" means "to be in pain" but it also implies the ability to tolerate, "to bear pain patiently." The Sfat Emet (the Gerer Rebbe ז"ל) explains that Hashem promised to liberate us not only from the burden of Egypt but also to take us away from the <u>patience</u> with which we bore <u>the oppressive yoke</u> of slavery and spiritual depravity. Patience is a great virtue if used in the right circumstances, it can, however, be the opposite. The ability to get used to the base culture of Egypt was a sign of degraded and corrupt spirituality. When Hashem saw the Jewish people sinking in *Tumat Mitzraim*[3] that they had reached the abyss of *Sivlot Mitzraim* "that they no longer cared to seek freedom, then He intervened and saved them." Consequently, the verse "I shall take you out from under the burdens of Egypt" means two things – firstly, that we shall no longer remain under their yoke, and secondly, "you shall no longer suffer them" (spiritually).

---

1. Have faith.
2. The Holy Language.
3. The impurity of Egypt.

We find such paradoxes also in Hashem's direction of history, two opposites at one stroke. For example, Joseph accused his brothers, the sons of Leah, that they called the sons of the erstwhile maid-servants "slaves," so measure for measure, he was sold as a slave. He also accused them of immorality – so he was suspected of misdeeds with the wife of Potiphar. His punishment, however, served as a blessing at the same time. First a slave and later a prisoner, he ultimately reached the highest office. He achieved this with the help of Hashem, by correctly interpreting the dreams of his fellow prisoners, the butler and the baker as well as those of Pharaoh's. This led to him saving not only his own family but also millions of other people from starvation.

Here we have a similar paradox. Hashem decided to entice Pharaoh and his army to pursue us, so that eventually they should be drowned in the sea. At the same time **we** had to be persuaded to leave Egypt; after all, four fifths of our people wanted to remain and they were killed in the plague of darkness (Midrash Tanchuma Beshalach 1). Hashem did both these tasks simultaneously. He enticed Pharaoh to give chase, although he had suffered the ten plagues. All these measures helped to achieve this task. First of all, we did not go by the short route, and we turned back for a while to make him believe that we were lost in the desert. Moshe Rabbenu only asked for three days, so that when we did not return after three days it was an additional reason for Pharaoh to pursue us. We went armed so Pharaoh should decide that Hashem does not fight our battles anymore. However, Moshe Rabbenu said "ה' ילחם לכם ואתם תחרשון" – "The L-rd will fight for you and you shall hold your peace" (Exod. 14:14). Finally Hashem wanted us to take lots of gold and silver from Egypt, so that Pharaoh would not be able to hire other workers. All these schemes caused him to make a headlong dash to his destruction.

At the same time all these manipulations helped **US** to leave Egypt. First of all, we did not sever our ties in one stroke but gradually, so we did not take the short route **because it was near.** We also turned round towards Egypt in order not to burn our bridges completely. That is why we only went for three days at first. We also left Egypt armed to give us more self-confidence. In addition, the fact that we had gold and silver created more self-assurance. Incidentally, all this was needed to help us to leave "סבלת מצרים" – "the burdens of Egypt." For all these measures were to the Egyptians what our great Rabbis called "שוחד לשטן" – "bribes to Satan." For us it was "ישועת ה'" – "Salvation by Hashem."

This reminds me of the following story. A Rabbi used to borrow an amount of money before Shabbat and return it after Shabbat. When a friend enquired from him the reason for this strange conduct he replied: "It gives me more self-confidence...." My Rabbi, the famous Rabbi Dessler ז״ל used to say: "When confronted by Satan, the evil inclination, our strategy should not be to engage in direct confrontation but to use the tactics of <u>gradual</u> disengagement. A direct battle with the *Yetzer Horah* is compared to the action of a coiled spring which shows more resistance the more one presses down on it. One should try, with cunning and shrewdness, to make rings around the enemy, even if it may mean taking a longer route. There is no short cut to Judaism. Of course, we must have faith in Hashem, but we must follow the path which Hashem has mapped out for us to save us from the burdens of Egypt from depravity and assimilation." אמונה[1] alone is not sufficient but "ויושע ה'" – "Hashem saved us and the people believed."

This leads us to my concluding story. A person was trapped in a flood. The waters reached to his chin. A canoe came past, "Jump in." "Thank you very much – I have faith in Hashem." The water reached his mouth. A motorboat came past, "Jump in." "Thank you very much – I have faith in Hashem." The water reached his nose. A helicopter threw down a rope. "Grab it!" "Thank you very much but I have faith in Hashem." Eventually he drowned. When he came up to Heaven he complained to Hashem. "I had such a lot of faith in You, why did You not rescue me?" Hashem replied: "I <u>sent</u> you a canoe, I <u>sent</u> you a motor boat, I <u>sent</u> you a helicopter, what more did you expect Me to do?" Yes – Hashem stretches out His hand to stop us from drowning in the morass of alien cultures by means of His Torah and Mitzvot. We must not rely on faith alone but acknowledge and make use of His wonderful help. "ויושע ה'" – "Hashem saved us by giving us his Mitzvot and "ויאמינו בה'" – "And they believed in Hashem."

Let us actively grab the "outstretched Hand" of Hashem, his Torah, and mitzvot with great enthusiasm combined with "בטחון".[2] That is the correct way forward.

---

1. Belief.
2. Trust.

George Bernard Shaw was once asked: "What do you think of civilization?" He replied: "It is a very good idea – someone ought to start it."

We the Jewish people can be immensely proud of the fact that we <u>did</u> start REAL CIVILISATION by accepting the Ten Commandments which were given to us by Hashem at Mount Sinai. They are the greatest documents given at the most important event in human history. They were presented in a desert, not in any particular country, in front of millions of people (unlike other religions) and are universal and timeless.

The following questions need to be addressed:

1. We find that the עשרת הדברות[1] were already revealed to us in Mara **before** we reached Mount Sinai

"שם שם לו חק ומשפט ושם נסהו"

"There He made for them a Statute and a Law" (Exod. 15:25).

Explains the Gemara Sanhedrin 56b:

Israel were charged with ten precepts in Mara. Seven, the sons of Noach had already accepted (Gen. 9:1-7) and three more were added: Shabbat, honouring of parents, and *dinim*[2] (law and order). Why were they handed over to us **before** Sinai?

2. The famous question of Kuzari: Why does the first Commandment start with "I am the L-rd who brought you out of Egypt" and not "who created the world?"

3. On what system are the Ten Commandments built?

Before trying to solve these problems, a little anecdote may be in place: When the Shaagat Arie was appointed Rav of Metz, he insisted that the Ten Commandments be included in the constitution of the Congregation. When

---

1. The Ten Commandments.
2. Laws.

asked for the reason, he replied: "In the course of my experience I have found that the *Kehillah*[1] often regard their constitution as being more important than the עשרת הדברות. Therefore they must be included in the rules of the Kehillah."

A fundamental classification of the Divine constitution is that seven of the commandments apply to **all** mankind, while three are meant **only for us.** These are:

Only for us: 1. I am Hashem your G'd who brought you out of Egypt.
               2. Do not serve idols.
               3. Do not take the name of Hashem in vain.
Only for us: 4. Observe Shabbat.
Only for us: 5. Honour your Parents.
               6. Do not murder.
               7. Do not commit adultery.
               8. Do not steal.
               9. Do not bear false witness against your fellow man.
               10. Do not covet.

The seven which are meant for all human beings are the minimum requirements, so that the Law of the Jungle should not be the norm. Therefore, they are meant literally. The tenth one, not to covet, is meant to refer to the lowest standard of coveting, namely, to cut off the limb of a living animal in order to eat it because one is hungry.... All have a common denominator. **Don't** ! The three mitzvot, however, which are directed to the Jewish People only are **positive** commandments. Their common demoninator is twofold:

Firstly,
1. **Gratitude** to Hashem for looking after our nation (who brought us out of Egypt).
2. For creating the **world** (Shabbat).
3. And for creating **us** (honouring parents and Hashem, the third partner in our creation).

Secondly,
1. Our unique partnership with Hashem:
   Just as Hashem revealed His Divine trait of justice by saving us from

---

1. Congregation.

our oppressors, the Egyptians, whom Joseph had saved, so are we bidden to act likewise, and pursue justice and help to preserve the world which Hashem has created. The Rabbis say that anyone who dispenses true judgment becomes a partner with Hashem in the work of creation.

2. Emulate our Divine partner by working for six days and resting on Shabbat.

3. Honouring the three partners who created us, which obviously includes Hashem.

We can now answer the first question as to why the outline of the Ten Commandments in general, and our three special mitzvot in particular, were already given to us in Mara **before** the revelation on Har Sinai.

Rabbi Meir Shapiro ז״ל, the Rav of Lublin, explains:

The angels claimed the עשרת הדברות by invoking the law of בר מצרא (Bava Metzia 108a). If a plot of land is about to be sold, the owners of neighbouring plots have the right of first refusal. So the angels, being neighbours of Hashem in heaven, wanted to keep the Torah in Heaven. Partnership, however, rules out this preference and we are Hashem's partners. The three precise precepts which we received in Mara, which are meant only for us, are exactly the three special commandments of the ten which make us partners with Hashem.

1) **DINIM – Law and Order,** which we received in Mara tallies with "I brought you out of Egypt." I dealt justly so you are my ***partners*** to preserve the world by pursuit of justice.

2) **SHABBAT** – partners by emulating Hashem in working for six days and resting on Shabbat.

3) **HONOURING** parents and Hashem, the partners in our creation.

Thereby the problem is resolved: In order to receive the Ten Commandments on Sinai we had to become associates with Hashem **before** that great event. By accepting the seven mitzvot of the sons of Noach and our three special ones, we did indeed become partners with Hashem and were entitled to receive the complete עשרת הדברות on Mount Sinai.

This answers the question of the Kuzari, too:

The first commandment states that G-d had brought us out of Egypt, but does not mention that He had created the world. As we have discovered now, it is the first commandment of the three which only concerns us and not mankind in general. Therefore, if it would have stated "I have created the world," it would have applied to all mankind and not only to us!

This goes further. Two standards prevail in the עשרת הדברות: the minimum standards of the מצות which apply to the world in general, and the entire Ten Commandments, the headlines of all the 613 מצות (Rashi Exod. 24:12) which are for us and which mean much more to us than their literal translation.

Incidentally, 613, six plus one plus three equals ten.

For example, for us "do not murder" includes embarrassment of a person in public. "Do not steal" includes stealing someone's mind by pretending to intend to buy expensive articles which are completely out of the person's financial range, and so forth. "Do not covet" means for us not to be coveting someone else's Rolls Royce if one is "**only**" the owner of a Jaguar.

However, there is another division in the Ten Commandments as well. One tablet contains מצות between us and Hashem whilst the other tablet refers to commandments how to conduct ourselves towards others. They are intertwined with one another and form one unit. Let us see:

1. <u>I am Hashem</u> on the first tablet is paralleled by <u>Do not murder</u> on the second. A human being is created in the image of Hashem (Gen. 1:27).

2. <u>You must not have other G-ds</u>, on the first, relates to <u>Do not commit adultery</u>. Taking someone else's wife is similar to worshipping other gods.

3. <u>You must not take G-d's name in vain</u>, on one, <u>Do not steal</u> on the second. A thief will inevitably find himself taking a false oath as stated in Lev. 19:11-12. "Do not steal," "do not swear falsely." One leads to the other.

4. <u>Remember Shabbat</u> is coupled with <u>Do not bear false witness</u>. By observing Shabbat we give testimony that Hashem created the world. Do not bear <u>false</u> witness by profaning it.

5. <u>Honour father and mother</u> (and the third partner Hashem) is connected with <u>Do not covet</u>. By appreciating the goodness of one's parents, one will not desire someone else's property, because just as the parents want the best for their children, and give each one his or

her full share – so does the other partner, Hashem, allocate a share which is fitting for that person and for which he or she should be grateful.

We see that the two tablets form one single unit comprising both aspects between man and Hashem and between man and man in equal proportions and in equal importance. **One can not be a proper observant Jew by fulfilling just one side of the tablets.** לחת אבן[1] (Exod. 31:18) is written without a 'Vav' to point out that these two tablets are in reality only one (Rashi).

We have now answered the third question regarding the systems on which the עשרת הדברות are based.

Looking round today's world we find that often even the minimal seven of the ten commandments are being broken. Violence, muggings, bombings and terrorism. Our task is to cultivate our special relationship and partnership with Hashem by observing gratefully, sincerely and joyfully the עשרת הדברות with all their 613 מצות, both tablets, and to serve as an example and teacher to our fellow Jews, and even to the world around us, showing that our Torah is the only real comprehensive civilization.

---

1. Tablets of Stone.

CIVIL LAW

משפטים

"ואלה המשפטים אשר תשים לפניהם"

"And these are the ordinances that you shall set before them."

(Exod. 21:1)

Our Sidra deals predominantly with social and ethical laws including a great deal of civil and criminal legislation. They are based on the Ten Commandments of the previous *Sidra*, which are the headlines of all 613 *mitzvot* (Rashi at end of this sidra, 24:12). Just as the Ten Commandments contain laws between us and Hashem and social laws, so our *Sidra* contains such a mixture, too. Dietary laws are interspersed between the social laws (Exod. 22:30), Temple offerings (Exod. 22:28) and festivals (Exod. 23:12-17). All the ordinances derive their validity from Sinai. There is no distinction between them in their importance. That is why the passage immediately preceding the civil laws gives particulars of the altar in the Temple (Exod. 20:21-23). Rashi explains that the highest Court – the Sanhedrin – is located next to the Temple (Exod. 21:1). The Maharal of Prague observes that the reason for this is that the Temple and the Court of Law fulfill a similar purpose. The altar creates peace between Israel and their Father in Heaven, and implementation of the social statutes bring peace into the world.

This reminds me of the story of a Jew who applied some years ago to become a member of the Communist Party in Russia. The Commissar gave him a test and asked him: "If you were the owner of two houses, what would you do?" "One for the Party," was the immediate reply. "If you possessed two cars?" "One for the Party," "Two shirts?" The applicant hesitated. "Why do you take so long to answer this question? After all, you were ready to give a house and a car to the Party." "I have two shirts," was the answer.

There is a great difference between THEORY and PRACTICE. The Ten Commandments in last week's *Sidra* were HEADLINES, but our *Sidra* deals in detail with the PRACTICAL applications of the *mitzvot*.

The first of these functional precepts pertains to the laws concerning a Jewish slave. These do not apply at the present time since we have no more יובל – Jubilee years – every fiftieth year – when all Jewish slaves were set free, even those who extended their period of slavery beyond the six year minimum period on a voluntary basis. יובל is only operational when all the Jewish people reside in Israel (Gemara Erechin 32b).

Two questions present themselves:

1. What can we learn from this law for our times?
2. What is the central theme of all these 53 varied social and ritual laws?
3. Why is our acceptance of the Torah with the famous words נעשה ונשמע – "We shall do and we shall listen" (Exod. 24:7) mentioned in our *Sidra* and not in the previous one, which deals with the great event of the giving of the Ten Commandments?

Let us preface the answers to all these questions with the following anecdote:

A coach driver once asked his passenger, who happened to be the famous Baal Shem Tov – the founder of Chassidism – to watch out while he "takes" some hay for his horse from a field. When the driver approached the bundle of hay with his sickle, the Rebbe called out, "Someone is looking!" Quickly, the coach driver dashed back to the coach and looked around. To his surprise there was nobody in sight. He turned angrily to his passenger to complain. "<u>The Owner is looking</u>," exclaimed the Baal Shem Tov pointing heavenward.

It has been said that the thread on which the different qualities of human beings is strung is the fear of Heaven. When the fastening of that fear is loosened, the pearls roll in all directions and are lost one by one....

The case of the Jewish slave is the only deprivation of freedom in the Torah laws. There is no prison but only temporary custody mentioned in two specific cases: One is the blasphemer of Hashem's name (Lev. 24:10-23) and the other one is "the gatherer of wood on Shabbat" (Num. 15:32-36). Both were taken into custody until their sentence was declared, which happened to be – execution.

Theft is such a degrading sin that the thief is called a "Hebrew slave" and not an "Israelite slave." He is only sold as a slave by the Court of Law if he stole a large amount of money or goods which can only be recompensated by six years work. However, he is regarded as a member of the family that bought him. This is in stark contrast to the manner of the Romans who treated their slaves with extreme brutality.

Tosaphot in Gemara Kidushin (20a) states that if there is only one pillow in the house, it must be given to the slave. In case of prolonged illness the master must look after him for up to four years! This puts him into a far better position than that of a contemporary worker.

There are many advantages to the Torah's treatment of thieves, compared with the modern punishment of putting criminals into prison.

1. Prisons are very expensive institutions which have to be funded by the taxpayer.
2. Prisons do not improve the character of the offenders. On the contrary, they often have the opposite effect. They learn more efficient methods of burglary, for example, from one another.

   In contrast: the Jewish slave lives with a family and learns to **work** for his living.
3. Prisoners do not pay any compensation to their victims. In Torah law, however, the money that is raised from the sale of the thief goes to the victim.
4. Today the family of the prisoner has to suffer, but in Torah law the family of the slave is looked after by his master.
5. The Biblical slave gets a "golden handshake" הענקה at the end of six years to help him start life as a free person....

There is, however, a strange ceremony concerning the Jewish slave which requires study:

When a slave wishes to extend the six years of slavery, his ear is bored through with an awl to the doorpost. After that he serves until the Jubilee year (Exod. 21: 5-6). This happens to be the only physical punishment of an offender besides מלקות – flaggelation of 39 lashes – for certain offences. The Gemara Kiddushin (22b) – based on the Midrash that all Jewish souls were present at Mount Sinai when the Torah was given (Shemot Rabba 28:4) – explains that:

The ear heard at that time "Do not steal" but he did steal, and so it has to be pierced. It also heard "Be servants unto Me" (Hashem), but he acquired a human master and, therefore, that ear has to be punched through.

The question arises: If these are the reasons, why was his ear not pierced immediately after he was apprehended for his theft? The answer is very convincing: At that time he was punished enough by being sold as a slave against his will. Now the door is wide open for him to be free but he **voluntarily** remains a slave – tied to the door of his master's house. Therefore, his ear is pierced to that door as a strong and permanent reminder not to steal and not to be a servant to a human master, but only to Hashem.

There is however another question concerning the ear piercing:

Why was this not done as a punishment for other sins? Surely the ear also heard on Mount Sinai not to commit other offences, and yet he did transgress them?

Our גדולים[1] give the following answer:

The ear is a very important instrument. The Gemara Baba Kama (85b) says: If one has caused someone's slave to become deaf, one has to pay the owner the full value of the slave. A slave directs this precious equipment to listen to his human "Master's Voice" rather than to the voice of Hashem. As we say in the Shema "....if you will listen to My precepts...." Therefore, his ear has become blemished. From this it follows that a Cohen, who must not have any blemishes because he performs services in the Temple, cannot have his ear pierced.

Other sins, however, are in a different category. The sinner **did** use his ear to hear the commandments on Mount Sinai, but he did not **observe** the laws he heard there. Therefore, there is no point in boring his ear to the door.

The thief wrongfully made himself the master over other people's property. His standard has become very low indeed. Therefore, he has to work himself up to reach the seventh year (the number seven is a very important figure – see essay on Bereshit). If he is still not "cured" then he works himself up until the Jubilee year – parallel to the fiftieth day after the Exodus from Egypt when the Torah was given. Just as the sound of the *Shofar* on Mount Sinai proclaimed our freedom from the oppression of Egypt, so the *Shofar* on Yom Kippur of the Jubilee Year announces his freedom. Now he will truly return to his real master.

---

1. Great Rabbis.

This is the central theme of the whole *Sidra*. Do not make yourself master over other people's bodies. They belong to Hashem, who made them in His image; do not kidnap people, nor cause them injury or damage their property. Do not be a master over your debtor. "Do not act towards him as a creditor" (Exod. 22:24). The Talmud says: "A debtor is a slave to the creditor" (Gemara, Gittin 14a, based on Prov. 22:7).

There are many more examples in this *Sidra* of wrongful mastery over other people. Do not oppress a stranger (Exod. 23:9). Similarly, ritual laws. Observe Shabbat (Exod. 23:12) to acknowledge that **Hashem** is master of the universe. Observe Shemita – do not work on the fields in the seventh years to recognise that **Hashem** is the owner of the land of Israel. The Torah continues: If you realize who the real Master is and conduct yourself accordingly then "I (Hashem) shall send an angel to guard you... but take heed of him and **hearken to his voice**" (Exod. 23:20-21).

Now we understand why נעשה ונשמע[1] (Exod. 24:7) appears here and not in the previous *Sidra, Yitro*. The Torah wants to give us an example of using the precious instrument of hearing in the correct manner, namely, to listen to our real Master's voice, the voice of Hashem.

In contemporary life many people who regard themselves as free people are, in reality, slaves in various ways: a worker or a professional to his employer and a businessman to his customers. Many succumb to their evil inclination and its very effective enticements. Many use their hearing to listen to the command of human masters.

"Who is free? He who busies himself with the study of the Torah" (Avot 6:2).

The message of our *Sidra* is: Let us free ourselves from the bondage of our various masters and attune our ears and our minds to the voice of our real Master – Hashem. נעשה ונשמע[2] to the קול תורה[3] then we will really be free.

---

1. We shall do and we shall listen.
2. Let us do and let us listen.
3. The voice of the Torah.

THE TABERNACLE

A speech is always beneficial to the listeners. Either they are inspired, or they wake up refreshed....

I hope that my talk on the *Mishkan* will be classified under the first category.

Midrash Tanchuma (2) gives the *Mishkan* major importance. It says that the Sanctuary is as significant as the creation of the Universe. The Baal Haturim adds the following to this statement: In this *Sidra* ten items of the Mishkan begin with the word ועשית – and you shall make – according to the ten expressions with which Hashem created the world. It is indeed a prototype of the Universe.

The Gemara Shabbat (28a) explains the origin of the top skin cover of the Tabernacle, the עורות תחשים – "*Tachash* skins." They come from an animal which rejoices in the many colours of its skin.

Many ideas, many symbols, indeed many colours are contained in the portable *Mishkan* – all of them are eternal teachings for all generations. I shall confine my talk today to just a few of them. Two questions are appropriate:

1. The Midrash אליהו רבה (17) connects the famous נעשה ונשמע[1] (Exod. 24:7) acceptance of the Torah which is mentioned at the end of last week's *Sidra* with the building of the Tabernacle in our portion by saying: "In the merit of saying נעשה ונשמע we were given the *Mishkan*." What is the connection?
2. What are the lessons we can learn for our times from the details of the *Mishkan* and its appurtenances?

To answer these questions let us share the following anecdote:

A member of a small *Beth Hamedrash*[2] was shown around a magnificent, large "modern" Synagogue in pre-war Berlin. The proud warden of that

---

1. We shall do and we shall listen.
2. House of Study and Prayer.

beautiful edifice put particular emphasis on the exquisite, splendid Holy Ark with its many Torah's scrolls clothed in majestic silver ornaments. To the warden's great consternation the visitor was not at all impressed. When asked for his reasons, the guest told him the following story: Two sisters got married, one to a very wealthy husband, the other to a poor man and they lived in different towns. When they met, years later, the poor sister looked very happy whilst the rich one was sad. "Why are you so unhappy?" asked the poor sister. "Surely you have all the luxuries that life can offer?" She received a surprising reply. "My husband treats me like a piece of furniture. He decorates me with fashionable clothes to act as a hostess at his home and his parties, but he does not pay any attention to my opinions. Your husband may not have much money to give you, but he regards you like a queen. Every word you say is his command...."

"In your palatial synagogue the Scrolls of the Torah may have beautiful mantles and decorations, but your congregants do not take any notice of their Divine contents in their daily lives. They violate every precept. Only the lions on top of your ארון הקדש[1] keep the Ten Commandments! In our Beth Hamedrash the Sifrei Torah may not have silver ornaments but their Divine teachings are being practised, studied and honoured very diligently by our members every single day. Judge for yourself: is the Torah not much happier in these simple surroundings?"

To answer the first problem regarding the connection between נעשה ונשמע and the Temple: Looking at the construction of the *Mishkan*, it occurred to me that it is built exactly on the principles of "we shall do and we shall listen." It is divided into two parts: Holy and Holiest of Holies, divided by a curtain. In the holy part there were three items of "furniture."

> **A Golden Menorah** (Candelabra) consisting of a middle shaft plus three branches on either side made from one piece of pure gold.
> **A Golden Table** with twelve showbreads, and
> **A Golden Altar** on which incense was burnt.

All these three pieces required נעשה – *Action*.

The *Menorah* required the action of replacing the oil and lighting it. The

---

1. Holy Ark.

actions required for the *Table* was to bake the showbread and the incense had to be made and burnt on the *Altar*.

The קדש קדשים – **Holiest of Holies** contained the Holy Ark with its tablets of the Ten Commandments covered with a golden cover and golden Cherubim – angelic golden figures which looked like a young man and a young lady joined together in marriage (Tractate Yuma 54a).

"I shall speak to you from above the Ark cover, from between the two Cherubim, all the things which I will command you the Children of Israel." (Exod. 25:22) Here we have נשמע – *Listening* to the voice of Hashem.

We now have a very convincing answer to our problem:

As a reward for our implicit trust in Hashem, by first accepting נעשה – to *practise* the Torah, and only afterwards נשמע, to listen, and expound its laws, to study and research them, we received the Sanctuary – נעשה and נשמע – doing and listening. נעשה the Holy part and נשמע the Holiest of Holies in a *concrete* form. There we can **practise** נעשה ונשמע.

If we go a little deeper into this subject we will discover that the three items in the Holy Part of the Tabernacle are the symbols of the three Pillars on which the world stands (Avot 1:2). על התורה ועל העבודה ועל גמילות חסדים.

The Golden Candlestick symbolises *active* performance of the *Mitzvot of our Torah*.

מצות מעשיות, the light which *Mitzvot* give, the light of the **Torah**.

The Golden Altar represents עבודה – *Service* to G-d by offering incense.

The Golden Table teaches us גמילות חסדים – *kindness* to people – by providing the כהנים[1] with showbread.

The Holiest of Holies part, however, is the symbol of the study of the Torah, listening to the words of Hashem and absorbing them by study. לימוד תורה[2] is the greatest of all (Mishna Peah 1:1).

Active performance of Mitzvot is **holy**, but **study** of **Torah** is **Holiest of Holies!**

There are still many more lessons to be learned from the pieces of "furniture" in the Mishkan. We can only discuss a few in this talk. Let us take the individual appurtenances:

The Golden Menorah: It was constructed from *one* piece of gold. It lights up

---

1. Priests.
2. The study of the Torah.

the material aspect of life symbolised by the Golden Table. It gives it the spirituality of our holy Torah. The shaft represents the written Torah and the six branches represent the oral Torah. The wicks of the six branches are pointing to the middle one. The Oral Law illuminates and explains the Written one. No foreign matter must be introduced into our Torah. It is **_pure_** gold. The Written and Oral Torah are one unit.

The Golden Altar: The odour of the incense rises up and joins the heavenly Pillar of Cloud protecting the Tent of Meeting. In our time, **_prayers_** take the place of incense and sacrifices. They are like יעקב's ladder going up to heaven and Hashem standing by him promising to protect him. So our prayers, if they are sincere, go up to heaven and help to provide us with the protection of heavenly "pillars of cloud."

The Golden Table: 12 showbreads were sufficient for all the כהנים[1] who were doing the service in the Temple. When one does one's best, Hashem will augment it.

"כל הבא לטהר מסייעין אותו"

"Whoever wants to purify himself, Hashem will help him" (Shabbat 104a).

This reminds me of the story of a wealthy man who gave a lot of money to charity. The more he donated, the wealthier he became. When people asked him "how does this come about?" he replied: "I shovel out and Hashem shovels in – Hashem's shovel is much bigger than mine...."

The Holy Ark: This consisted of three boxes which fitted into one another. The outer and inner ones were made of pure gold, whilst the middle one was made of wood from the cedar tree which יעקב – our forefather – planted in Israel. It is a model of balance, honesty and integrity. If it had been just one Ark of pure gold, people would identify the Torah with wealth, therefore, wood was put inside. Gold is permanent but not alive, whereas wood is a "tree of life for those who grasp it" (Prov. 3:18). Gilded would not do because it would create a false impression, therefore, two boxes were made from pure gold.

    The Holy Ark had two poles which shall "not be removed from it." The Torah must be carried from generation to generation and who are the carriers? Our youth, symbolised by the two Cherubim. It is noteworthy to mention that the

---

1. Priests.

voice of Hashem did not come from the Golden Table, Menorah or the Golden Ark, but it was heard coming from between the two Cherubim. It came from our youth who are our future (Dayan Swift ז"ל).

The Cherubim were made from one piece of gold, together with the lid of the Holy Ark and its Ten Commandments. One looked like a young lady and one looked like a young man. This proves conclusively the Torah teaching that men and women when they are married are **one** piece of pure gold – both are equally important but have different tasks. We have "women's liberation" since Sinai and even before that time. Men and women should, however, protect the Torah with their golden wings and be attached to the Holy Ark.

Finally, the *Mishkan* is a prototype of the Jewish Home. It is well known that in the tent of שרה and later in the tent of רבקה three miracles occurred (Rashi Gen. 24:67).

"A lamp burned from one Shabbat Eve to the next, the dough was blessed and a Divine Cloud overhung the tent" (Bereshit Rabba 60:16).

The Ramban points out that the very same miracles also happened in the Sanctuary. The seven lamps of the Golden Menorah contained the same input of oil. Yet, the "Western light," which was the nearest to the Holiest of Holies, carried on burning until the next evening, whilst the others had gone out in the morning. One could relight the others from the western light in the evening. That is why we have a נר תמיד[1] in our synagogues. The twelve showbreads were blessed. There were enough for all the priests serving on Shabbat in the Temple. The *Mishkan* was also protected by a Heavenly Pillar of Cloud. All these treasures inside the *Mishkan* were covered over with skins like a tent, which is a symbol of modesty.

A Jewish home should model itself on the Temple, and so, of course, should synagogues, which are the small Temples of our times. It is not sufficient to put a lot of silver on the Torah Scrolls, although it is commendable to make them look beautiful, but it is much more important to **act** according to their precepts and to study both the Written and Oral Laws thoroughly. Learning Torah is the Holiest of Holies – "We shall listen and learn." In addition, we require the holy part of the Mishkan, consisting of three pillars: Torah, service to G-d and service to the people, both in our everyday lives and in our homes.

---

1. An everlasting light.

We should use the model of the three boxes of the Holy Ark to practise honesty and integrity in our lives. We should also think of the Cherubim and protect the Torah in our homes, men and women in equal measure. All this has to be done with modesty, then we can hope and pray that our lives will be blessed with all three blessings of the tents of שרה and רבקה.

כפה – HEAD COVERING

"ועשית בגדי קדש לאהרן אחיך לכבוד ולתפארת"

"And you shall make holy garments for Aharon your brother, for splendour and for beauty" (Exod. 28:2).

Our *Sidra* is dealing to a great extent with the special clothing which the כהנים[1] and the כהן גדול[2] had to wear when they were doing the service in the משכן.[3] My subject today, however, is an item of clothing which **every male** has to wear all the time, namely, the Kippa.[4] This is a most respected tradition of ours. Any deliberate deviation is an insult and disloyalty to our Jewish way of life, and an adoption of secular modes of conduct!

The question we must ask is: What is this wearing of a כפה all about? Is it a דין – a law of the Torah or from the Rabbis? Is it a מנהג[5] or merely מידות חסידות – a voluntary practice which is worthy but not obligatory?

To introduce the answer, a charming anecdote is in place. A Jewish American tourist entered the Mea Shearim district of Jerusalem to take some photographs. Suddenly a little chassidic boy challenged *"Wu is dein Yarmulke?"* "Where is your Kippa?" The tourist realised that he had committed the ultimate faux pas by not covering his head in this very orthodox district. He was stunned for a moment. Suddenly, looking up at the sky he found the answer. "The heaven is my Kippa." Not to be outsmarted, the little boy looked up at the sky, stared for a moment at the tourist's bare head then retorted: *"Dos is zu grois a Yarmulke far so a klein keppele."* "This is too big a Yarmulke for such a small head."

Yes, it is sad that this duty to wear a כפה is often not observed. The caption

---

1. Priests.
2. The High Priest.
3. The Tabernacle.
4. The Yarmulke.
5. Custom.

under a photograph of the Pope meeting the Israeli Prime Minister speaks volumes: "The one with the כפה is the Pope...."

Now to answer the question on what do we base this tradition of head covering? To arrive at an answer, let us consider the significance of clothing in general. The origin of human dress is related to us at the beginning of human history in the Torah. After their sin, Adam and Eve discovered that they needed clothing.

The question is:

1. What connection is there between sin and clothing?
2. It is recorded in the Torah (Gen. 3:21) that "Hashem made garments of skin and He clothed them." Why did Hashem give them newly made clothes and nothing else? No furniture, no housing, no ready baked bread, etc.?

Rabbi S. R. Hirsch ז"ל gives the following remarkable explanation:

Man's unique position in nature is בחירה.[1] All other natural forms, such as planets, plants, and animals, do not have this distinction. They can do nothing but carry out the will of Hashem. Unlike the rest of creation, men and women consist of גוף[2] and נשמה,[3] either of which could dominate them. At first, they did follow the dictates of the Soul. Their body was a source of pride to them "ולא יתבששו" (Gen. 2:26) "they were not ashamed of being naked." There was nothing to hide. However, the bodily desires became dominant and they sinned. They realised their failure to be superior to the rest of creation, and they felt a sense of contrition. They were ashamed that their desirous body triumphed and that they were now **_below_** the rest of creation. They became aware that they alone acted **_against_** the will of their Creator. All other beings in nature do carry out G-d's will. This shame, however, now became the means of their elevation "כל הבא לטהר מסייעין אותו" (Shabbat 104a). "Anyone who wishes to purify himself, Hashem will help him." Hashem helped them rise again above the rest of nature by **_covering_** their bodies. Therefore, **_He, Himself_** gave them ready made skins to put on. Nothing else was given ready made! They had to build their own houses, construct their own furniture and bake their own bread. Consequently, clothing is a positive **_declaration_** that man is **_higher_** than the rest

1. Free choice.
2. Body.
3. Soul.

of creation. It is a sign of distinction and a symbol that man controls his bodily desires and is indeed a consecration of mankind.

We find other coverings, too, in the Torah:

תפילין, which men wear at the morning service are also signs and symbols of distinction. They control and guard our intellect, they direct our hearts and our hands to the service of Hashem and to guide us on the right path.

So are ציצית, our uniform as soldiers in the army of Hashem. They are also signs of distinction of a higher kind than ordinary clothing.

Similarly, the clothing of the כהנים was worn "לכבוד ולתפארת" (Exod. 28:2) – "For Honour and for Glory."

An ordinary כהן[1] wore four items of clothing:

Trousers, tunic, girdle and a mitre (a kind of head covering). All these were essential coverings for Service to Hashem.

The High Priest wore another four items:

An Ephod (kind of pinafore), a robe, a breastplate with twelve precious stones (to symbolize the twelve tribes) and a head-plate of gold on his forehead which was engraved with the words "Holy to the L-rd" (Exod. 28:36). All these symbols gave him further distinction above the others and a sense of responsibility for the Jewish People, by wearing the names of the twelve tribes on his breast-plate and on his shoulders.

This brings us to a better understanding of the tradition to wear a כפה.

Just like clothing, which covers the nakedness of the human body in a spiritual sense, the head-cover expresses the realisation that the intellect must be covered and controlled. It can be a source of evil if it is not covered with a symbol that the Divine Presence is above us and bids us to use the brain for good purposes. Bare-headedness symbolises misguided free thinking. We cover our heads to show that there is something higher than our limited intelligence. The Gemara in Kidushin (31a) tells us that Rav Hunna did not walk four cubits without a head covering because he said "the Divine Presence is above my head."

The Gemara in Shabbat (156b) narrates a story about the mother of Rabbi Nachman. Astrologers had told her, "Your son will be a thief." So she would not let him go without a head covering. She said, "Cover your head in order that you

---

1. Priest.

shall have fear of Hashem." We see that the כפה has a role similar to that of תפילין.

We can now solve the problem we set. Is כפה a דין[1] or is it a מנהג[2] or a worthy voluntary practice.

In Gemara Brachot (60b) it is stated:

When a person puts on a head-cover he should say the Bracha

"עוטר ישראל בתפארה"
"Who crowns Israel with glory."

In the *Shulchan Aruch* by Rabbi Joseph Caro (25:3) it says:

The Rosh (a famous Rabbi) used to put on Tefillin and say this blessing. We do not do that. However, some people tap their Tefillin when reciting this blessing (Mishna Brurah). We see that both תפילין and כפה are crowns of Israel. This also proves that covering the head is a דין[3] and not a מנהג.[4] It requires a blessing just like any other Mitzvah.

The *Mishna Brurah* (written by the renowned Rabbi Yisrael Meir Hacohen ז"ל, the Chofetz Chaim) remarks that of all the fifteen blessings which we say in the morning, only two mention Israel.

"אוזר ישראל בגבורה" "who girdles Israel with might" (referring to the belt separating the top and bottom part of the body for prayers) and "עוטר ישראל בתפארה" "who crowns Israel with glory." (In order that we realise that there is a Divine Presence above us.) All the other *Brachot* refer mainly to ALL mankind, such as "He who clothes the naked" or "He who raises up those who are bowed down" etc.

The Tas in *Shulchan Aruch* (Chapter 8, small paragraph 3) goes further, by deciding that in our time it is **_forbidden_** by the **_Laws of Torah_** to walk about bare-headed. It comes under the prohibition

"ולא תלכו בחקת הגוי אשר אני משלח מפניכם"
"Do not walk in the traditions of the nations that I expelled from before you" (Lev. 20:23).

---

1. A law.
2. A custom.
3. A law.
4. A custom.

Non-Jews use bare-headedness as their mode of worship. It was introduced to change from the Jewish practice of having the head covered.

The accepted דין[1] in the *Shulchan Aruch* (2:6) is that one may not walk four cubits without any head covering. Less than four cubits it is voluntary – מידות חסידות – a voluntary, worthy practice to wear the כפה.

According to the Tas, however, it is forbidden by the laws of the Torah to walk even less than four cubits bareheaded.

Finally, how big must a כפה be? Rabbi Shlomo Kluger ז"ל says: "It must cover the whole head," but Rabbi Moshe Feinstein ז"ל decided that even if one part is covered, it is sufficient. He proves it from the law that in an emergency situation, if one has no כפה, and one wants to daven – someone else can put his hand on the person's head and then he can daven. Surely one hand cannot cover a whole head! (even a *"klein keppele"*)

In contemporary times it is often the **_lack_** of material that makes a lady's dress so expensive. At some functions it appears as if one has returned to the good old days of Adam and Eve before the sin, in the Garden of Eden. Dignity, modesty and morality are a lost art. ציצית, תפילין and כפה are being honoured in the breach rather than by fulfillment. Yes! Our head is very small in comparison with the greatness of Hashem. Our task is not to swim with the current of our surroundings, but to realise at all times that

"שכינה למעלה מראשנו"
"The Divine Presence is above our heads."

We must strive to restore modesty in general and our special symbols of distinction in particular, to their rightful and honoured place.

"כי עם קדוש אתה של אלקיך"
"Because you are a Holy People to Hashem your G-d" (Deut. 7:6).

---

1. Law.

כי תשא   THE GOLDEN CALF – עגל הזהב

The Portion of כי תשא contains the most puzzling episode of our history. Only forty days after accepting the Ten Commandments, some of the Jewish people danced round the golden calf, just because Moshe Rabbenu was delayed in his return from Mount Sinai, according to their reckoning. Worship of the golden calf was a popular form of ritual at that time, which was imported from Egypt by the mixed multitude – the *Erev Rav* – who joined us at the Exodus. In Egypt they used to worship sheep, but here they substitued a calf for a sheep. This caused Moshe to break the precious tablets. The three thousand dancers were killed by the לוים[1] and the golden calf was destroyed by Moshe Rabbenu.

Before dealing with a number of problems concerning this narrative, I would like to share with you the following relevant anecdote:

Reb Shmelke, who was a very observant Jew, had attended synagogue and Shiurim[2] every day for twenty years, decided to make a break "for a change." His *Yetzer Horah*[3] succeeded in making a chink in his armour. Just three days in Las Vegas for a little gambling spree – after all what are three days compared with twenty years? So he dressed in Bermuda shorts, flowered T-shirt, Stetson hat and dark sunglasses and flew off to Las Vegas. Upon his arrival he hailed a taxi, but he stumbled and broke an arm, a leg and a few ribs.

While he was in hospital he lamented to G-d: "Oh why should this have happened to me after twenty years? You didn't even give me a chance to get started." A heavenly voice rang out, "Schmelke, is that you? We didn't recognise you...!"

Four questions present themselves:

    1.   G-d already told Moshe Rabbenu on Mount Sinai that the People had

---

1. Levites.
2. Lectures.
3. Evil inclination.

made a golden calf (Exod. 32:7-10). If so, why did Moshe not leave the tablets there instead of bringing them down and breaking them?

2.   How could Moshe have broken the most holy object in the world and get a *Yasher Koach*[1] for it? (Gemara Shabbat 87a).

3.   The tablets were divided: five Commandments towards Hashem and the other five towards people. Why did he break both tablets? He should only have broken the first tablet, which contained the law "you shall not make for yourself a graven image."

4.   Finally, what message can we take away from this event for our times? Surely we do not dance around a golden calf today!

To introduce the answers to these questions I would like to narrate a remarkable story from the Kalisher Rebbe:

A prominent Jewish businessman told the Rebbe that he was about to complete an important business deal but in order to clinch it, it was necessary to engage in some sharp practices. Not outright thievery, just some shady dealings. The Rebbe was appalled and pointed out that it says in the Torah,

"כתבים משני עבריהם"

"The letters were engraved through and through" (Exod. 32:15).

Since that was the case, the final *Mem* and the *Samech* could only exist by miracle – they had nothing to hold them in place (Gemara Shabbat 104a). There was another miracle on these tablets, namely, that the writing could be read on both sides. Therefore, continued the Kalisher Rebbe "whichever way you turned the tablets, לא תגנב[2] stares you in the face. Even if you do not commit an overt act of stealing, you must not violate the spirit of the Commandment."

Now to answer our question. Rabbi Zalman Sorotzkin ז"ל says:

Moshe Rabbenu did not leave the Tablets in heaven but took them down because he hoped that their divine authority would be recognised by their wondrous nature. As the verse (Exod. 32:16) says

"והלחת מעשה אלקים המה"

"The Tablets were Heavenly work."

However, over three thousand people continued dancing even after seeing the

---

1. A thank you.
2. You shall not steal.

tablets. That was when Moshe Rabbenu decided that they were beyond hope. But what about the millions of bystanders who watched them dancing? These were dithering whether to join in or not. They probably thought that the "modern" Egyptian way of service could be combined with the Torah. Therefore, Moshe had to take drastic action to remedy this explosive situation. Speeches would be useless. There was only one possible option: Shock treatment! He broke the heavenly Tablets, thereby, proclaiming forcefully: Torah **cannot** be combined with the golden calf!

Torah is pure, through and through, written on both sides! That saved the Jewish people and therefore ״יישר כחך ששברת״ – "Thank you for breaking them."

This leads us on to the next question: Why did he break **both** tablets?

After all, they had only sinned against G-d, not against other people? The answer is very convincing: As demonstrated in the talk on the Ten Commandments, in the *Sidra* יתרו: For us, the Jewish People, the five commandments between us and G-d and the five between man and man form an inseparable unit – breaking one is breaking all of them.

Similarly, in the Haftarah we find Eliyahu the Prophet confronting eight hundred and fifty idolatrous priests on Mount Carmel. There too, the people were dithering and Eliyahu told them: "How long will you loiter between two opinions?" Drastic action was called for there, just like it was here, so he challenged them to make a fire come down from heaven to consume their sacrifices. Eliyahu also prepared one. Fire came down on his, but not on theirs. Then they all exclaimed "Hashem is G-d" (Kings I 18:20-39).

This brings me to the final question. Surely we do not dance around the golden calf nowadays? But don't we? Many dance around the **modern** golden calf in the form of money, power or honour. Others "dance" to the tune of *Wissenschaft* – Bible Criticism – thus putting human clothing on our Torah. What a travesty! In Sanhedrin (99:a) the Gemara states:

״ואפילו אומר כל התורה כולה מן השמים חוץ מפסוק אחד הוא דבר ה׳
בזה אין לו חלק לעולם הבא״

"Even if someone says that the whole Torah is from heaven except
one verse, he has despised the word of Hashem and has no portion
in the world to come."

The eighth of our Thirteen Principles of Faith is that the Torah was given to

משה רבינו in its entirety. We need no proof. It is however, interesting to note how so many predictions in the Torah have come true. We can now look back three thousand three hundred years and ***What do we see?***

For example, the destruction of the first Temple and seventy years of exile in the *Sidra* בחקתי. The destruction of the second Temple and the exile following it, even the Holocaust, in כי תבא, as well as the repossession of Israel after the dispersion throughout the whole world, in נצבים. No human being could possibly have made such predictions. And there are many more, the details of which we shall discuss in the talk on the *Sidra* כי תבא. What about the archaeological discoveries which tally exactly with the Torah account? For example, the Flood which was discovered only recently by the famous archaeologist Sir Wooley. He found traces of marine life in many places far from the sea, in Iran. They were buried deep in the ground.

What about so many Mitzvot which have come to be admired by mankind as a whole with the advance of science. Circumcision, Shabbat, the Jewish marriage laws and laws of morality, to name but a few. The last two are being seen as the only way to combat the modern plague of AIDS. The recent discoveries by computers of secret codes permeate the ***whole*** Torah. They could not have been invented by different authors.

The letters of אמת[1] have two legs to stand on. It stands firm whilst the letters of שקר[2] have only one leg and cannot endure (Gemara Shabbat 104a). Our wonderful תורה הקדשה is תורת אמת.[3] It cannot, by way of analogy, be dressed up in any human clothes, with imaginary modern Stetson hats, and coloured T-shirts and the like, nor can it be combined with any kind of golden calf, such as illegal profit-making schemes or introducing into it so called "human inspiration" or false Bible criticism. All these would make the Torah unrecognisable. Torah is pure and is מן השמים – heavenly through and through.

It is "written on both sides" (Exod. 32:15).

"אשרנו מה טוב חלקנו"

"Happy are we, how good is our portion," and we are its proud adherents.

---

1. Truth.
2. Lie.
3. Torah of Truth.

THE CHERUBIM

"ויעש שני כרבים זהב"

"And he made two gold Cherubim."   *(Exod. 37:7-9)*

This week's *Sidra* deals mainly with the actual construction of the משכן[1] in the desert.

I shall confine myself to just one item of all the articles mentioned, namely, the most mysterious one, the Cherubim. They were angel like figures, looking like a young male and a young female (Gemara Yuma 54a), made from one piece of gold together with the lid covering the Holy Ark which contained the Ten Commandments in the Holiest part of the משכן.[2]

Let us deal today with one question of the Lutzker Rav, Rabbi Zalman Sorotzkin ז"ל. Why were the Cherubim placed here in the Holiest of Holies, whilst similar Cherubim were put outside the Garden of Eden, after the expulsion of Adam and Eve to "guard the Tree of Life" (Gen. 3:24)? According to Rashi, they were in fact מלאכי חבלה – Angels of Destruction.

Before quoting his answer I would like to share with you the following anecdote:

Three grandmothers were sitting on a bench in Hyde Park discussing their grandchildren. One said proudly:

"My grandson is only twenty-six years old and he is already the Director of a Public Company." The second one boasted, "My grandson is only twenty-two years old and he is already on the Board of a West End Firm." The third one said: "My grandson is only sixteen years old and he is already helping the police with their enquiries...."

Rabbi Sorotzkin ז"ל gives the following answer: "If our young people are

---

1. Tabernacle.
2. Tabernacle.

connected with Torah observance and cover the Holy Ark and the Ten Commandments with their wings and if their faces are directed towards one another – denoting unity in their service to Hashem, then they are truly the Holiest of the Holy. However, if they are not connected with the Torah (Heaven forbid), then they are potential מלאכי חבלה – now more commonly known as "Hell's Angels," which we sadly see all around us. They are the ones who might eventually have to help the police with their enquiries. Not only might they become vandals and destroy other people's property and even lives, but their empty lifestyles might bring about their own destruction, through confinement in prison or through drugs and AIDS, the modern plague.

However, they could be and *should* be our most precious asset – our קדש קדשים[1] provided they receive a Torah education past their Bar and Bat Mitzvah age. They should not only study for a higher level secular qualification, but more importantly, for a higher level of Torah education, leading up to Yeshiva and Seminary. If not, then they will become giants in secular wisdom but remain dwarfs in Jewish knowledge and culture.

I would like to illustrate this point with the following charming anecdote:

A father was always troubled by his little boy after returning tired from work. He hit upon the idea of taking out a page from a magazine containing a map of the world and cutting it into small pieces to form a jigsaw puzzle. He had counted on at least an hour or two of peace and quiet. Ten minutes later the little boy came back with the completed puzzle. "How did you do it so quickly?" asked the father. His little son replied:

"Daddy, I discovered that the back of that page consisted of the picture of a young person. That was easy to put together."

Once youth is put together and educated in the Torah way, the Jewish world falls into place....

There are other important teachings emanating from the Cherubim. The Cherubim had youthful faces but mature bodies. Every Jew should be young in spirit. There is so much Torah to learn and so many Mitzvot to perform – it is not age that matters but attitude.

Finally, the construction of the Cherubim teaches us the Torah guidelines concerning the problem of equality between men and women. This problem is *needlessly* agitating the Jewish press and public at the present time. The young

---

1. The Holiest of Holies.

man and young lady figures of the Cherubim are made of one piece of pure gold together with the lid covering the Holy Ark. Does this not clearly indicate that our תורה הקדשה[1] regards married men and women as equal partners? One piece of pure gold! No problem of women's lib! Our women have always enjoyed equality. However, *Vive La Difference!* Men and women have different tasks in life, which are equally important. They should keep to the different duties and Mitzvot given by Hashem and interpreted by the great Rabbis and not mix them up.

The message of the כרבים therefore is as follows:

Both men and women, the young and the young in spirit, should protect our Torah by adhering to its way of life firmly through intensive study and observance and by harmony with one another, each helping the other in his or her own special way. Spiritually and materially, each can make individual contributions to put together the fragmented Jewish world. That places one's life in the קדש קדשים.[2]

---

1. Holy Torah.
2. The Holiest of Holies.

ACCOUNTS PRESENTED BY MOSHE RABBENU

There are a number of problems contained in our *Sidra*. It is appropriate to introduce them by way of the following charming anecdote:

The Head of a Primary School put the following notice up on the wall of his office:

"If you will not believe all your child tells you about us, we will not believe all your child tells us about you...."

Our *Sidra* seems to suggest that the Jewish people did not believe משה רבינו, so he had to give an exact account of what he did with the donations for the משכן, although the Torah says, "in My entire house, he is the trusted one" (Num 12:7) and "Never again has there arisen in Israel a prophet like Moshe" (Deut. 34:10).

Furthermore, in the Gemara (Ta'anit 8b) it states, "A blessing is only found in something which is hidden from the eye" – not by displaying wealth to the public gaze.

Another question arises: Why were no accounts demanded and given for the gold used for the golden calf?

The answers are as follows:

עין הרע – the evil eye is not a mystical concept but has its rational side, too... A person who flaunts his wealth becomes an object of envy. This can cause enmity between the "haves" and the "have-nots." It might result in vandalism, theft and even violence. However, this only applies to **personal** wealth. That is what the Gemara refers to when it says: "Blessing comes only in something which is hidden," but accounting of **communal** wealth is a completely different matter. Everyone benefits from it, even the "have-nots." Therefore, accounts of the משכן are matters of **sharing** by the public. Instead of envy there is appreciation, because here the blessing lies in the accounting of the donation

(Rabbi Bulka שליט״א). This explains why there should be accounting for public wealth.

However, why could this not have been left out in this case, as משה רבינו showed right at the beginning of his leadership that "Not a donkey of theirs did I take" (Num. 16:15). To go from Midian to Egypt he did not even deduct traveling expenses (Rashi).

Furthermore, while the rest of the Jewish people were busy taking "vessels of gold and silver" out of Egypt by command of Hashem, Moshe Rabbenu took the bones of Yoseph (Exod. 13:19).

Rabbi Sorotzkin ז״ל, by solving the third problem – why were no accounts given at the golden calf? – answers this question, too. He quotes the famous רמב״ם's statement concerning a husband who refuses to grant a divorce to his wife. The Beth Din forces him until he says "I want to" (Laws of Divorces 2:20). There the רמב״ם asks: "Surely a GET (divorce document) must be given only with the full consent of the husband? It cannot be forced. He answers: A Jewish person does want to do the right thing in his innermost heart, but outside influences, fueled by evil inclination, try to stop him; therefore, the Court forces him until his real will comes to the surface."

Here we have a similar case: A Jew wants his money to be used for Holy objects and not for a golden calf. Outside influences make him give money for the calf against his better judgement. If this donation does not reach its destination, but goes into the pocket of the collector, so be it. But a person who donates for the building of the משכן wants _all_ his donation to be used for that purpose, not for expenses, etc. That is why משה רבינו had to reassure them that _all_ their gold was used for the Holy Building. No suspicion was implied by this of any misappropriation of the donated gold and silver.

This reminds me of the story of a Rabbi who collected funds for a Yeshivah. When the wealthy would-be donor saw that the fund-raiser came by coach and horses, he refused to give anything, saying: "I do not want to pay for your transport." The collector replied: "The money of those who donate with a full heart goes to the Yeshivah, whilst the funds of people who only give because they are pressed for a donation, goes to pay for the necessary transport." משה רבינו did not take off any expenses from his collection.

The Midrash, however, views this matter in a different light. It says: Scoffers mocked משה רבינו, saying:

"How fat is the neck of the son of Amram. One who is in charge of the work of building the משכן should not become rich." Overhearing this arrogant remark, משה רבינו said, "I shall give an account of every donation" (Midrash Shemot Rabba 51:4).

Rabbi Joseph Salanter remarks in his work, Be'er Yoseph, what made them suspect Moshe Rabbenu and what triggered this scoffing? As we mentioned before, משה רבינו did not take any silver or gold out of Egypt. He only took the bones of Yoseph. Therefore, the mockers wondered how משה רבינו became rich straight after the start of the erection of the משכן. In Nedarim (38a), the Gemara states that Hashem rewarded משה רבינו with the residue of the broken tablets. It would not have been right for all the ordinary people to become rich and for משה רבינו to remain poor (Midrash Shemot Rabba 46:2). Therefore, straight after Hashem commanded, "Carve for yourself two tablets of stone" (Exod. 34:1) some people noticed that משה רבינו appeared wealthy. They concluded that it must have been from the funds of the משכן. However, in reality, it was generated by some pieces of the broken tablets. We can see from this, how strong ridicule can be. The sin of taking anything belonging to the Tabernacle is very serious indeed. The Gemara Sanhedrin (81b) states: "He who steals a vessel of service belonging to the משכן, may be killed by zealous people on the spot. Just as a person who is intimate with a non Jew may be executed immediately." (Which is what Pinchas actually did.)

We see the enormous power of scoffing at the beginning of the *Sidra* תולדת (Gen. 25:19). There the Torah emphasises that אברהם is the father of יצחק by stating this fact twice in the same verse. Rashi explains: The reason is that the mockers of that generation said that Avimelech, the King of Geror, was the father of יצחק. After all, שרה was married to אברהם for many years and they had no children. Yet, after having been taken to the palace of Avimelech, she became pregnant with יצחק. This was an extremely serious accusation that could only have been rebuffed by Hashem Himself. Hashem made יצחק's features so undeniably similar to אברהם's that even the scoffers had to admit that יצחק was אברהם's son (Rashi Gen. 25:19). Here too, the ליצנות[1] had to be nipped in the bud by משה רבינו's accurate accounts.

Consequently, the messages of our *Sidra* are as follows:

A) Private wealth must not be flaunted but kept "hidden from the eye."

---

1. Mockery.

B) One tenth of it should be used to support Torah institutions and poor people with a full heart; then the donations will reach those for whom it is meant and not used for expenses.

C) Public money should be accounted for to defeat the mockers. The maxim should be: "You shall be vindicated from Hashem and from Israel" (Num. 32:22). That applies to all our actions in life.

May we merit to deal with all our problems in that manner, then Hashem will give us His blessing.

VAYIKRA

HUMAN DIGNITY

"וסמך ידו על ראש השעיר ושחט אתו במקום אשר ישחט את העלה
לפני ה' חטאת הוא"

"He shall lean his hand on the head of the goat and he shall slaughter it in the place he would slaughter the elevation offering before Hashem, it is a sin offering." *(Lev. 4:24)*

By way of introduction to the above subject, I would like to share with you the story of a little boy who was crying very bitterly in *Cheder*.[1] His teacher asked him, "Why are you crying?" "Someone called me a חמור."[2] The teacher tried to calm the young pupil saying: "Surely that is no reason to cry?" "I don't care about myself, but he insulted צלם אלקים"[3] (Gen. 1:27).

Three questions present themselves:

1) What is the reason that the חטאת – the sin offering has to be slaughtered in the same place as the עולה – the elevation offering?

2) Why were special sign-posts set up in Israel giving directions to the City of Refuge for those who killed by mistake? (Rashi on the verse "prepare the way" Deut. 19:3).

3) Why were so many soldiers sent back from the front-line by the משוח מלחמה – the Cohen anointed for battle – supported by officers, including those who had built a house, planted a vineyard or betrothed a wife (Deut. 20:5-8).

All these questions have a single answer, which can be illustrated by the following anecdote:

Rabbi Yisroel Salanter ז"ל, the founder of the *Mussar* Movement,[4] was once

---

1. Hebrew classes.
2. An ass.
3. The image of G-d.
4. Ethical teachings.

invited for a Friday evening meal. The host noticed that the two *Challot*[1] on the table were not covered with the *Challah* cloth. He flew into a rage at his poor wife in front of the Rabbi. "It is a disgrace. How could you have forgotten a thing like that?" The wife apologised and rectified her oversight by quickly placing a beautiful *Challah* cover over the *Challot*. A flush covered her cheeks. Rabbi Yisrael did not say a word. After the meal, however, the Rabbi called the host aside and asked him: "Can you tell me what is the reason why the *Challot* must be covered?" The host replied: "In order that the loaves should not consider themselves slighted that Kiddush over wine precedes them." Rabbi Salanter rebuked him in a gentle manner:

"You were concerned with the imaginary feelings of two pieces of baked dough, but you did not take into consideration the real pain that your dear wife suffered when you were insulting her in public...."

Human dignity occupies a great deal of space in the written as well as the oral Torah.

In Genesis 9:6:

"שפך דם האדם באדם דמו ישפך כי בצלם אלקים עשה את האדם"

"Whosoever sheds a man's blood, by man shall his be shed, because
in the image of G-d did He make man."

Our great Rabbis spoke about another kind of murder: **Disgrace and shame in public.**

"המלבין פני חברו ברבים אין לו חלק בעולם הבא"

"He who insults his fellow man in public loses his share of life in
the world to come" (Avot 3:15).

Literally מלבין means **whitening**. One can see the blood of a person who has been disgraced draining from his face. That is the interpretation of shedding blood of a man **within** the man. The Gemara Sotah (10b) continues to tell us that it is better to throw oneself into a fiery furnace rather than putting someone to shame in public. The Gemara asks: "from where do we know this?" From Tamar, the daughter-in-law of יהודה,[2] the son of יעקב,[3] who was accused by יהודה

---

of immorality, since she was pregnant and was sentenced to be executed by fire. She did not say, "You are the father!" but she produced a seal ring, a wrap and a staff and said, "To whom do these belong?" She was very well aware what could happen to her if יהודה did not admit his paternity; however, he told the truth and Tamar gave birth to twins, one of whom became the ancestor of King David and משיח.[1]

Now we have the answer to the first question:

Why the elevation offering (עולה) has to be slaughtered in the same place as the sin offering (חטאת). The עולה was a **voluntary** sacrifice which was completely burned on the altar (except the hide). עולה means going up in flames.

According to Rabbi S. R. Hirsch ז"ל, to raise – עולה – the owner from a low state to a high state, to a spiritual elevation in order to bring himself nearer to Hashem. קרבן comes from קרב – nearness.

According to the Midrash Vayikra Rabba (7:3), the עולה is to atone for sinful thoughts that come up in a person's mind or imagination. This happens to everyone. חטאת[2] is for a sin which one committed – בשגגה – in error (Lev. 4:27-35). However, had he been more careful, this would not have occurred. People might see a person bringing a חטאת[3] and shame or ridicule him. Therefore, the Torah requires that the **voluntary** elevation offering be slaughtered at the same place, so that on-lookers do not know which kind of sacrifice the person had offered.

We also have the answer to question number two, why special sign-posts were set up to direct people to the ערי מקלט.[4] People who have killed inadvertently should not be put into the embarrassing situation of having to ask directions from others how to get to the ערי מקלט, where they will be safe from the wrath of the murdered person's family.

The third question is also answered in a similar vein:

Why were so many soldiers sent home from the battlefield? Rashi (Deut. 20:8) quotes the Talmud (Sotah 44a) on the verse:

---

1. Messiah.
2. The sin offering.
3. A sin offering.
4. Cities of Refuge.

"מי האיש הירא ורך הלבב ילך וישב לביתו"
"Who is the man who is fearful and fainthearted? Let him go
and return to his house."

Rabbi Akiva says that the verse is to be taken literally, that **cowardly** people should leave the field immediately. They are not worthy of a miracle because they lack faith in Hashem and would affect the morale of the others.

According to Rabbi Yosef Haglili, however, the declaration was directed at the **sinners** who know they were not worthy of Hashem's help.

In order to protect such people's dignity, additional soldiers were freed; namely, those with new houses, or those who just got married, and so forth. In this way, onlookers would not be able to ridicule the sinners and put them to shame because they would not know why the soldiers went home.

So great is the dignity of man, according to the philosophy of the Torah. That is the reason why the main prayer, the *Amidah*, should be said silently, not to show up those who have sinned (Sotah 32b). It also has to be in the **plural**.

Similarly, the על חטא[1] on Yom Kippur is recited silently and in the plural. If one would confess one's sins loudly and in singular, the neighbour in the synagogue would have a field day. He could tell his friends:

"Oh, boy! What I heard in the synagogue today, what the person next to me confessed!"

One must always be conscious of the teachings of פרקי אבות (Ethics of the Fathers 2:15).

"יהי כבוד חברך חביב עליך כשלך"
"Let the honour of your fellowman be as dear to you as your own."

The Mishna Sanhedrin (4:5) says: the human being is a whole world.

Let us conclude with the teaching of Rabbi Akivah (Avot 3:18).

Beloved is man for he was created in the image of Hashem, but it was by special love that it was made **known** to him that he was created in the image of Hashem, because it is said in the Torah (Gen. 1:27):

"In the image of Hashem He created them."

---

1. Confession of sins.

GRATITUDE

צו

A Chassidic Rebbe once said, "A Jew must live with the times." Was he referring to the Times newspaper? Certainly not! He meant, of course, the weekly *Sidra*. Let us see what we can gather from our *Sidra* which deals with various offerings in the Temple. We shall concentrate on one:

"אם על תודה יקריבנו"

"If he shall offer it for a thanksgiving offering" (Lev. 7:12).

The Talmud says (Berachot 54b).

"ארבעה צריכין להודות יורדי הים הולכי מדברות ומי שהיה חולה ונתרפא
ומי שהיה חבוש בבית האסורים"

"Four categories of people are required to bring a Thanksgiving offering: Those who survived a sea journey, those who survived a journey in the desert, someone who was ill but has now recovered and someone who was imprisoned." (Nowadays one says ברכת הגומל.[1]

Torah is based on gratitude. The Ten Commandments begin with:

"אנכי ה' אלקיך אשר הוצאתיך מארץ מצרים"

"I am the L-rd your G-d who brought you out of Egypt"
(Exod. 20:2).

<u>Not</u>, who has created the Universe. Rashi remarks: This is sufficient reason to be subordinated to Hashem. As a matter of fact, the three Mitzvot of the Commandments which only apply to us the Jewish People, in contrast to the other seven which are the basis of the שבע מצוות בני נח[2] have gratitude as a common factor.

<u>**The First Commandment**</u> is our special relationship as a nation with the

---

1. A blessing of Thanksgiving to Hashem which is said in Shul.
2. The seven commandments given to the Sons of Noach, the gentile world.

Creator. Gratitude to Hashem that He looks after us and took us out
of Egypt.

The Fourth Commandment teaches gratitude that He gave us the
Shabbat and

The Fifth Commandment commands gratitude to our parents, and by
implication, also to the third partner – Hashem. All the other seven
Commandments have a common denominator, namely, that there
must be no "law of the jungle" in the world – one should not steal or
murder, etc.

The contrast between הכרת הטוב[1] and the reverse can be illustrated by the
following story:

Two people pass one another in the street. One wears a big smile, and gives
thanks to Hashem. The other one is a picture of gloom. Let us find out what
happened to them:

The second one is a wealthy businessman who bought a house for £100,000 and
sold it for £150,000, but an estate agent told him afterwards that he had a buyer
for £200, 000! The other one, a poor porter, stood in a long line, in the cold, in
the marketplace until he got a job carrying sacks of grain. He brought home
money for food for his hungry family. He praised Hashem for giving him "Bread
from Heaven."

"קרוב ה' לנשברי לב"

"Hashem is nearest to those with a broken heart" (Psa. 34:19).

The business man, being a conceited person thinks to himself:

"כחי ועצם ידי עשה לי את החיל הזה"

"My strength and the power of my hands made this wealth for me"
(Deut. 8:17).

One who says, "I got this wealth through my own strength" – is a person that is
never satisfied.

As the great חפץ חיים ז"ל said: "It is easier to see Hashem when one's 'ego' is
not in the way."

Pharaoh showed extreme ingratitude to יוסף who not only saved Egypt from

---

1. Gratitude.

starvation, but made it a very wealthy country. Yet, "אשר לא ידע את יוסף" "Who did not know Joseph" (Exod. 1:8), in the end he denied the goodness of Hashem.

"מי ה' אשר אשמע בקולו" "Who is Hashem that I should listen to His voice?"

"לא ידעתי את השם" "I do not know Hashem" (Exod. 5:2).

The denial of the goodness of someone else leads to the denial of the goodness of Hashem; an ungrateful person cannot draw a line between people and the Creator in this matter.

Similarly:

"לא יבא עמוני ומואבי בקהל ה'...על דבר אשר לא קדמו אתכם בלחם
ובמים בדרך בצאתכם ממצרים"

"Amonrites and Moabites shall not enter the Assembly of Hashem forever, because they did not meet you with bread and water when you came out of Egypt...." (Deut. 23: 4-5).

The question arises: "Surely we had plenty of מן[1] and the well of Miriam?"

The answer is as follows: Our ancestor אברהם[2] risked his life to rescue their ancestor לוט[3] and through his merit, לוט was saved from סדום.[4] Therefore, be a מכיר טוב – show your gratitude by inviting us in for "a cup of tea!" But they were ungrateful and did not return any favours. That is the reason why an Amorite or Moabite cannot marry a Jewish girl (Ramban).

On the other hand, משה רבינו possessed the opposite quality of character. He did not even smite the River Nile with his staff to produce the first and second plagues – blood and frogs – but left it to his brother Aharon, because his life had been saved in the water. According to Gemara Baba Kama (92b),

"אמרי אנשי בירא דשתית מינה לא תשדי בה קלא"

"People say: A well from which you drank water, do not throw a stone into it."

Obviously water has no feelings, however, character traits are not only influenced by reason but by emotions. These would have been blunted by

---

1. Manna.
2. Abraham.
3. Lot.
4. Sdom.

smiting the water, which was instrumental in saving him. That solves the following problem, too:

When משה רבינו was told by Hashem to liberate the suffering Jews, he did not go straight away but returned to יתרו, his father-in-law, and asked permission to go to Egypt (Exod. 4:18). The question arises: How could he stand on ceremony at a time when he was told to rescue millions of his people?

But the Midrash Tanchuma Shemot 16 explains: יתרו welcomed משה רבינו when he fled from Egypt. Gratitude demanded that he return to יתרו and tell him of his plans before leaving and to get his permission.

However, that poses another question: Why is the name of משה רבינו not mentioned prominently in the הגדה? This looks like ***ingratitude***.

The Vilna Gaon ז"ל gives the following answer in his commentary on the הגדה: "Gratitude must be directed to the ***source*** of the goodness – to Hashem who redeemed us, as stated in the הגדה:

"לא על ידי מלאך ולא על ידי שליח אלא הקדוש ברוך הוא בכבודו ובעצמו"

"Not by an Angel or a Messenger but by Hashem Himself!"

This explains why in the *Amida* prayer, as well as in all brachot, all the attributes of Hashem are in the third person – "***He*** listens to our prayer," for example – except for the blessing for giving thanks.

"הטוב שמך ולך נאה להודות"

"Your name is good and to ***you*** it is becoming to give thanks"
(Quoted in the name of my son-in-law, Yisrael Learman נ"י)

The importance of gratitude is clearly shown by the fact that only מודים אנחנו לך is said by the congregation itself, whilst all other blessings in the repetition of the *Amidah* is only recited by the reader. That is why in Mishna Avot (6:7) it says that a person who says something in the name of the person who originally said it brings redemption to the world. It says in the Megilla that אסתר[1] told of Bigtan and Teresh's assassination plot against the King, in מרדכי's[2] name (Esther 2:22). אסתר could have taken the credit herself, but she did not because she possessed the quality of truth. That is required for one to be involved in the process of

---

1. Esther.
2. Mordechai.

redemption – to place credit where credit is due. So did משה רבינו when the daughters of יתרו said: "An Egyptian man saved us from the shepherds" (Exod. 2:19). The question arises:

Did משה רבינו look like an Egyptian? Surely his looks were different? The *Midrash Tanchuma* (Shemot 11) explains this verse with a story: A man bitten by a snake ran to the water to bathe his foot. There he found a child on the point of drowning and he saved him. When the child thanked him, he said, "do not thank me but the snake, because it was the bite of the snake which caused me to dash to the water." Here משה רבינו said, "I did not save you, but the Egyptian ***whom I killed*** was the reason I had to flee from Egypt and eventually meet you and save you from the shepherds. He saved you!" That is what the daughters of Jetro told their father: Who caused Moshe to come to our aid? The Egyptian whom he killed. Now we understand why משה רבינו was fit to be the leader at the exodus from Egypt. Unlike Pharaoh, who was very conceited and said, "I have made the River (Nile)," משה רבינו was the most humble of men.

"והאיש משה ענו מאד מכל האדם אשר על פני האדמה" "And the man Moshe was very humble indeed from all the men who are on the face of the earth" (Num. 12:3) and also possessed the quality of truth, both of which are absolutely essential.

After all, the aim of the Exodus is clearly stated:

"וידעו מצרים כי אני ה' בנטתי את יד על מצרים והוצאתי את בני ישראל מתוכם"
"And the Egyptians shall know that ***I am Hashem*** when I stretch out
my hand over Egypt and I shall take the children of Israel from among them"
(Exod. 7:5).

Now we clearly understand the reason why משה רבינו's name is not prominently mentioned in the הגדה.

In conclusion, I would like to share with you the following remarkable anecdote:

A former student of a famous Rosh Yeshiva became a very wealthy man. His Rebbe visited him one day and asked him, "What are you doing?" The reply was: "Quite well, thank you, my business has prospered." After some time the Rosh Yeshiva asked the same question again. "Thank you Rebbe, I have a nice family." Surprisingly, the Rebbe inquired a third time. "Please forgive me Rebbe, but why did you ask the same question for the third time?" "You have not even answered the question once. You tell me about your prosperity and your lovely family. but I asked, what are _you_ doing? Those are not your doing but Hashem's. I wanted you to tell me what _you_ are doing with all the gifts Hashem has given you. What learning are you doing in your spare time? What education are you giving your children? What charity do you support with your money?"

We must ask ourselves these questions too. Hashem has given us a lot to be thankful for. We would have to offer up innumerable thanksgiving offerings if the בית המקדש would be still standing. So what are we doing with all these wonderful heavenly gifts? Are we חס ושלום[1] ungrateful like Pharaoh, or are we מכיר טוב, recognising His great goodness not only in our minds but also in our hearts and feelings by translating them into prayers, Torah, Mitzvot and good deeds, like משה רבינו?

Such gratitude will help to bring redemption to the world – במהרה בימינו – Speedily in our days!

---

1. Heaven forbid.

KASHRUT

"להבדיל בין הטמא ובין הטהר ובין החיה הנאכלת
ובין החיה אשר לא תאכל"

"To distinguish between the contaminated and the pure and between the animal that may be eaten and the animal that may not be eaten."

(Lev. 11:44)

The latter part of our *Sidra* is devoted to the dietary laws of the Torah, and that will be the subject of this talk.

By way of introduction, I would like to share the following anecdote with you:

An observant Jew once passed a MacDonalds restaurant. He was very thirsty, so he entered the non-kosher eating place and ordered an orange juice. However, the smell of the fried food tempted him into having an hors d'oeuvre as well, which led to a hamburger and a dessert. To his surprise, he noticed the Rabbi of his synagogue standing outside and looking at him. He went up to the Rabbi and asked him: "Did you see me having my hors d'oeuvre?" "Yes, I did," replied the Rabbi. "What about the hamburger?" "I observed that too." "And the dessert?" "I saw you eating that as well." "Thank you Rabbi, now I have eaten under Rabbinical supervision...."

Our problem today is:

1) What is the great importance of the dietary laws that they require ___real___ Rabbinical supervision?

2) What reason can we find for some of the details of this fundamental part of Torah life? Obviously, our thoughts cannot compare with those of our Creator, and we are not able to go into the very depths of these laws, just as we cannot possibly comprehend the 613 מצות in their Divine profundity.

However, certain teachings are open to us which we are at liberty to find. טעמי המצות – reasons for the commandments – can only give some טעם – flavour – to the מצות but can not reveal all their Divine teachings.

Before we answer these questions, I would like to share the following story with you:

Once, a Chassidic Rebbe went with some of his Chassidim to a town they had never visited before. The Chassidim made numerous enquiries about the religious suitability of the local שוחט[1] in order to ascertain the כשרות of the local meat. This led, unfortunately, to לשון הרע.[2] The Rebbe admonished them saying: "You are so careful concerning what comes _into_ your mouths. This is very important indeed. However, you must be equally watchful and cautious about what comes _out_ of your mouths...." The very first law in the history of the world was a dietary one given by Hashem in the Garden of Eden. However, the tempter's evil talk was the cause of its transgression with dire consequences.

Let us try to investigate why Kashrut laws occupy such an important place in the life of a committed Jew. Some scholars would answer by saying that these laws are not unusual since in the Orient such rules were widespread.

How wrong they are! The ancient people believed that unclean animals were **enemies** which had to be hunted down. We do not do that. Hunting for these reasons or for sport is cruel and forbidden to us under the laws of צער בעלי חיים[3] (Gemara Bava Metzia 32b).

In the Torah only Nimrod (Gen. 10:9) and Esau (Gen. 25:27) were hunters and were looked upon with disfavour, as Rabbi Meir of Rothenburg writes: "He who hunts game with dogs will not enjoy life in the world to come." Also, the ancient peoples used to regard horses, dogs and foxes as clean animals. We do not! However, for us there is nothing intrinsically unclean – all creations are made by Hashem; only some of them are forbidden to us to be used as food.

But other points can be considered: רמב"ם[4] in his מורה נבוכים – _Guide to the Perplexed_ – puts forward this reasoning: "Kashrut furthers physical hygiene." Latest discoveries show that certain non-kosher fish are poisonous; oysters

---

1. Slaughterer.
2. Evil talk.
3. Causing unnecessary pain to animals.
4. Maimonides.

sometimes contain typhoid germs and shell-fish breed diseases. Toads (one of the eight impure שרצים – swarming things) in tropical countries have poison under their skin. South American Indians use this poison for their arrows. Furthermore, we know that שחיטה, our way of slaughtering animals, causes a virtually painless death, because it reduces blood pressure in the brain to zero, and it takes two to three seconds to convey pain messages to the brain, which is dead by then. It also drains the blood, and so helps to preserve the meat, which other methods do not.

The examination of the animal's lungs by the שוחט prevents illnesses. We have had food hygiene inspectors – שוחטים – for thousands of years. We were immune, to a great extent, to the Black Plague in the Middle Ages because of washing our hands before handling food and because of כשרות. People at that time accused us of poisoning their wells.

The famous Abarbanel, however, was very much at odds with the רמב"ם. He says: If so, the Torah would be reduced to a medical text book. Furthermore, why does the Torah not forbid us eating from poisonous plants? What about antidotes against ill effects? Surely Hashem leaves secrets about nature for us to discover.

"ומלאו את הארץ וכבשה"
"Fill the earth and subdue it" (Gen. 1:28).

We are commanded to protect ourselves against poison, etc. in the verse

"ונשמרתם מאד לנפשתיכם"
"And you shall guard your souls very much" (Deut. 4:15).

This leads us to another explanation:
The Torah says "אל תשקצו את נפשתיכם" (Lev. 11:43) "You shall not defile your souls."

There is a verse in תהלים – (Psa. 51:12):

"לב טהור ברא לי אלקים ורוח נכון חדש בקרבי"
"A pure heart create for me G-d and a steadfast spirit renew within me."

Only Hashem knows what is good for our souls and what is not.

The Sefer Hachinuch adds that the body is a vessel for the soul. What is good for the body favourably affects the soul which is contained in the body. A tree produces better fruit on a better soil. Hashem, who created both, knows best what food is good for both, the body and the soul.

Rabbi S.R. Hirsh ז״ל writes: By not eating the meat of aggressive predators we are protected from the transmission of cruel traits into our personality. We eat the meat of passive grass eaters who are nearest to plant life, who are vegetarian. (Feeding cows with sheep meat is the main cause of mad-cow disease.)

Others say that כשרות laws are designed as a barrier to separate us from other nations; as the Torah clearly states:

"ואבדיל אתכם מן העמים להיות לי"

"And I shall separate you from the other nations to be mine" (Lev. 20:26).

Our Rabbis extended this to wine, which must be Kosher, in order that we should not join with other people in their parties. Also "בשר שנתעלם מן העין" – meat which is hidden from the eye (of a Jew) is forbidden (Gemara Chullin 95a).

This reminds me of a story of Don Isaac Abarbanel, the renowned commentator on the Torah, who was invited to dinner by King Alfonso of Portugal. Obviously, Abarbanel had brought his own kosher food. The King ordered identical treifa food for himself. Before sitting down at the table, however, the king called Abarbanel to view the royal gardens from the window of the dining room. In the meantime, the king had the revolving table turned so that the treifa food was in Abarbanel's place. When they returned from the window, the king invited his guest to start partaking of his meal. However, Abarbanel replied: "Sorry, your Majesty, I cannot do that because my meat was "hidden from the eye" and our שולחן ערוך[1] does not allow me to eat this meat." The king admitted "I was only trying to test you. Halacha[2] guards you. How wonderful is your שולחן ערוך...."

There is still another point to consider: כשרות teaches us self control. Seeing tempting foods in treifa restaurants and being able to withstand the temptation – unlike the person at MacDonalds – is a very important part of our character training. The Midrash puts this teaching very succinctly: Why did Hashem command Adam that he may eat from all the trees in the Garden but forbid him the fruit of one of them? That was in order that he should see it all the time,

---

1. Book of Laws.
2. Jewish Law.

should remember his Creator, recognise that the yoke of his Maker is on him, and he should not be too proud. We see that there is an educational function to the laws of כשרות as well as discipline. Adam and Eve, however, could not withstand the temptation and had to suffer expulsion from Gan Eden and death.

This brings me to the final point:

A person should not say, "I cannot eat pig meat." I certainly can, but what should I say instead? That my Father in Heaven has decreed that I must not eat it (Midrash Sifra Lev. 20:26).

Just as Hashem made laws of nature, so He made Statutes which are absolutely beyond our understanding. What is very interesting in this connection is the following: Only Hashem could possibly say that there are only four kinds of animals which have only one sign of the two required to declare an animal kosher – chewing the cud and having cloven hooves. The camel, the rock-badger and the hare chew the cud but do not have cloven hooves. The pig has a cloven hoof but does not chew the cud (Lev. 11:4-8).

When the Torah was given, America and Australia, as well as many other parts of the world, had not yet been discovered. Even now, when we know about so many animals which are found only in these places, the above-mentioned four are still the only ones which have only one sign of purity. This is stated in Gemara Chullin (59a): The Ruler of the World knows that there is no other animal which has a cloven hoof and yet is impure except a pig, and that is why the verse only mentioned the pig (Ibid, Gemara and Tosaphot). The same applies to the other three animals mentioned in the Torah.

To sum up: Kashrut contains *biological* elements: a diet for wholesome and healthy living.

> *Spiritual Health* – namely the correct diet for both body and soul which only the Creator can know. Also that no cruel qualities of animals are absorbed into our system.

> *Historical Elements* – continuity and unity for our people. It acts as a barrier from the non-Jewish world. The knowledge that what we eat today is the same as what our ancestors ate makes history come alive. It also creates unity with our present Jewish brothers and sisters all over the world.

Ethical Teaching – namely that of self-control. Knowing that we cannot eat just any food anywhere and at any time we choose. We must not eat dairy foods immediately after meaty ones. We also have special foods like Matzot, as well as fast days.

Furthermore, we have the obligation to share our food with the needy. Our table is an altar. We say blessings before and after food. We are careful with what comes out of our mouths, too. Above all there is the *Educational function* of absolute obedience, and attachment to our Maker all day and every day.

"בכל דרכיך דעהו"

"In all your ways you should know Him" (Prov. 3:6) even whilst eating.

We see now what a wealth of teaching is contained in this מצוה. That is some טעם המצוה[1] – and that is just what we know! But what about the deeper insights which we do not know? The mystical elements? Thus Kashrut falls into line with all other מצות.

"לא נתנו מצות אלא לצרץ את הבריות"

"Commandments were only given to refine people"
(Midrash Bereshit Rabba 44:1).

Kashrut elevates the act of eating from a basic bodily requirement into a holy act.

"והייתם קדשים כי קדש אני"

"And you shall be holy because I am holy" (Lev. 11:44).

---

1. Some flavour of the commandment.

WHAT IS צרעת – LEPROSY?

רבי יוחנן בן ברוקא אומר
"כל המחלל שם שמים בסתר נפרעין ממנו בגלוי"

Rabbi Yochanan Ben Berukah says: "Whoever profanes the name
of Heaven in secret, will suffer the penalty for it in public."

(Ethics of the Fathers 4:5)

These two *Sidrot* deal mainly with leprosy, infections of the skin, clothing and houses, and require a great deal of explanation. Before attempting to throw some light on these difficult subjects, I would like to share the following anecdote with you:

Someone once visited a friend who had opened a tailor's shop on the main road of Vienna. The tailor complained bitterly that someone else had done likewise and had put a sign, 'The Best Tailor in Austria.' Another one opened a new shop later accross the street and had called his business 'The Best Tailor in the World.' Yet another competitor appeared under the name 'The Best Tailor in the Street.' "What can **I** do now?" His friend counselled him: "Put up a sign saying "MAIN ENTRANCE." He did and was very successful....

The "Main Entrance" to these complex topics can only be built up by our great Sages who provide us with the correct guidelines.

Various questions present themselves:

1. What is the connection with last week's *Sidra, Shemini,* which dealt in part with impurities of animals carcasses as well as with forbidden foods?
2. What is this צרעת?[1] Is it a medical or a spiritual problem?

---

1. Leprosy.

3. What have the various types of צרעת, namely skin, clothing and houses, in common?

4. Why does the Mishna quoted above say that if a person profanes the name of Hashem in secret, he will be punished in public? What about the principle of מדה כנגד מדה?[1] This seems to be disproportionate.

The answers are best introduced by the story of Dayan Abramski ז"ל who was the Head of the London Bet Din. He was often invited to people's houses but he never partook of a meal that was offered. What was his excuse? "I am under doctor's orders." When one of his friends asked him privately what the doctor's orders were, he confided: "I'm under the great doctor's orders, namely the famous רמב"ם...."[2] (Referring to problems of Kashrut). We shall also consult the רמב"ם (who was a doctor) regarding the solution to our queries.

The first one: What is the link with the previous *Sidra*?

The great חתם סופר gives the following elucidation: "Man was created last because if he merits it, he is the pinnacle of creation. The Rabbis say, however, that if he does not merit it, a fly was created before you" (*Bereshit Rabba* 8:7). Animals only create impurity when they are dead, but man, even while he is alive, can become a מצורע[3] if he commits serious sins, as we shall see.

Rabbi Yisrael Salanter ז"ל, the famous בעל מוסר[4] gives another explanation:

Some people are very careful not to eat the tiniest insect (in previous *Sidra*) yet they swallow others whole with their vicious tongue by evil tales, resulting in leprosy....

These explanations already point to the solution of our second question. What is צרעת? Is it a medical or a spiritual problem?

Since time immemorial there has been a tendency amongst the denigrators of the Torah to reduce the purpose of our divine laws to the level of a text book of medicine and hygiene. The regulations laid down in our two *Sidrot* of the three types of צרעת have been the subject of a great deal of speculation. Until recent times, leprosy had always been considered highly contagious, hence the

---

1. Measure for measure.
2. Maimonides.
3. A leper.
4. Master of Ethical Teachings.

isolation of the leper, it was mistakenly claimed. Tacitus, the Roman historian, even stated that the Exodus from Egypt was nothing more than the expulsion of the "Jewish Slaves" because of their leprosy to prevent an epidemic in Egypt. What a perversion of the truth! It can be compared to the denial of the Holocaust in our times.

It is true to say that the skin is an important protector of the body. It also plays the role of a thermostat. If one loses most of one's skin by burns, for example, one cannot live. Yet, our greatest doctor, Maimonides, confirms at the end of the laws of צרעת, in his monumental work Yad Hachazakah, based on Gemara Erachin (15b and 16a), that צרעת is not a medical condition. We are under his "orders."

He quotes the verses (Deut. 24:8-9): "Take heed of the plague of צרעת – Remember what Hashem has done to מרים." מרים said about her brother משה רבינו, mistakenly, that he had neglected his wife because of his many public duties. Her brother was very humble and did not take exception to her well meant reproach; after all, everything he did was by the command of Hashem. Still, Miriam was punished with צרעת for seven days. This shows the importance of refraining from לשון הרע![1]

We can now clearly see that צרעת was a punishment from **Heaven**, to deter people from speaking לשון הרע.

First the person with צרעת discovers some ominous signs on the walls of his or her house. If the person repents, well and good, but if not, his clothes and eventually his skin will be affected (Rambam, Laws of impurities of "Leprosy" 16:10).

There are many proofs for this.

Soforno, the famous commentator, who was also a doctor, wrote that leprosy is a swelling of a brown colour while צרעת is of a white colour.

Samson Raphael Hirsch ז"ל refutes the health theory with a number of pertinent questions:

1. If the laws of צרעת are meant to prevent infection, why did an afflicted person have to leave only those cities which had a wall around them at the time of the conquest by יהושע (Mishna Kelim 1:7), but not any other cities?

---

1. Evil talk.

2. Why are non-Jews exempt from the laws of leprosy (Rambam, Laws of "Leprosy" 9:1)?

3. Why during the time of the greatest possible crowds, namely during the three Festivals and wedding feasts, were no צרעת examinations carried out by the כהן (Rambam, 9:7)?

4. Why is the city of Jerusalem immune from צרעת on houses (B. Kamah 82b) (Rambam, 14:11)?

5. Why were articles removed from the suspected house before the כהן examined it, in order to spare the owner their loss? Surely, they might be contaminated, but the rule is that the law affecting our health goes beyond forbidden food. חמירת סכנתא מאיסרא To avoid danger is more strict than forbidden things (Gemara Chullin 10a).

All this points clearly to the Rambam's interpretation that צרעת has no physical or sanitary effect.

After all the above, it remains for us to examine these laws in more detail. *Klei Yakar* divides צרעת into three groups:

I)   *Evil tales* – Miriam – (Num. 12:10)

II) *Haughtiness of Spirit* – Naamon (Kings II 5:1) – He was a Syrian General who suffered from צרעת and was ordered by the Prophet Elisha to dip into the River Jordan. He did so under protest and was eventually healed.

III) *Jealousy* – Gehazi (Kings II 5:27) – He was a servant of the Prophet Elisha, who asked Naamon for payment, against the express orders of Elisha, and was stricken with צרעת as a consequence.

Now we understand why the Torah commands a כהן and not a doctor to deal with this condition (Lev. 13:3).

כהנים do not suffer from any of the above faults

Evil tales: אהרן, the High Priest, loved and pursued peace (Avot 1:12).

Haughtiness of Spirit: אהרן and משה רבינו said "who are we"? (Exod. 16:8)

Jealousy – כהנים had no share in the land; instead they received gifts from the other tribes, therefore, the more the other tribes possessed, the greater the gift! (The opposite of jealousy.) That is why כהנים bless us. They are certainly well disposed to the congregation and besides, they are the teachers of the people.

However the following question remains to be answered:

How do the laws of צרעת correct these imperfections? The answer is twofold:

A) The affected person is being taught the power of a word. **_One_** word from the כהן declared him impure; similarly, **_one_** word from the כהן declares him pure when his condition improves.

B) He is excluded from the society which he wanted to harm. His exclusion teaches him how much he misses society.

Let us now deal with the third question, namely, what is the common denominator of all these types of צרעת?

They are all **_coverings_**, skin, clothes and houses. All need special signs of holiness: מילה, ציצית and מזוזה.[1] The sinner had desecrated all these coverings and, therefore, had become impure.

Which leads us to the final question. Why should a person who desecrated the name of Hashem in private (through evil tales, for example) be punished in public? Where is the principle of מדה כנגד מדה?[2]

Rabbi Chaim of Volozhin, in his book *Nefesh Chaim* says: חלול ה'[3] comes from the word חלל – emptiness. However,

"מלא כל הארץ כבודו"

"The whole world is full of His glory" (Isa. 6:3).

Therefore, whoever profanes the name of Hashem tries to make a part of it empty – חלל. He tries to push the Divine Presence away from it by his evil talk or deed. That leads to severe consequences.

When Joseph was put into a pit, the Torah says "it had no water" (Gen. 37:24) but it did contain snakes and scorpions (Gemara Shabbat 22a). How do the Rabbis know this? The Vilna Gaon explains: Nature abhors a vacuum, therefore, if there was no life-giving water then deadly snakes and scorpions took over. Here, too, if holiness is removed then impurity takes over and spreads to the

---

1. Circumcision, tzitzit and mezuzah.
2. Measure for measure.
3. Profanation of the name of Hashem.

public. Evil tales cannot be contained and eventually become public. Therefore, he is punished in public.

In modern times לשון הרע[1] has become very powerful through the media. Propaganda for evil reaches millions of people. It truly has cosmic repercussions! A clothes plague is also prevalent in the form of immodest dress. צרעת of the house is visible in the shape of living beyond one's income. This reminds me of the story of an East Ender who moved to a fashionable London suburb. In the East End, he had lived **above his shop** whilst in the suburb he lived **above his means**....

What is required of us in order to remain in the rightful place, the top place of the universe, is to use our unique power of speech, with which Hashem has endowed us for its most exalted purpose, the study of Torah and prayer; our clothes should be adorned with ציצית to remind us of all the מצות of Hashem, and our houses should have מזוזות to help us create a קידוש השם[2] by having a happy family life and using it as a בית ועד לחכמים[3] (Avot 1:4).

In this way we can attempt to emulate the example of משה רבינו whose face shone (Exod. 34:35). His inner spirituality and happiness of soul radiated outwards.

---

1. Evil talk.
2. Sanctification of the name of Hashem.
3. A meeting place for the wise.

WHAT IS HOLINESS?

The common theme running through these Sidrot is the קדושה – holiness of the Jewish people and the need for its preservation and protection. In אחרי מות we are told not to conduct our lives in the depraved manner of the Egyptians and Canaanites (Lev 18:3).

There is a list of forbidden marriages, which are the opposite of קדושה with which we are exhorted to lead our lives in the *Sidra* of קדשים. In קדשים we find fifty *Mitzvot* based on the Ten Commandments and which are the basis of real civilization.

"קדשים תהיו כי קדוש אני ה' אלקיכם"

"You shall be holy because I, the L-rd your G-d, am holy" (Lev. 19:2).

This is our distinction. As the Torah says in V'etchanan (Deut. 7:6), "You are a holy nation to Hashem and Hashem has chosen you to be an עם סגולה."[1]

This reminds me of the story of a Rumanian Jew who applied for naturalisation as a United States citizen. He was asked a number of questions which he answered correctly. Finally he was asked: "Will you support the Constitution of the United States of America?" He replied: "With regret, I cannot do this as I have a wife and four children to support in Romania...."

Let us delve into our divine constitution, which we are proud to support joyfully.

Three questions present themselves:

1. What is the meaning of "....You shall be holy...?" Does it mean one should be a holy person, a monk or a guru?
2. Why is "ויראת מאלקיך" – "you shall fear your G-d" mentioned here so frequently?
3. We find the law of פגול – rejected offering – mentioned here. It refers

---

1. A treasured people.

to a כהן who slaughters a sacrifice with the intention of eating the meat outside the Temple; or not during the prescribed time limit of one or two days. That makes the sacrifice פגול – rejected and disqualified (Lev. 19:7).

The laws of שעטנז – not wearing a mixture of wool and linen – are also found here.

What have these אסורים[1] to do with our civilization and constitution, which is the main subject of the *Sidra* קדשים?

Before attempting to answer these questions, a little anecdote on one of the precepts in the *Sidra* will be in place:

Rabbi Susse of Anipoli once put ten roubles in a *Chumash*[2] at the page where it mentions ״לא תגנבו״ – " you must not steal" (Lev. 19:11) for safekeeping. Later, he found five roubles on the page of ״ואהבת לרעך כמוך״ – "you should love your fellowmen as yourself" (Lev. 19:18). Rabbi Susse exclaimed: "Here we can see the difference between me and the thief. I wanted to keep all ten roubles for myself, but he, a merciful person, the son of merciful people, only took **half** in order to fulfill the מצוה of ״ואהבת לרעך כמך״ – " you should love your fellowmen as yourself." However, this story does not have a happy ending. Next day he found the Chumash open at ״לא יניח ממנו עד בקר״ – "You must not leave anything until the morning" (Lev. 7:15). (This refers to the meat of a Thanks-Offering.) There were no roubles left there at all....

I would like to share with you the most precious commodity, our constitution, which is infinitely more valuable than any amount of roubles – namely our Torah – and so fulfill ״ואהבת לרעך כמך״.[3]

The following Gemara (Baba Batra 74b) should shed light on our problem. Rabbi Joshua and Rabbi Eliezer once went on a sea journey. In the middle of the night, Rabbi Joshua woke Rabbi Eliezer: "I can see a great light in the ocean." "It is only the gleam of the eyes of the giant Leviathan fish," replied Rabbi Eliezer. What a beautiful and descriptive story, in an allegorical manner, of a dispute between two great philosophers.

---

1. Forbidden things.
2. Torah book.
3. You should love your fellow man as yourself.

Rabbi Joshua was very poor (Talmud Berachot 28a) whilst Rabbi Eliezer was the son of a very wealthy father, namely, Hirkanus. He fled to Jerusalem to study Torah and become a great Rabbi (Shabbat 130a). He was able to see right through the elegance and winged words of the Romans of his time.

Underneath the surface of their "civilization" were cruel and barbaric practices of conquest of guiltless foreign nations, as well as immoral conduct, revenge, hatred and scandals.

Rabbi Joshua, being poor, was so impressed by the external comfort and wealth. The sea represented the sea of nations. Rabbi Joshua called out: "I see a light!" Massive beautiful buildings, statues, Olympics, etc.

Rabbi Eliezer replied: "Do not be deceived. The lights are just the large eyes of Leviathan." They stare with avidity in their desire to swallow powerless nations elegantly and smoothly. They are never satisfied. Their proud temples are dens of iniquity and immorality.

Now we have the answer to all three questions:

קדשים – <u>Kedoshim</u>: Holiness does not mean having to separate oneself from the world, like certain religions prescribe, but to <u>elevate ordinary life</u>. Rashi comments: One should keep away from immorality, incest and sin, which is described in the previous *Sidra* of אחרי מות.[1] For example, relations between men and women should be ennobled and uplifted by marriage – קדושין – holiness. If not, they lead to destruction, AIDS and other plagues, as well as to criminal conduct of their children. Everything in the world can be utilised for good or for bad. Bricks can be used for קדושה to build a ישיבה[2] or a בית המדרש[3] or, G-d forbid, to build gas chambers. On the surface they may look alike, but in reality they are completely different. The difference is in one important point: יראת ה'.[4]

The two goats in אחרי מות, on which lots were cast on יום כפור[5] looked exactly alike. However, one was sent to Azazel – a hard cliff in the desert – and pushed from the summit to its destruction. The other was used as a sin offering in the Temple (Lev. 16:7-11).

One of the many explanations is given by Rabbi S. R. Hirsch ז"ל:

---

1. Acharei Mot.
2. Talmudical college.
3. House of study.
4. Fear of Hashem.
5. The day of atonement.

Every person must choose between good and evil and no one has the luxury of being neutral. Those who do not choose to move towards holiness are inexorably pushing themselves towards a wasteland of spiritual destruction. When Abraham came to Egypt he said that his beautiful wife was his sister. "Why?" "Because there is no fear of Hashem in this place and they will kill me because of my wife" (Gen. 20:11). What a civilized country! Look at the civilized Nazis! Civilization without "Fear of Heaven" leads to swallowing up other nations, just like Leviathan! Many of the Nazis said, "We had orders from on high." However, look at the Jewish midwives! They also received orders from on high, yet "the midwives feared Hashem and did *not* do as Pharaoh told them" (to kill the babies) (Exod. 1:17).

Now we have the answer to the second question. Why is "Fear Hashem" mentioned so many times?

This is the basis of real civilization and of our constitution. The five commandments "between man and his fellow man" are based on the five commandments "between man and Hashem." They are one unit!

This leads me to solve the third problem, too: Why are פגול and שעטנז mentioned here? A person may offer a sacrifice and yet deserve a very severe punishment:

> פגול – **_Disqualification_** – a כהן may not make his private rules when dealing with sacrifices. If he does, then the sacrifice is פגול.[1] Fear of Hashem and **_HIS_** rules must be the basis of everything.
>
> שעטנז – **_Shaatnes_** – The Midrash (Tanchumah Bereshit 9) tells us that Cain, who was a farmer, brought flax as his sacrifice, whilst Abel, his brother, who was a shepherd, brought wool. Cain became jealous when Hashem accepted the gift brought by Abel and not his own, so he killed his brother. Both brought sacrifices, but they became the cause of a murder. Why? Because Cain had no fear of Hashem, only jealousy and greed. This may be one reason why we do not wear any garments which contain wool and linen – שעטנז – to keep this in mind. The Midrash (ibid) puts it in this manner: "It is not right that a gift of a sinner should mix with one of an innocent person."

"קדשים תהיו" – "Be holy" – Fear Hashem. Therefore, after it says "Do not

---

1. Disqualified.

hate your fellow man – love your fellow man" the Torah tells us not to wear שעטנז.

As we said once before: "The thread on which the different qualities of human beings is strung as pearls is the fear of G-d. When the fastening of this fear is loosened, the pearls roll in different directions and are lost one by one."

What can we learn from these two *Sidrot*?

Things which may look alike on the surface may be completely different in reality. Everything can be used for good and for evil. What we have to do is to elevate our actions to the state of holiness.

"Be holy because I am holy."

We must try to elevate our deeds and emulate Hashem. Without that, outward behaviour may look very polished, refined and civilized, but even a sacrifice can lead to a terrible disaster.

In international relations, elegant speech making and enlightened, fashionable conduct may hide the desire to swallow weaker nations smartly and gracefully. This is the trouble in the contemporary world. One sees the eyes of Leviathan everywhere and very little fear of Hashem.

Let us not be dazzled by the polish, the light and refinement of modern civilization, but let us rather enjoy the real light, the light of Torah combined with קדושה and Fear of Hashem!

THE COUNTING
OF THE OMER

The *Sidra* אמור contains special laws concerning כהנים[1] and the כהן גדול.[2] It mentions that sacrifices have to be perfect, and not have any blemishes. It concludes with the ימים טובים[3] and their varied commandments. One of them is the מצוה of ספירת העומר,[4] which we perform every night between פסח and שבועות (Lev. 23:15). What always puzzled me was, what is the significance of this מצוה which is, after all, one of the 613 מצוות?

However, there are many wonderful and exciting teachings contained in the מצוה. Space permits me to offer only three of them. They are simply amazing. Let me introduce the first one with an anecdote:

A man rushed into a doctor's surgery and said to the lady receptionist, who happened to be very tall, "I must see the doctor at once, I am shrinking all the time!" The receptionist looked down on him and said: "You cannot just barge into the doctor's surgery. Sit down and be a **little patient.**"

A great miracle, perhaps the greatest of all at the exodus from Egypt, was that we, a brutally enslaved people could reach the spiritual heights of נעשה ונשמע, of the giving of the Torah, within seven weeks. What was the magical means we had to do this? ספירת העומר – to count every day. It teaches us that no challenge is so great that it cannot be overcome successfully, if it is only broken down into manageable morsels. One only has to worry about how to elevate one's lifestyle **today.** One must **be a little patient!** The Angels in יעקב's dream did not *fly up*, they went up the ladder step by step. This piecemeal approach makes today's challenge manageable. It provides the means to advance tomorrow

---

1. Priests.
2. The High Priest.
3. Festivals.
4. Counting the Omer.

towards נעשה ונשמע.[1] Make each day count! No one should ever say: The Torah expects too much from me so I will not even start (Rabbi A. Twerski שליט"א).

The second point is given by Rabbi Samson Raphael Hirsch ז"ל. ספירת העומר connects חרות הגוף[2] with חרות הנפש[3] at שבועות. One without the other is of very little value. To be physically free and not to know what to do with one's life is not freedom. One is still a slave to one's יצר הרע.[4] Without Torah one <u>shrinks</u> rapidly in one's spiritual stature. That is why שבעות is called עצרת – the final festival of פסח, because on שבעות we received the תורה, which was the aim of the Exodus from Egypt. It is also called חג הבכורים – the first spiritual fruits of פסח. On פסח Hashem took Israel out of slavery, whilst on שבועות He took slavery out of Israel. The two are tied together by ספירת העומר.

The third point is illustrated by the following parable of the חפץ חיים. A bricklayer at a seaside resort by the Pacific Ocean went out every lunch break to observe the tide. One day he saw plenty of oysters with lots of pearls, left by the outgoing tide. He did not want to "waste" his lunch break collecting the oysters. When he told this to his mates, they reproached him severely, saying, "You fool! If you spend one hundred years picking up heavy bricks, you will still never be able to earn as much as half an hour of picking up pearls." Time moves on and seems to be beyond our control, yet man's influence over time is unlimited. It is highly elastic, depending on how much or how little one puts into it. But people are busy counting assets, if any, and liabilities, etc. Calculators and computers can count far better. However, people forget to count the most precious asset of all – *TIME!* Many kill time. The normal rules of arithmetic do not apply to them. Two hours plus two hours equals zero. ספירה bids us to <u>make time count</u>. Now we readily understand the words עת and זמן. Both words mean ***preparation.***

The person who took the goat to the desert on יום כפור is called in the Torah "איש עתי" – "the prepared appointed man" (Lev 16:21). זמן also means preparation as in "הנני מוכן ומזומן" – "I am prepared." The Mishna tells us that time is meant to be used for preparation in this world for the world to come (Avot 4:21).

---

1. We shall do and we shall listen.
2. Freedom of the body.
3. Freedom of the soul.
4. Evil inclination.

There is even more to this. The word וספרתם comes from the word ספיר –
sapphire (Exod. 28:18) which was one of the twelve precious stones on the
breastplate of the כהן גדול. Time is a precious jewel, and we should use this jewel
וספרתם לכם – and you should count for yourselves – by using time correctly for
Torah and מצות, not like an accountant who counts someone else's assets.

These are only some of the beautiful and exciting ideas behind this seemingly
insignificant מצוה of counting the עומר.

To sum up: The daily counting of the עומר bids us not to embrace too much too
soon, but to live and count one day at a time. Then the impossible becomes
possible. Secondly, the physical freedom of פסח must be intertwined with the
spiritual freedom of שבעות. The counting brings these two together. That is the
proper way to grow in one's spirituality. Finally, it bids us to stop wasting our
lives by scooping up bricks, but rather collect the precious pearls of limited time
and convert them into hours, days, months and years of unlimited
accomplishment through Torah study, observance of מצות, and doing good
deeds.

How true is the well known saying:

"אדם דואג על איבוד דמיו ואינו דואג על איבוד ימיו, דמיו אינם עוזרין
וימיו אינם חוזרין"

"A man worries about losing his money but does not worry about losing
his days. His money does not help and his days do not return."

I will conclude with Rudyard Kipling's famous saying:

"If you can fill the unforgiving minute
With sixty seconds' worth of distance run,
Yours is the Earth and everything that's in it,
And – which is more – you will be a man, my son!"

THE SHABBAT YEAR

"וידבר ה' אל משה בהר סיני לאמר: דבר אל בני ישראל ואמרת אליהם
כי תבאו אל הארץ אשר אני נתן לכם ושבתה הארץ שבת לה'"

"And Hashem spoke to Moses on Mount Sinai saying: 'Speak to the
Children of Israel and say to them: When you come to the Land that
I give you, the land shall observe a Shabbat rest for Hashem."

(Vayikra 25:1-2)

The subject of this talk is the מצוה[1] of שמיטה[2] details of which are given in
this *Sidra* and also mentioned in בחקתי.[3] Before discussing this very
perplexing מצוה, I would like to share with you the story of a person who loved
trees and had some tall ones planted in his garden. His neighbour, however,
sued him for ***"daylight robbery***...." Every Jewish person should love trees, but of
a different kind.

"עץ חיים היא למחזיקים בה" – "A tree of life (Torah) for those who grasp it."

"ותומכיה מאושר" – "And those who uphold it are rendered happy" (Prov. 3:18).

This kind of tree has the opposite effect. It ***provides*** daylight and ***illuminates*** our
path through life. Let us try to make use of this light to provide some insight
into the מצוה of שמיטה.

The following problems present themselves:

1. What reasoning is there behind the precept of שמיטה? (This is the
   law forbidding work on the land in Israel every seventh year.)

---

1. Commandment.
2. The Sabbatical year.
3. My Statutes.

2. Why does the Torah give such a severe punishment for non-observance of שמיטה, namely, expulsion from the land of Israel?

"The land will be appeased for its שמיטה years, while you will be in the land of your enemy" (Lev. 26:34). This came to pass with seventy years of exile to Babylonia. As Rashi explains (Lev. 26:35): During the existence of the First Temple in Jerusalem, we did not observe the seventy שמיטה and יובל years which occurred during that period, therefore the exile lasted exactly seventy years. An amazing prediction which came true, together with many more which we shall discuss in the *Sidra* כי תבוא.

3. What is the explanation of the statement in Gemara Shabbat (118b): "If the Jewish people would observe two Shabbatot, they would be redeemed immediately?"

שמיטה is the example par excellence of absolute trust in Hashem. The Torah itself mentions a question (Lev. 25: 20-21) "If you will say what will we eat in the seventh year? Behold! We will not sow and not gather in our crops? I will ordain my blessing for you in the sixth year and it will yield a crop sufficient for the three year period" (until the crops grow in the eighth year). However, obviously we have to work as well.

"You should work the land for six years and the seventh year shall be a complete rest for the land" (Lev. 25:3-4).

This is beautifully illustrated in the parable of an old ferryman who painted the word אמונה[1] on one oar and מלאכה[2] on the other. To cross a river one needs both; one without the other would make the boat go round in circles....

שמיטה is the most difficult of national duties. According to the Chatam Sofer ז"ל, the explanation of Rashi's remarks point to these difficulties (Lev. 25:1). Rashi says: What is the connection between שמיטה and Mount Sinai? It is to teach us that, just as שמיטה was given on Mount Sinai, so were all the other מצות (*Sifra*). What is the meaning of this statement?

No human leader could have issued such a commandment that all work on the land must cease every seventh year. The people might starve. This could only have come from Hashem Himself. So all the other מצות also only have come from

---

1. Faith.
2. Work.

Hashem. Although the actual fulfillment of this מצוה only applies in Israel, its message is timeless and unlimited.

What is the message? There are many aspects in connection with this מצוה.

> **Rambam:** It is an agricultural device for increasing crops by letting the soil rest.
>
> **Abarbanel** violently disagrees. He says, if that were so, why a three fold harvest in the sixth year and why such a severe punishment?

However, the first question can be answered by saying the three fold harvest is not quantative but qualitative. As the Rashi says "He eats little but is blessed" (Lev. 26:5).

> **Ibn Ezra:** It is meant to be a sabbatical year for Torah study.
>
> **Chinuch** points to the verse itself: "The land belongs to Me" (Lev. 25:23).
>
> Therefore, just as no work must be done on Shabbat to acknowledge every seventh day that Hashem is Master over nature, so, no work must be done on the land every seventh year, to acknowledge that the owner of the land is Hashem. Furthermore, שמיטה is the prototype of complete אמונה[1] in Hashem. Our Rabbis call it יסוד האמונה – the foundation of faith. American research discovered that man's toil only produces five per cent of the harvest. The rest is produced by Hashem. In the sixth year we receive three harvests for five per cent toil!
>
> **Rav Kook:** It is meant to be a spiritual break for the **nation** just like Shabbat is for the **individual**. It promotes peace between people because it removes the jealousy of wealth. It gives a new start for debtors – שמיטת כספים – the cancellation of all debts at the end of the שמיטה year. The יובל[2] year removes the monopoly from the great land owners. The land goes back to the original owners and all Jewish slaves are set free.
>
> **Urim Vetumim:** The earth carried on producing during Shabbat and Yom Tov during the six years; therefore it needed a שמיטה year of rest

---

1. Trust.
2. Jubilee.

to make up for the Shabbat and Yom Tov periods. During the six years there are

6x7 Yamim Tovim =	42
6x52 Shabbatot =	312
	354 days which equal one lunar year exactly.

Malbim: During the שמיטה year the land reverts to its state of the first man before the sin. No need to work it.

Lubavitcher Rebbe: There is nothing lower in human endeavour than working the soil. No grosser labour than tilling it, but by command of Hashem man brings holiness even to this aspect of life by refraining from all this work.

שבת לה׳ – "A rest to Hashem" (Lev. 25:2). Even the earth celebrates!

Yalkut Yehudah: Only what you toil for is yours (during the six years) but when you do not work the soil, all are equal to acquire what grows by itself. The fields become ownerless and revert to the real owner – to Hashem.

"כי לי הארץ" – "The land belongs to Me" (Lev. 25:23).

There is still more to it! We can clearly see that there is a striking parallel between the counting of the Omer for forty nine days from *Pesach* to *Shavuot* and forty nine years between counting the years (by the *Bet Din*) and the Yovel[1] year, the fiftieth year. Every seven days we thank Hashem for granting us חרות הגוף[2] so every seventh year we are free, too. Just as after *Pesach* there are seven שבתות when we enjoy freedom of the body – leading up to חרות הנפש[3] by receiving the Torah, so the seven שמיטות lead us to the ultimate חרות הנפש – the blowing of the *shofar* on *Yom Kippur* of the *Yovel* year. **The Summit!** Then any sins towards G-d are forgiven as well as any injustices towards people. Furthermore, just like חרות הנפש of *Matan Torah* required <u>our own</u> נעשה ונשמע "we shall do and hear" acceptance, so *Yovel* requires <u>our own</u> actions in blowing the *shofar*, sending away the slaves and returning the fields to their original owners. Without the acceptance of נעשה ונשמע there would have been no *Matan Torah*,[4] and without the blowing of the *Shofar*, and freeing the slaves and returning the land, there is no *Yovel* (Rambam, Laws of Shmitta 10:13).

---

1. Jubilee.
2. Freedom of the body.
3. Freedom of the soul.
4. Giving of the Torah.

Our Rabbis tell us:

"הכל בידי שמים חוץ מיראת שמים"

"Everything is in the hands of Hashem except for the fear of Hashem"
(Gemara Berachot 33b).

At the counting of the Omer we elevate ourselves by our own effort from the impurities of Egypt to the real freedom of the giving of the Torah. So here we raise ourselves from the bondage to the soil as well as to creditors, from שמיטה up to יובל when complete freedom from slavery is attained and the family fields are returned to their rightful owners. *Yom Kippur* atones for sins towards Hashem and since

"אין יום כפור מכפר עד שירצה את חבירו"

"Yom Kippur cannot atone until one has pacified one's fellowman"
(Mishna Yoma 8:9).

This is being done too. Therefore, *Yovel* is truly the **summit** of real physical and spiritual freedom both of individuals and of a nation as a whole.

Furthermore, the son of the Sokochover Gaon, the *Or Hachayim*, writes in *Bereshit*: Every Shabbat is a renewal of the Lease of the creation to mankind; so every שמיטה is a renewal of the lease of Israel to us, the Jewish people. "אשר אני נותן לכם" – ... which I **give** to you... not which I **have given.** It is renewable all the time.

Now we have the answer to the second question: Why such a severe punishment for non-observance of שמיטה? שמיטה is not only a biological blessing for the land but also an **educational** opportunity to study the Torah, as well as the **religious** acknowledgment of Hashem and of complete trust in Him. It is also a spiritual break for the nation, freedom from slavery to the soil and to the creditors. It contains all the ingredients of the three pillars on which the world stands:

> *Torah* (Sabbatical) service to the L-rd
> *Avodah* (ability to serve to Hashem by freeing ourselves from slavery to the soil)
> *Gemilat Chasadim* (kindness to others)

"והיתה שבת הארץ לכם לאכלה לך ולעבדך ולאמתך ולשכירך
ולתושבך הגרים עמך"

"The Shabbat produce of the land shall be yours to eat, for you, for your servant, for your maidservant, for your labourer and for the resident who lives with you" (Lev. 25:6).

That is also a condition of the renewal of the lease. All these matters apply to Shabbat, too. That is why שמיטה is called שבת לה'. We have now seen the importance of the מצוה of שמיטה. If one does not trust Hashem and does not do this mitzvah with all its aspects, then our lease will not be renewed and we might have to leave Israel – Heaven forbid!

Deeper still, what does Rashi say at the beginning of *Bereshit*? Why does the Torah start with the creation of the world and the stories of the book of Bereshit and not with the laws of Pesach? This is so that the nations of the world should not come and say that we are robbers because we captured Israel. Hashem created the world and has given Israel to us. Our right to Israel is, therefore, **solely** on the grounds that the freeholder, Hashem, has given us the lease. If we do not comply with its conditions then we really are robbers – Heaven forbid!

Now we also have the answer to the final problem: What are these two Shabbatot? As we have seen, the six days of work and the six years of the *shmitta* period are interconnected (Num. 25:4). So are Shabbat and *Shmitta*. The Torah calls *Shmitta* – שבת שבתון – a complete rest. Both contain similar teachings and blessings, and so, if Jews kept these two Shabbatot, then redemption would come immediately because it would cement our claim to Israel.

At the present time the phrase "you are robbers...." is bandied about a great deal amongst the nations of the world. Our task is to do our bit to silence this false charge by using both our faith **and** our work in the crossing of rivers and other obstacles. It is also our duty to use our days and years meaningfully in the service of the Creator and Master of the World, the freeholder and owner of our precious land of Israel, and to observe both Shabbat and שמיטה in practice as well as יובל's timeless message. Then the verses (Lev. 26: 3-6)

"אם בחקתי תלכו ואת מצותי תשמרו ועשיתם אתם ..... וישבתם לבטח
בארצכם ונתתי שלום בארץ"
"If you will follow My decrees and observe My commandments and perform them, then you will surely dwell in your land ...and I will give peace in the land" (Lev. 26:3-6).

BAMIDBAR

CENSUS OF THE JEWISH PEOPLE

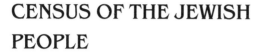

"שאו את ראש כל עדת בני ישראל למשפחתם לבית אבתם במספר שמות
כל זכר לגלגלתם"

"Take a census of the entire assembly of the Children of Israel, according to their families, according to their father's household, by number of the names, every male according to their headcount."

(Num. 1:2)

H ere is a little anecdote by way of introduction to this subject:
A lady had a photograph taken at a fashionable studio. "Good heavens!" she exclaimed to the photographer, "Do I really look like that?" The photographer smiled at the lady and replied: "Madam, the answer is in the NEGATIVE...."

There are a number of questions on this *Sidra* which we shall try to answer in a POSITIVE manner.

1. What is the significance of this count? Surely there was no need to ascertain how many portions of food were required. Didn't everyone receive the Heavenly Manna?
2. What can we learn from the way the Jewish people were organised during their travels in the desert?
3. What is the connection with the previous Sidrot?

Before answering these questions we have to realise that the people had to establish their יחוס[1] by documents or witnesses (Rashi on Num. 1:18). However, the Radziner Rebbe used to say:

---

1. Genealogy.

"יחוס is great, but it is like an umbrella, it is only useful if a person is under it." When someone repeated the well known proverb "an apple does not fall far from the tree" to the great חפץ חיים, the famous Sage replied: "Yes, if the wind does not carry it away."

How often do the very strong winds of our surroundings carry many away from the trees of the wonderful Zeidas – grandfathers – as well as from those of their fathers! However, for the census in the desert, tracing ancestry was essential for affiliation to individual tribes, and the headcount was significant for many reasons:

a) It is called "שאו" – "uplifting." Being part of the count makes everyone feel like a proud soldier of the צבא ה',[1] and like part of עם סגולה.[2]

b) "According to their families" signified that each individual is not an insignificant name amongst 603,549 others, but that every person retained his identity.

c) The השגחה פרטית[3] was also evident in the מצוה of the census, because, as Rashi comments (Num. 1:1): Hashem revealed His infinite love of the Jewish people by counting them frequently. When they left Egypt (Exod. 12:37), after the sin of the Golden Calf, to see how many were left (Exod. 38:26), and now, when He rested His Presence amongst them (Num. 1:46).

d) To give us the opportunity to demonstrate our gratitude and to show how miraculously we had **grown** as a nation. We came to Egypt as a family of only seventy people, but within two hundred and ten years, we had expanded to a few million people (Ramban).

e) The census was eventually needed to prepare for the military campaign to capture Israel. It is true to say that originally there was no need of a military count because the occupation of the land would have taken place without war immediately, had the Jewish people not sinned, unfortunately, at the episode of the spies (Rashi, Deut.1:8). However, this was not to be....

---

1. The army of Hashem.
2. A treasured people.
3. The Divine Providence.

f) The census also revealed how many people were eligible to receive portions of land in the Land of Israel (Ramban).

The count was accomplished by everyone contributing half a shekel. This prompts us to ask: "Why was this not achieved by a headcount?" The answer is: We have a principle in the Gemara (Betza 3b):

"כל דבר שבמנין לא בטל"
"Anything which is counted does not become forfeit."

For example, eggs which are counted are important products and, therefore, they do not become בטל even in a thousand if one of them happens to be טריפה.[1] So figuratively speaking, every Jewish person is unique, a whole world of his own (Mishna Sanhedrin, Chapter 4:5). Therefore, he does not become nullified in a multitude. He is not just a number. However, the half shekel contribution towards the silver sockets of the משכן[2] is a means of emphasising that everyone has an **_equal_** share in the foundation of the משכן. (At the first count before the building of the משכן, Rashi, Exod. 30:15.)

Here, in the second year, the half shekel donations were used to buy public sacrifices, so that everyone would have an equal part in them. These were collected every subsequent year.

There is another reason for this census. The verse says:

"תפקדו אתם לצבאתם אתה ואהרן"
"You shall count them according to their legions, you and Aharon"
(Num. 1:3).

This created our opportunity to **_personally_** receive the blessings of the Father of the Prophets and his brother, the High Priest, and since everyone is a world of his own, משה רבנו and אהרן הכהן could not bless all of them together but gave each one a blessing tailored to his individual requirements. Incidentally, there is a Chassidic custom to present a "Quittel" – a paper with special requests to a Rebbe. Here we may have had the first "Quittels," and what distinguished Rebbes!

Now that we have answered the first question concerning the necessity for a

---

1. Non-kosher.
2. Tabernacle.

census, let us try to give a <u>positive</u> reply to the second one about the lessons to be learned from the way our people were organised in their travels through the wilderness.

Just like in an intricate machine, all the various components must form a unit in order to function perfectly; so all members of the "Army of Hashem" must be united to form an effective spiritual force. In the desert, the organisation of the twelve tribes with the Tabernacle in the centre created this unity. In this way, the potential of each tribe and each individual was combined for achieving perfection.

"איש על מחנהו ואיש על דגלו"

"Everyone by his camp and by his flag" (Num. 1:52).

The Divine camp in the middle was surrounded by the camp of the Levites and the camp of the ישראלים. The centre of all the camps was the Tent of Meeting, the spiritual heart of the Jewish people. This solves the second question. Now we have a truly convincing answer to the last question, namely, "what is the connection with the previous Sidrot?"

Time is very precious and one must count each day as a jewel. "וספרתם" – and you shall count – (ספירת העומר) comprises the word ספיר – sapphire, followed by counting שמיטה and יובל years and the counting of the precious individuals of the עם סגולה.[1]

As the זוהר[2] says in בראשית:

"צלותא דסגיאין סליך קמי קודשא בריך הוא בגוונין סגיעין צלותא דיחיד
רק גון חד"

"The prayers of many are in front of Hashem like many colours but
the prayer of one is only one colour."

This is the importance of תפלה בצבור.[3] Similarly, in studying תורה and working together for the furtherance of תורה Judaism, everyone should contribute his or her special talents and qualities for the benefit of all. Furthermore, we have seen that although יחוס[4] is important, we must realise that it is not the most

---

1. The treasured people.
2. Mystical book.
3. Prayers with a congregation.
4. Genealogy.

important thing in life. This reminds me of the story of the שמש[1] of the Chassam Sofer ז״ל, one of the famous Rabbis of the last century. He used to boast to his friends that he had a rich uncle in America and that he was the butler to the great Chassam Sofer. The friend told him: "I would understand your pride if you had the learning of the Chassam Sofer and your uncle's money. But the fact is that you possess your uncle's learning and the Chassam Sofer's money.... There needs to be a man under the umbrella...."

Furthermore, we must not allow the winds of our surroundings to carry us away from the עץ חיים[2] our תורה.

What is required of us is that everyone should stand up to be counted and lend his support to the Tent of Meeting. In our times, these are the בתי מדרש[3] Jewish schools, yeshivot and seminaries which take the place of the משכן and its successor, the great Temple. There no winds can move us and we can look forward to a continued upsurge of true תורה Judaism in our life's travels until the rebuilding of the בית המקדש[4] in ירושלים[5] and the coming of משיח.[6]

May it be speedily in our days!

---

1. The butler.
2. The tree of life.
3. Houses of study and prayer.
4. Temple.
5. Jerusalem.
6. Messiah.

THE BLESSINGS OF THE COHANIM

נשא

"דבר אל אהרן ואל בניו לאמר כה תברכו את בני ישראל אמור להם...
יברכך...."

"Speak to Aharon and his sons saying: This is the way that you
shall bless the Children of Israel. Say to them... May Hashem bless
you....

(Num. 6:22-27)

T he Vilna Gaon and the Dubno Magid were great friends. One day the Vilna
Gaon asked the Dubno Magid: "How do you always find such fitting
parables to illustrate your sermons?" The Magid replied: "I shall answer your
question with a משל."[1]

A king sent his son to a military academy to learn the art of sharp-shooting.
After having completed his course the prince passed through a village. To his
great surprise he saw many "bulls-eyes" in the centre of the circles on a wall.
After having made enquiries, he discovered that the master sharp-shooter
happened to be a little village boy. The prince asked him: "Where did you
acquire your sharp-shooting skills to be able to hit the centre of the circle every
time?" The village lad replied: "Your Excellency! I did not shoot my arrows into
the circle like you do. First I shoot, then I make a circle to go round it." The
Dubno Magid continued: "First I find a nice story then I encircle it with my
sermon."

Let us *"shoot"* a number of questions on the subject of the blessings of the
כהנים[2] in our *Sidra* and put the answers round them....

1. We always put great emphasis on scholarship and piety as the most
    important of human attributes. If so, why does the תורה appoint

---

1. A parable.
2. Priests.

כהנים,[1] some of whom may not have these qualities, to bless the people? Why are scholars and strictly G-d fearing people not the **_only_** people to perform this important task?

2. Why are these ברכות couched in the singular? Surely the כהנים bless the whole congregation?

3. Why does the Mishna Sotah (Ch. 7:2) insist that the ברכות כהנים[2] **_must_** be in Hebrew whilst *Shema*, prayers, or grace after meals can be said in **_any_** language (if one cannot say them in Hebrew) (Ch. 7:1)?

4. In each of the three ברכות the name of Hashem is in the centre because obviously Hashem gives the ברכות, and the כהנים are merely His agents. However, why does the first blessing consist of two words, the second of four words, and the third of six words (Abarbanel)?

5. **Finally**, why do כהנים not "duchan" (referring to the platform on which the כהנים stand whilst they bless the people) at night (Talmud Yerushalmi, Chapter 1 of Ta'anit)?

Let us introduce the answers to these problems with the following anecdote:

A student at the yeshiva of the famous חפץ חיים (Rabbi Yisrael Meir HaCohen, 1838-1933) in Radin who had been diagnosed as having an incurable, life-threatening illness, came to his Rebbe, the חפץ חיים, to ask for a blessing. The Rosh Yeshiva told him that he would give him advice provided that he never revealed it to anyone. The yeshiva student readily agreed.

"Go and see a certain תלמיד חכם[3] who lives in a small town and ask him for a ברכה.[4] He will give you a ברכה and, with G-d's help, you will recover. The student did so and in an incredibly short time he became well. Eventually, he even married and raised a family. Many years later, he became ill again and was extremely concerned. He immediately traveled to his former Rebbe who was, by then, old and frail. The חפץ חיים remembered their past encounter but told him, " I wish I could help you but what can I do? When you first had the illness I was young and I fasted for **_forty_**! days on your behalf, so that you would be healed. Today, I am too old and I cannot fast like that anymore...."

---

1. Priests.
2. Blessings by the Priests.
3. Torah scholar.
4. A blessing.

What is incredible here is not only that the גדול הדור[1] fasted for forty days on behalf of one of his students, but that he used a subterfuge of telling the young man to go to a תלמיד חכם in another town to get a blessing, so that when the student became well the חפץ חיים would not get the credit for it!

We see that a blessing from a כהן involves the utmost concern with the plight of the person he blesses – the חפץ חיים happened to be a כהן ("The Maggid Speaks," by Rabbi P. Krohn).

כהנם who pronounce Hashem's blessings for the benefit of their congregations, even though they are not world famous scholars still have good will – טוב עין (Sotah 38b) and genuine concern for those they bless. They used to depend on the contribution of ordinary people for thir livelihood. Therefore, they are bound to the rest of the nation with a bond of gratitude and they wish their congregations well with all their heart (Rabbi Wolkin). The Talmud Yerushalmi says that a blessing given by someone who loves a person will be fulfilled, even if the person who receives it is totally wicked. That is the reason, explains Ralbag (a 14th century commentator), that יצחק requested עשו to bring him venison before being blessed. This is due to the fact that יצחק knew that עשו was a bad son. Therefore, in order to arouse in himself feelings of love towards Esau to make the blessing more effective, he commanded Esau to bring him venison. When יצחק blessed יעקב later, no preliminaries were required, since he loved him (Gen. 28:1). That is also the reason why the כהנים **face** the congregation, unlike the חזן[2] as an indication of love. Similarly, the כרובים[3] faced **one another** (like man and wife) – when Jews were performing Hashem's will, but when they were not (Heaven forbid), the Cherubin faced **away** from one another (Gemara Bava Basra 99a). That is why the כהנים conclude the ברכה, which they pronounce before their three priestly blessings with "באהבה"[4] a word which we do not find in any other ברכה.

This answers the first question of why כהנים were chosen to perform the "duchaning."

We now move on to the second question. Why do they bless in the singular? After all they address the *whole* congregation?

---

1. The greatest of his generation.
2. The Reader.
3. Angel-like figures above the Holy Ark.
4. With love.

The answer can be found in the Mishna Sanhedrin (4:5), "He who preserves *one* human soul, it is as if he has preserved a whole world...." and to tell the greatness of Hashem. A human king mints many coins from one seal and all are alike, but the King of Kings, Blessed be He, mints all human beings with the seal of the first man, and no one is exactly the same as any other person (in appearance, talents, character, ability, education and so on in any generation). Therefore, everyone is duty-bound to say "for me the whole world was created!" That is the **thrill of life**! Everyone can reach a unique standard of קידוש ה'[1] by performance of מצות and good deeds which **no one else** can possibly achieve, because no one else is like him or her! Truly, "for me the whole world was created!" (Gemara Sanhedrin 37a).

That is the reason why everyone requires a special tailor-made blessing fitting to his or her circumstances, and consequently the duchaning has to be said in the singular.

How can, however, the blessings of the כהנים – who are the agents of Hashem – be fitted to each individual?

By pronouncing them in Hebrew. Only the Divine Hebrew language can be interpreted in many ways:

"כפטיש יפצץ סלע"
"Like a hammer hitting a rock it produces many sparks" (Jeremiah 23:29)
(Gemara Shabbat 88b).

Now we have answered questions two and three.

This leads us on to explain the question of the nature of the blessing themselves. Why does the first blessing consist of two words, the second consists of four and the third of six? Rashi explains the first ברכה: "May Hashem bless you...." this refers to material prosperity. The second blessing, "May Hashem illuminate His countenance for you," refers to the light of Torah as in Proverbs 6:23.

"כי נר מצוה ותורה אור"
"For the commandment is the lamp and the Torah is the light."

Material blessing, although important, consists of only two words. It is only a **means** towards the spiritual blessings of Torah life which are *doubly* important.

---

1. Sanctification of the Holy name.

If a person's life is so conducted – two plus four – then all six words together give you שלום real peace! This is the proper balance between the needs of the body and the higher duty to the soul!

Finally, we should discuss the reason why duchaning is not performed at night! In Leviticus 9:22 it says:

"And אהרן lifted up his hands towards his people and he blessed them (with the priestly benedictions – Rashi)... and came down after carrying out the sin, elevation and peace offerings."

We see here clearly a link of the duchaning with the Service in the Temple. During the night there were no sacrifices. Therefore, there were no blessings from the כהנים either. That also sheds light on the custom not to look at the כהנים during duchaning. It is a reflection of the activity that took place in the בית המקדש.[1] There the שכינה[2] rested. So we may not look at the כהנים. As Rashi explains (Talmud Haggiga 16a), the שכינה is resting on the tips of their fingers.

With these insights, many aspects of this great מצוה are now clearly understood. כהנים who love their congregation and are concerned for them pronounce these ברכות. They are in the singular and in Hebrew, because everyone needs a special ברכה, since everyone is different and unique.

The blessings themselves teach us the right way of life. Material prosperity is only a means to the doubly important spiritual elevation through תורה. By re-enacting the blessings in the Temple, the כהנים bring the שכינה of Hashem to bless us.

May Hashem give us all these ברכות and grant us perfect peace!

---

1. Temple.
2. Divine Presence.

"FAREEBLES" – "UPSETS"

FAMOUS YIDDISH EXPRESSION

בהעלותך

This *Sidra* contains many varied and diverse subjects. It begins with the kindling of the Candelabra by אהרן the High Priest (Num. 8:2). Then it continues with the consecration of the לוים, followed by the laws of פסח שני, the "Second Pesach" for those who could not offer the Pascal lamb at the proper time. After that we read about the way the Jewish people journeyed in the desert, guided and protected by the Heavenly cloud. Then we have two verses which are enclosed in two upside-down "Nun" letters (Num. 10:35-36). This is followed by the people complaining about their fate and being punished by fire. Then the *Sidra* relates the episode of the "meat revolution," when some of the Jewish people bemoaned the fact that they had no meat, "only" the מן, culminating in many being buried in the "graves of lust." Finally, the לשון הרע[1] of מרים, the sister of משה רבינו, against her brother, resulting in her being afflicted by "צרעת",[2] for seven days.

The question arises, of course, what is the connection between all these subjects? Secondly, what is the meaning behind the upside-down "Nuns"?

Before attempting to answer these questions I would like to share the following anecdote with you. The great חפץ חיים once approached a wealthy person for a donation for his Yeshiva. However, he was told: "I have already given and fulfilled my obligations." The חפץ חיים replied: "There are several ways to fulfill one's obligations. Some people eat "bread with salt." Some have ten people living in one room and wear very simple sandals and second-hand clothing and so "fulfill their obligation" to survive. You, fortunately, do not lead such a life. Hashem has given you a life of luxury to enjoy. Since your lifestyle is not limited by your "obligation," so your donations to תורה must not be limited either. What will happen after one hundred and twenty years? You will be taken

---

1. Evil talk.
2. A divinely imposed skin condition.

to the Heavenly Court on High and subsequently to גן עדן[1] where תורה giants and great supporters will sit at golden tables and נהנין מזיו השכינה – enjoying the glow of the שכינה.[2] But you will be allocated standing room in a corner, where no one will notice you. There you will wave your wad of receipts and claim that you have "fulfilled your obligation." However, you will be told: Take it easy Reb Yid. Why are you protesting? You gave only enough צדקה[3] to "fulfill your obligation," so we, in turn, also give you just enough גן עדן to "fulfill **our** obligation!"

This will help us answer our questions:

All the topics contained in this *Sidra* deal with people who were greatly upset. They have one common denominator: "Fareebles" – "Upsets." However, up to the verse containing the upside down "Nuns", the people concerned were complaining about __spiritual__ matters. They clamoured to go **beyond** their minimal obligations and do more than was required, because of their love for Hashem and His מצות. However, after the upside-down "Nuns" the situation turned literally upside-down. They complained about their __physical__ state and demanded more. Whilst the first "complainants" were rewarded by Hashem's protection with the Heavenly clouds, the second group were heavily punished.

Let us see what Rashi (Num. 8:2) says:

"אהרן was not called upon to donate gifts to the משכן like the twelve princes who gave identical offerings (in last week's *Sidra*) to dedicate the new משכן. This upset him (because he thought that his involuntary involvement in the Golden Calf was the cause of it). However, he was given a greater מצוה, namely, the lighting of the מנורה. The candelabra is the symbol of the written תורה (the centre shaft) and the six branches representing the six orders of the משנה.[4]

The מנורה revealed that the שכינה[5] was in Israel (Talmud Shabbat 22b) by the miracle of the one light to the west of the seven which had the same amount of oil as the other six. Yet, whilst the others went out in the morning, the western light continued to burn until the evening and one could kindle the other six from this one. (That is why we have a נר תמיד[6] in the synagogue). Furthermore, the Ramban comments that the descendants of אהרן, the High Priest, namely

---

1. Paradise.
2. Divine Presence.
3. Charity.
4. The Oral Law.
5. The Divine presence.
6. Continuous light.

the חשמנאים[1] rekindled the light of Judaism which was nearly extinguished at חנוכה time. What a remarkable prediction!

The לוים[2] were upset. "What about us? Why were we left out?" So they were inducted into service, and they brought about the return of the שכינה, namely:

"שובה ה' רבבות אלפי ישראל"

"Return Hashem amongst the twenty two thousand of Israel" (Num. 31:36).

That was the total number of all לוים!

Some who were impure because they dealt with the dead were upset that they could not offer the Pascal lamb, particularly those who carried the bones of יוסף. After all the Midrash says:

"וינס ויצא החוצה"

"Joseph *fled* outside" (from the entreaties of Potiphar's wife) (Gen. 39:15).

Therefore,

"הים ראה וינס"

"The sea saw and fled" (Psa. 114:3).

"מה ראה הים וינס" – "What was it that the sea saw that caused it to *flee* – at the splitting of the sea? It was the casket of יוסף who had *fled*...." (Midrash Hagadol 14). Therefore, they complained: since we are carrying the bones of יוסף whose merit enabled us to leave Egypt, why should we be excluded from offering the Pascal lamb, the symbol of our exodus from Egypt? They were consequently given פסח שני, the opportunity to offer it one month later.

All this great display of love for מצות *beyond their obligations* was instrumental in receiving the special protection of the Heavenly clouds by day and the pillar of fire by night.

"על פי ה' יחנו ועל פי ה' יסעו"

"According to the word of Hashem they encamped and according to the word of Hashem they would journey" (Num. 9:23).

"ויהי בנסע הארן ויאמר משה קומה ה' ויפצו איביך וינסו משאניך מפניך

ובנחה יאמר שובה ה' רבבות אלפי ישראל"

---

1. The Hasmoneans.
2. The Levites.

"When the Ark would journey, Moses said: 'Arise, Hashem, and let Your
foes be scattered and let those who hate You flee from before You.'
And when it rested, he would say 'Reside in tranquillity, O Hashem,
among the myriad thousands of Israel" (Num. 10:35-36).

These are the two verses between the upside-down "Nuns." However, this very
protection from Hashem led to the meat revolt, with disastrous consequences.
The people said: "We remember the fish which we ate in Egypt free of charge"
(the Midrash explains this as 'free of מצות'). They did not like the wonderful
miracle of manna which gave them a great deal of leisure time to study תורה.
That is why seventy Rabbis were appointed to teach them תורה – to provide them
with spiritual freedom.

"There is no free person except one who occupies himself with the study of
the תורה" (Ethics 6:2).

That is why we have the upside-down "Nuns." נעשה ונשמע[1] (Exod. 24:7) has
two initial "Nuns." The people turned them on their heads. They failed the test.

"למען אנסנו הילך בתורתי אם לא"
"So that I can test them whether they will follow My teachings or not"
(Exod. 16:4).

How would they react to the fact that food came to them from Heaven without
toil (Seforno)? They hankered after freedom without תורה discipline and after
excessive luxuries which led them to קברות התאוה – the graves of lust (Num.
11:34).

מרים also complained that her brother, משה רבינו neglected his wife because
he was so occupied with looking after the Jewish people. She did not take into
account that משה רבינו acted on the instructions of Hashem, and that is why she
was punished.

This is the connection between all the various subjects. Devotion, love and
acting **_beyond_** one's obligations leads to Divine protection, but pursuit of
physical desires **_in excess_** leads to the grave. Similarly, evil talk leads to צרעת.[2]
There are good and bad complaints. נעשה ונשמע must be followed and not be
turned upside down.

---

1. We shall do and we shall listen.
2. Skin affliction.

This reminds me of the following remarkable story: In Israel the son of a Russian immigrant once celebrated a סיום[1] at a Yeshiva. With difficulty the father was prevailed upon to attend. When he arrived he was struck by the very joyful atmosphere at the event. Eventually, he asked to be called upon to speak. He explained that despite his assimilation to the Russian culture, he was sent to Siberia. There a friend told him the following parable which he only began to understand now.

Two gardeners tending an apple orchard decided to do away with the "old fashioned" methods and turned the apple trees upside-down to produce even better apples. Their philosophy? "If dirty roots can produce such delicious fruits, how much more so would nice branches." Of course nothing happened. They tried again and again until only one apple was left and the orchard was saved by its seed. "Now I understand," said the father. "My generation in Russia tried to overturn נעשה ונשמע, our roots, to produce a more modern youth based on communism, the "culture" of the country at the time. It has not worked but one apple was saved. You are the apple, my son. You are the future of our family and of our people. I am proud of you!" Then he embraced his son and wept.

The message of our *Sidra* is now clear. During the historic times we find ourselves in, our lifestyle must not limited by obligations, but we enthusiastically follow the guidelines of our תורה **beyond** our obligations with love and devotion. That should be the order of the day.

Just as Hashem tested us in the desert, so we are being tested now as to how we use our more plentiful leisure time – thanks to Hashem. Will we dull our brain with the ceaseless flow of tripe from "that box" and other media, or by cheap thrills of social and moral delinquency by overturning our precious mark of distinction – נעשה ונשמע?

"הילך בתורתי?"

"Will they go in the ways of My Torah" (Exod. 16:4)?

Will we use the extra time for study of the תורה and observance of מצות? The former leads to קברות התאוה – "graves of lust," AIDS, and similar disasters – Heaven forbid – but the latter leads to Divine Clouds of protection from Hashem. The choice is ours!

---

1. A party at the conclusion of the study of a tractate of the Gemara.

VIEWING AND INTERPRETING EVENTS · שלח לך

O ur *Sidra* deals with the viewing and inspection of the most wonderful country on earth, the physical and spiritual centre of the universe – ארצנו הקדושה.[1] Yet ten מרגלים – spies, or better still, surveyors, out of the twelve משה רבינו sent, reported: "We found giants there and cities which are greatly fortified...we cannot conquer it" (Num. 13: 28-31). Their report caused a terrible disaster. Nearly all members of that generation had to die in the desert, only their children entered Israel.

This reminds me of a Polish Jew who, while visiting his relations in London, was shown round the sights. At each beautiful home he saw he exclaimed enthusiastically, "I would like to live here." However, when they looked at Buckingham Palace he did not utter a word, just stared glumly at the palace. His relations asked him: "Why are you so silent? Would you not like to live here?" "No, for heavens sake, no. The cost of מזוזות alone would ruin me!...."

The ten bad spies exclaimed:

"לא נוכל לעלות"
"We cannot ascend" (Num. 13:31).

The cost of capturing the palace of the world is too great! It will ruin us....
However,

"ועבדי כלב עקב היתה רוח אחרת עמו"
"My servant Caleb because a different spirit was with him...
therefore, I shall bring him to the land" (Num. 14:24).

Similarly, יהושע would also enter the land of Israel.
I shall confine myself to three points only:

---

1. Our "holy land."

1. In which way was their approach and spirit different?
2. What is the connection with ציצית at the end of the *Sidra*?
3. What lessons can we learn from this episode for our times?

To answer the first question I would like to share the following anecdote with you....

A mischievous member of a congregation discovered that their Rabbi was partial to cherry brandy. He offered him a number of bottles of his favourite beverage as a gift, provided that it would be published in the synagogue magazine. Surprisingly, the Rabbi consented. In due course the following notice appeared in the synagogue paper: "Rabbi Chaskel thanks Mr. Shmelke for the gift of fruit in the **_spirit_** in which it was given...."

Let us now see the difference in the spirit of the good versus the bad spies.

There are a number of ways to view things. First of all the human eye. What wonderful instruments Hashem has given us! The eye is highly complex, consisting of many millions of seeing elements, plus lens and retina! A fantastic televisual apparatus opening up for us nature, holy books and scrolls, and protecting us. A million nerve cells connect it to the brain. Yet it is limited – it only catches a few of the many wavelengths. We cannot see infra-red light because its wavelength is too long. Neither can we see ultra-violet rays because their wavelength is too short. We can see lots of things, but there are many things we cannot see.

The mind's eye is a thousand times more wondrous. It contains hindsight, insight, foresight, accumulated knowledge of the past, the ability to think and draw conclusions, calculate and invent, but it is also limited. What is **_not known_** is by far the greatest vision of all. This is in the province of the soul's eye. Einstein once said: "To know that what is impenetrable to us really exists, the mystical, the secret (and we can add, the Divine), this knowledge is the highest wisdom and the most radiant beauty, this feeling is the centre of true religiousness" (Rabbi E. Pilchik).

The following analogy will convince us of this fact. When we travel in a jumbo jet, our eyes can only see the magnificent plane and nature, etc., around us, but the pilot knows about another world. The world of radar keeps him in contact with flight control, or in the case of a spaceship, with mission control. We do not see it but it is there!....

In human life we also live in two worlds – גשמיות ורוחניות.[1] תורה combines and blends these two worlds into one. It is the heavenly Pilot which guides us safely in this *multi*-dimensional world!

That is the answer to the first question. The other ten spies viewed Israel with their physical and mind's eye whilst כלב and יהושע penetrated into the multi-dimensional, unseen world of the spirit! They saw with the *soul's eye* which gave them an entirely different outlook. For example, the ten bad spies said:

"ארץ אכלת יושביה"
"The land consumes its inhabitants" (Num. 13:32).

Everywhere we went we saw funerals! Survival of the fittest (Darwin's theory), only the giants survive. However, as Rashi explains, these funerals were engineered by Hashem, so that the people would be busy with funerals and the spies should remain unnoticed.... Giants? They were only shadows. Even a small person can cast a large shadow!

The good spies said:

"סר צלם מעליהם"
"Their shadow has departed from them."

"לחמנו הם"
"They are our bread" (Num. 14:9).

What bread did they have? מן[2] which melted in the sun, and their strengths would also melt away.

We find the same idea in the Haftarah. Forty years later יהושע sent two spies to Jericho who reported to him on their return:

"וגם נמגו כל ישבי הארץ מפנינו"
"And also all the inhabitants of the land have melted before us"
(Josh. 2:24).

That leads us to the answer to our second question, concerning the connection between the story of the spies with the chapter on ציצית. There, the תורה

---

1. Body and spirit.
2. Manna.

commands us to place blue threads at each of the four corners of a garment, so that "you may see it and remember all the commandments of Hashem" (Num. 15:38-39).

In Midrash Rabba (Num. 17) the following is stated: Rabbi Meir explains: "Why blue?" Because blue is the colour of the sky and the sky is similar to the throne of Glory as it says:

"They saw the G-d of Israel and under His feet was the likeness of
sapphire brickwork and it was like the essence of the heaven in purity"
(Exod. 24:10).

What is the idea behind this statement? It seems clear to me that we are bidden by the sight of the blue colour of the ציצית to view things more deeply. To look up to heaven and to admire the immense, incredible, vast expanse of space leading to its source – the Heavenly Throne, namely Hashem.

"השמים מספרים כבוד קל"
"The Heavens tell the glory of Hashem" (Psa. 19:2).

ציצית is consequently a means of encouraging us to view things with a view of the נשמה.[1] The right view!

"ולא תתורו אחרי לבבכם ואחרי עיניכם"
"And do not explore after your hearts and after your eyes" (Num. 15:39).

Do not follow your own spies! Do not go after your own hearts (minds), your eyes, after your physical vision of things, but

"וראיתם אתו"
"And you shall see Him" (Hashem) in everything in nature.

"למען תזכרו ועשיתם את כל מצותי"
"In order that you shall remember and perform all My commandments"
(Num. 15:40).

All מצות are a means towards the same aim! That is the connection with the story of the מרגלים.

In contemporary society many forces in nature which have been hidden up to now are being laid bare by modern science. The vision of the eyes has been

---

1. The soul.

greatly enhanced by telescopes and microscopes and the mind's eye by computers, books and study. Therefore, one would have thought that the spiritual vision of the soul should come to the fore – but that is not the case! Many people still live in a three-dimensional world and fail to see anything more than ארץ.[1]

"וראיתם את הארץ"
"And you will see the land" (Num. 13:18).

Their main interest in life is to pamper their ארציות – their earthly needs, and their גשמיות[2] – to the complete exclusion of the רוחניות.[3] We, who aspire to be בני תורה[4] have our task clearly set out in front of us.

"וראיתם אותו"

To see things as they really are – to acquire a רוח אחרת[5] a spirit of תורה and מצות, and to give our utmost support to our beloved Land of Israel. However, "Israel without תורה is like a body without a soul." The palace of the world – Israel – requires a lot of "מזוזות" which contain the שמע, the sovereignty of Hashem, the King of Kings. They also incorporate the promise that if we observe the מצות of Hashem, and if we love and serve Him with all our hearts then we shall live long lives with our children in the land that Hashem has sworn to our forefathers.... (Deut 11:13-21).

Maimonides remarks on the verse in our *Sidra*:

"אשר עין בעין נראה אתה ה'"
"That you, Hashem, appeared eye to eye" (Num. 14:14).

The more we see Hashem, the more He sees us – and looks after us.

In these historical times, when the future of our beloved Israel is at stake, we must never be swayed by the majority secular opinion, with their superficial three-dimensional views, but we should acquire a deeper spiritual multi-dimensional soul's view of life and of Israel by observance of מצות and deeper insights into our תורה. Then we will be able to exclaim, with Hashem's help:

---

1. Land.
2. The material and mundane part of life.
3. Spiritual dimension.
4. Scholars of Torah.
5. A different spirit.

"כי יכול נוכל לה"

"We can surely do it" (Num. 13:30).

We shall overcome the enormous difficulties with which we are faced at the present time, because

"ה׳ אתנו אל תיראם"

"Hashem is with us, do not fear them" (Num. 14:9).

KORACH'S REVOLUTION

קרח

Our *Sidra* contains the story of the rebellion of קרח against משה רבינו and אהרן, resulting in קרח being swallowed up by the earth, together with his supporters. These were earth shattering events indeed!

Furthermore, two hundred and fifty leaders who offered incense were consumed by a heavenly fire. Resentment at the death of קרח caused further complaints to which Hashem responded with plagues. These were stopped by אהרן by taking similar incense among the people. Finally, Hashem commanded משה רבינו to take twelve staffs, representing the twelve tribes, and put them into the משכן[1] overnight. The next morning only the staff of אהרן blossomed and almonds ripened on it. Any complaints about אהרן's appointment as High Priest were clearly seen to be unjustified and אהרן's elevation was finally unchallenged. This episode is truly what the Mishna (Avot 5:20) describes as

"מחלקת שלא לשם שמים אין סופו להתקיים זו מחלקת קרח ועדתו"
"A controversy which is not for the sake of Heaven does not lead to
a permanent result, this is the quarrel of Korach and his group."

This is in contrast to the controversies between הלל and שמאי, which were in the name of heaven and which did lead to a permanent result.

The מחלקת of קרח brings to mind a different kind of quarrel, this time between a husband and his wife. The husband consulted a doctor who prescribed that he should do some physical exercise, in the form of jogging ten miles every day for seven days. He asked the patient to let him know at the end of seven days how things were. After one week, the doctor received the following telephone call: "It was very hard at the beginning but I got used to jogging long distances eventually!" The doctor replied: "Now the $64,000 question, how is your relationship with your wife at present?" "How should I know? I am seventy miles away!".... That husband dealt with his problem in his own special way.

---

1. Tabernacle.

The questions are:

1. How did קרח go about *his* מחלקת?
2. Why did קרח get such a spectacular punishment, while his followers received other means of heavenly chastisement?
3. Why was the test of the staffs necessary, too?

Let us illustrate the answer to the first question with the following anecdote: A Jewish passenger desired preferential treatment at Ben Gurion airport when the passengers disembarked, so he told the steward that he was ill. They made way for him. A friend asked him later: "What was the nature of your illness?" He replied: "חוצפה!"[1]

In our times many people suffer from this "illness." קרח suffered from the affliction of חוצפה – bare-faced cheek – when he took on משה רבינו and אהרן the High Priest. Like most quarrels, קרח's rebellion originated from *personal* grievances! As Rashi, quoting Midrash Tanchuma (Num. 16:1) says: He was jealous that his cousin, Elizaphan, son of Uziel was placed in charge of בני קהת – the sons of Kehat (Num. 3:30). קרח said: "There are four brothers (Exod. 6:18), the sons of Kehat: Amram, Yitzhar, Chevran and Uziel. Amram's two sons (משה and אהרן) *"took "* the best positions – one became "king" and the other became the High Priest. Who should get the next best appointment? Not I, the son of Yitzhar, the second brother after Amram, but משה appointed the son of the youngest brother, Elizaphan, the son of Uziel. Therefore, I object and I shall cancel his words...." (Rashi, Num. 16:1). However, he could not tell the public about this personal complaint. They would just say "hard luck" and not take sides in this matter. Therefore, he put forward the slogan

"כל העדה כלם קדשים"

"The whole congregation are *all* holy!" (Num. 16:3). No need to have leaders!

Democracy! That was sweet music to the ears of the people.

However, if that was the case, why did he not start his campaign at the time when the leaders were chosen? קרח was an astute politician – he did not make a revolt then, after the Exodus from Egypt because at that time the Jewish people were extremely happy to be freed from slavery. No one would have taken any notice then. But now, after they were told that they would have to die in the

---

1. Arrogance.

desert, the people were disgruntled and in the right mood for a revolution (Ramban). That is why קרח decided to make a "cover up" of his real complaint and to rouse the masses to revolt in the name of "democracy" – "We are all holy and do not need משה and אהרן!"

How did he go about it? He used his "חוצפה" to scoff at משה רבינו. He clothed his two hundred and fifty followers in *Taleitim*[1] which were completely blue (in the Chilazon fish's blood which is used to colour one of the four strands on each corner of the *Tallit*) and asked משה רבינו:

"Do these *Talleitim* require the four strands too?" משה רבינו said: "Of course they do!"

Afterwards he asked: "Supposing you had a room full of of the תורה scrolls – would this room require a מזוזה on its doorpost?" "Of course it does!" replied משה רבינו. קרח then scoffed and ridiculed משה רבינו. "If four threads of blue ציצית are sufficient even if the garment is white, surely if the **whole** garment is blue it should be even more acceptable, and if one מזוזה which contains two paragraphs of שמע is in order, how much more so if the room is **full** of ספרי תורה – scrolls of the תורה, each of which contains these two chapters!"

What did he mean by these שאלות?[2] There are various points which קרח wanted to convey:

a) We are all "blue", we are all scrolls of the תורה – all of us are holy and great – what do we need משה and אהרן for? We want democracy!

b) Ignorant people require blue colour (which resembles the blue skies pointing to the blue throne of Glory) and מזוזות to remind us of Hashem. But these are not required for the elite who are conscious of Hashem and have a house full of holy scrolls and books!

However, if we dissect קרח's arguments we would find that they are flawed. No nation can exist without leaders, and no one is so perfect that he does not require מצות. On the contrary:

"כל הגדול מחבירו יצרו גדול"

"Anyone who is greater than someone else possesses a greater יצר הרע"[3]
(Sukkah 52a).

---

1. Prayer clothing.
2. These religious questions.
3. Evil inclination.

Everyone has a point of בחירה[1] the higher his standard may be, the higher the counterweight must be (the יצר הרע) in order to balance free choice. This goes even further.

Rabbi Soloveichick ז"ל calls קרח's revolution "<u>COMMON SENSE REVOLT.</u>" קרח's philosophy was that no central authority was needed, only common sense. Accordingly, he developed his argument as follows:

Since the blue ציצית are meant to make us aware of the Divine presence (blue Throne of Glory) why not extend it to the whole garment? Similarly, since the מזוזה is designed to invoke His protection over our homes, why restrict it to the doorpost, why not extend it over the whole room which is full of תורה scrolls? However, this line of reasoning is equally flawed. There are two levels in a מצוה:

רחמנא ליבא בא – The תורה requires the heart (Sanhedrin 106b). That is true, but it also requires the objective outer מצוה. Feelings ___and___ deeds. Feelings and devotion alone depend on the mood that prompts them. They cannot be trusted on their own because there are volatile and fickle. Therefore, they must be combined with the ***performance*** of the מצוה. The ***practice*** of Halacha must be paramount! "נעשה" – "We shall do" before "נשמע" – "We shall listen!" Furthermore, the word מצוה comes from צוותא – companionship with Hashem. It provides the link to the Highest Authority! Only Halacha can provide this link to the Divine. No amount of human "common sense" can do that. We must bow to the infinitely superior will of Hashem as expressed by מעשה המצות – the performance of the commandments.

After having discussed the responses to the wrong rationale of קרח, we can now move on to the second problem: Why such a spectacular punishment? There are two points to be considered here.

i) Since קרח used scoffing and mocking as his weapon, Heavenly intervention had to be used to quell this kind of behaviour. "Satire" is a most deadly weapon against which there is little, if any, defence.

ii) The תורה was given in a public manner in front of millions, unlike "visions" of individuals in other religions. "Did any people hear the voice of Hashem speaking from the midst of fire as you have heard and survived" (Deut. 4:33)? קרח's rebellion implied refutation of this fact. Therefore, swift, spectacular and ***public*** punishment was

---

1. Free choice.

essential. This was done "measure for measure," the punishment fitting the crime. He wanted to swallow too much, so the earth swallowed him. He opened his mouth too wide, so the earth opened its mouth. He tried to make himself ten feet tall, so he was made very small indeed. He was prepared to swallow others "alive" to achieve his goals, so the earth swallowed him alive. This was reinforced by the fire which consumed his two hundred and fifty followers who had offered incense. Yet the same censor with incense which אהרן offered stopped the plague which followed קרח's rebellion and saved millions of lives. Everyone could see that only commands of Hashem are decisive!

However, all this was not sufficient! Punishment by itself does not convince, it merely makes people resentful. They wait for the day when *they* will be on top! How can one really convince an adversary? Not by **_negative_** punishment but by **_positive_** revelation that real Judaism blossoms and blooms, as symbolised by the staff of אהרן! Yes! One should run away from מחלקת as fast as one can. One should not use satire or mockery in one's arguments. Neither should one be a בעל חוצפה[1] nor should one cover up one's grievance. One also must not be a בעל גאוה[2] and above all, one should not employ one's "common sense" to judge מצות and Halacha which are far beyond human understanding but are a link to Hashem Himself.

Pride and ridicule were employed by the revolutionary קרח. And what was his end?

The Midrash says: "From under the earth came out the cries of קרח and his followers:

"Moshe is true and the Torah is true and we are liars!" (Targum Jonathan)

What we should do is to take part in the blossoming of true תורה Judaism and use this positive fact to convince our opponents. Above all we should be happy to fulfill our מצות and duties with great enthusiasm in whatever position in life Hashem has placed us.

May Hashem give us His help to accomplish this wonderful aim in our lives!

---

1. An arrogant person.
2. A conceited person.

THE RED HEIFER – פרה אדומה   חקת

"זאת התורה אדם כי ימות באהל כל הבא אל האהל וכל אשר באהל
יטמא שבעת ימים"

"This is the teaching: If a person dies in the tent anyone who enters
the tent and anything that is in the tent shall be contaminated for
seven days."

(Num. 19:14)

That person has to be purified on the third and the seventh day by being sprinkled with spring water into which ashes of the red heifer has been put. Then he has to immerse in a מקוה[1] and become pure. However, the one who **burns** the cow becomes **impure.**

I would like to introduce this very mysterious subject with the following anecdote:

During the Middle Ages a priest who was well versed in the Hebrew language challenged the Jews to a contest in the Central square of his town. They were to provide an opponent able to compete with his knowledge of the Hebrew language. If one of the competitors could not answer a question put to him, he would be beheaded immediately by the soldiers present.

There were no volunteers except for one עם הארץ.[2] People tried to dissuade him, but he insisted that he could look after himself. The ignoramus started the dialogue by asking, "What does איני יודע mean?"

The priest promptly and correctly answered, "I do not know." As soon as the soldiers heard this, they carried out their duty.... When the "hero" returned in triumph he was asked: "What made you ask this excellent question?" He replied: "Many years ago, when I was at Cheder, I asked my Rebbe what איני יודע meant. The Rebbe answered, 'I do not know.' Well, if the Rebbe does not know, how could that Priest know?...."

---

1. Ritual bath.
2. A simpleton.

We certainly do not know the hidden depth of the law of the Red Cow, but we shall try to bring it a little closer to our understanding.

This is a most puzzling and mysterious חק. It is so difficult to grasp that even King Solomon, who was so wise, exclaimed:

"I said I am clever but it is far from me!" (Eccl. 7:23).

Only משה רבינו understood it fully (Midrash Rabba 19:4). Therefore, we must be extremely wary in proposing even partial explanations. Yet, although they are decreed by Hashem, there are also reasons for מצות. These are called טעמי המצות. What does טעם really mean? A taste or a flavour! Obviously, one cannot exist by eating spice and sugar alone, yet they have their place, too. The following questions need to be addressed:

1. Can one find some rational explanation for this statute?
2. How can one explain the paradox of this חק? It cleanses the impure people but makes unsullied people impure?
3. What flavour can we contribute to this statute?
4. What is the reason of *Tosaphot Harosh* who claims that this chapter, by Torah law, must be read in public, just like the פרשה of "זכור את עמלק" "Remember Amalek" (Deut. 25:17-19) which we read on שבת זכור, the שבת before Purim?

Let us start with a rational approach by one of the *Baale Tosaphot* – Rabbi Yosef Bechorshor:

This ceremony was designed to discourage association with the dead and excessive grief! One becomes impure just by being in the same tent as a dead body (Num. 19:14).

In order to emphasise this, the תורה prescribes the expensive ritual of the "Red Heifer" – a very rare animal. I would add that the כהן must not make himself impure over the dead for that very same reason. After all, his task is to serve and teach the living! This solves the first problem.

However, this reasoning does not explain the paradoxical laws of the "Red Heifer" – our second problem. To answer this difficult question, it is well worth noting the fact that some medications beneficial for a sick person may be deadly to a healthy one. That applies to spiritual "remedies" too. The Gemara (Brachot

5a) states as follows: One should always battle with one's יצר הרע[1] if one defeats it, well and good, but if not, one should study תורה. If one wins, that is all very well, but if not, one should read the שמע. If one defeats the יצר הרע, that is very good, but if not, one should remember the day of death. The question is asked: If remembering the day of death is the best weapon against the יצר הרע, why not use it in the first place?

We can learn the answer from Esau. When יעקב wanted עשו to sell his birthright, עשו replied: "I am going to die in any case, what do I need the birthright for" (Gen. 25:32)? We can clearly see that remembering the day of death can have the opposite effect: Since one has to die, one may as well enjoy all of life's pleasures, legitimate or otherwise.

This paradoxical decree can best be illustrated by the story of a gentile Russian who invited three of his friends to a party. Afterwards, he discovered, to his great sorrow, that his valuable silver candelabra was missing. Obviously, each of his friends denied any involvement in this theft. No one could help him. However, he was told that there was a world-famous Rabbi who lived in Vilna who might be able to recover the candelabra. This Rabbi happened to be the Vilna Gaon ז"ל. The three friends were summoned to his house and questioned by the great Gaon. Of course they all denied taking it. So the Vilna Gaon had them blind-folded. He told them that in a dark room there was a magic candlestick. They would have to touch it. The guilty one would scream, but nothing would happen to the others. They all agreed to this course of action and went into that room, but **_no one_** screamed! Then the Gaon asked them to show their hands to him. Two pairs were soiled with soot and one was perfectly clean. Immediately the Vilna Gaon confronted the one with the clean hands. "You took the candelabra!" He confessed and returned it. The "magic" candlestick was covered with soot. The thief did not touch it whilst the innocent ones did! Here we have the same item performing two contradictory functions:

It soils the pure and innocent, and reveals the impure, the guilty one! It caused the thief to repent. This settles the second problem.

Now let us deal with the third problem, namely, what can we learn from the flavour of this baffling law? In order to do so, I would like to relate the well known parable of Rabbi Moshe Hadarshan who is quoted by Rashi (Num.

---

1. His evil inclination.

19:22). He narrates the story of the son of a maid-servant who soiled the palace of a King. The officials said: "Let the mother come and clean up the dirt!" So the (red) **cow** is intended to atone for the **calf**. Therefore, it must be a cow, not a bull as is usual in connection with sacrifices. The colour red denotes sin. Who deals with this service? Eliezer, the son of אהרן, but not אהרן himself who was involved (against his will) with the sin of the golden calf. "No accuser can be a defender" (Rosh Hashana 26a), say our sages. The cow had to be burnt just as the calf was destroyed and burned, and just as the golden calf made impure all those who were "busy" with it, so the cow makes those who deal with it impure. And just as they became purified by the ashes of the golden calf, as it is stated "משה רבינו spread them over the water" (Exod. 32:20), so here too, the ashes of the red heifer made the impure pure. The Kotsker Rabbi remarked: How fitting this parable is! The maid-servant was not expelled because her services were needed and the minor has no mind of his own yet. We were not expelled by Hashem because Hashem wants us, especially since we committed the sin of the golden calf unwittingly, like that baby... we still wanted to serve Hashem. We only intended to use that calf as a visible intermediary (Ramban).

However the famous Maharal asks in his *Gur Arye*: "How can the cow atone for the sin of the calf! Surely, the תורה says that it purifies those who have been in contact with the dead?

The Slabodker Rosh Yeshiva gives a convincing answer. What was the real trouble which caused the sin of the golden calf? Surely, it was conceit! Like that of the first man when he was told by the serpent, "Be like G-d!" Here they wanted to make their own intermediary to G-d! The worship of the all powerful intellect! The *statute* of the Red Heifer is the antidote: Our human intellect is limited! We do not grasp its deeper meaning. Furthermore, the burning of the cow is a "shock treatment" for conceit. The body of an animal is similar to that of a human being. It gets reduced to ashes! As אברהם אבינו[1] exclaimed: "I am dust and ashes!" (Gen. 18:27). Our distinction is the soul that Hashem gave us. The ashes go down when put into water but the living waters (the soul) go up (Rabbi Samson Raphael Hirsch).

One tries to make oneself ten feet tall like a cedar tree, but one must deflate one's ego to the size of a little herb – the hyssop (Num. 19:6). We should

---

1. Abraham our father.

cultivate our soul and not pamper the body. That is the atonement for the sin of the golden calf!.... That is why even King Solomon could not grasp the meaning of this statute, because he mistakenly relied on his intelligence when he said: "The law that a King should not have too many wives does not apply to me." We know what happened when he married too many wives.... But משה רבינו who was "the most humble of all men" (Num. 12:3) *did* understand this law, says the Midrash (Bamidbar Rabba 19:4).

This leads us on to answer the last question: Why do some פוסקים[1] hold that, by Torah law, the chapter of the Red Heifer has to be read in public (by the תורה law), just like the chapter of "Remember what Amalek did to us?"

In Deuteronomy 9:7 there is a מצוה to remember the sad story of the golden calf:

"Remember and do not forget how you provoked Hashem in the desert!"
(Referring to the golden calf)

However, our Rabbis delicately did not initiate a שבת זכור for the golden calf to remind us of that great disaster and embarrass us, but rather we should remember the **_atonement_** for the sin and so fulfill the מצוה of remembering the golden calf for the process of healing rather than by re-opening the terrible wound.

Is it not amazing what a wealth of important lessons this statute teaches us? First of all: Not to indulge in excessive grief and association with the dead. Secondly, to realise that sometimes a healing factor must be used with great caution, because it may do grievous harm to a healthy person. "It purifies the impure but contaminates the pure!" Thirdly, it teaches us the necessity to banish any trace of conceit from one's life-style by being aware that our intellect is very limited compared with the greatness of our Creator who gave us this statute which we cannot penetrate. Everyone of us should admit – איני יודע – I do not know.

Finally, our bodies are "dust and ashes." Eventually they go down, but our everlasting souls, the distinction which our Creator bestowed on us – they go up! Therefore, we need to pay far more attention and care to our נשמות[2] in our

---

1. Rabbis who decide the law.
2. Souls.

way of life, by תורה observance and study. Then our lives will be blessed by Hashem with "מעלין בקדש" – going up in our holy work – both for ourselves as well as for כלל ישראל.[1]

---

1. The Jewish nation as a whole.

THE MYSTERY OF THE "PROPHET" BILAM

בלק

In our *Sidra* we have the enigmatic story of the heathen prophet Bilam who was hired by Balak, the King of Moab, to curse the Jewish people. However, he ends up blessing us.

Let us try to solve some of the mystery of Bilam by commencing with the following story:

There was a delay at the airport. The stewardess said: "The pilot did not like the sound of the engine so we are waiting for **another** pilot...." I trust that you **will** like the sound of the words of תורה to pilot us through the great puzzle surrounding the baffling personality of Bilam.

The following questions require solutions:

1. What powers did this prophet really possess?
2. Why did he not bless Moab since he could not curse us?
3. Why did Hashem have to stop him?

"יקללו המה ואתה תברך"
"Let them curse, but You (Hashem) will bless us" (Psa. 109:28).

4. Why did Hashem change his instruction to Bilam?

"ויאמר אלקים אל בלעם לא תלך עמהם"
"And G-d said to Bilam, do not go with them" (Num. 22:12).

However, when more emissaries were sent by Balak to persuade the Prophet to change his mind, the instructions of Hashem were changed:

"אם לקרא לך באו האנשים קום לך אתם"
"If the men have come to summon you, arise and go with them"
(Num. 22:20).

Does this mean a change of heart on the part of G-d? Surely Bilam himself proclaimed:

"לא איש אל ויכזב ובן אדם ויתנחם"

"Surely Hashem is not a man to change His heart" (Num. 23:19)?

In any event, two verses after permitting Bilam to go with them, we read that Hashem was *angry* that he went (Num. 22:22).

To illustrate the answer to the first two questions, let us use the following parable:

A tiger and a lion were drinking at a water hole. The lion was roaring. The tiger admonished the lion forcefully. "Why are you so foolish as to make such a noise and give your position away?"

"I am not foolish!" replied the lion. "I am not called the 'King of the Beasts' for nothing. I have to advertise."

A little rabbit overheard this conversation. It quickly ran home and tried to roar. However, it could only produce a little squeak. A fox went to investigate and...had it for lunch. If you want to advertise, you need to possess the goods.... Bilam, despite all his advertisements, roaring and boasting, did **not** have the goods.

All his blessings were **from Hashem**. They were not his own. That is the reason why we start our davening in Shul with the words uttered by Bilam:

"מה טבו אהליך יעקב משכנתיך ישראל"

"How wonderful are your tents O Jacob and your dwelling places O Israel!"
(Num. 24:5)

The following parable by Rashi on Numbers 22:12 confirms this assertion. One says to a bee: "We do not want your honey and we do not need your sting!" That means that we do not want Bilam's blessings or his curses. Why is honey kosher? Because it is not part of the impure bee but comes from plants. But the sting is a component of the bee. This shows that Bilam could only 'sting' but could not bless. That is why he could not bless Moab.

Now that we have discovered that Bilam was not so powerful after all, the third question is even stronger. Why did Hashem have to thwart his plans to verbally condemn us? The answer is two-fold:

In order to help us, Hashem lowered the morale of our enemies in the forthcoming battle to conquer Israel. They looked up to Bilam whom they regarded as their leader. He had to be seen for what he really was, namely, "a little rabbit," a "fish on a hook" (Gemara Sanhedrin 105b), "a puppet on a string." Therefore, he was deflated in front of his colleagues.

a) The ass which carried Bilam saw an angel and stopped. Bilam hit the donkey and then it spoke: "Did I not always serve you?" Until he *himself* saw the angel with the sword to abort his mission.

b) He admitted that he needed the sword if he intended to kill the obstinate ass. He could not kill it with a curse (Num. 22:29).

c) Furthermore, he hit the donkey which had saved his life and Hashem made the donkey speak to teach him that, if He can make an ass speak, how much more so can He make Bilam say only what He wants him to say. Besides, if Hashem could make a donkey speak, He could certainly stop Bilam from speaking altogether. Also, Bilam had to have a dialogue with a donkey instead of with kings and ministers.

e) Eventually he was forced to admit to the angel: "I have sinned because I did not know that you were standing opposite me."

What a climb down! All these events would eventually become known to his public! Now it becomes clear why Hashem had to thwart his evil plans. However, it not only helped us in the short term but also had important consequences in our *future* history. Whenever unfortunate events might occur – G-d forbid – our people might ascribe them to the curse of Bilam rather than to our own actions. Therefore, he was not allowed to pronounce a curse on the Jewish people.

In the light of the foregoing, the answer to the third question falls into place. Since Hashem manipulated Bilam to such a degree, why did He have to change His instructions? At first He told him not to go with the princes, then He did allow him to join them but became angry when he did so. A very strange story indeed! The Vilna Gaon ז״ל solves this dilemma as follows: We should note that there are different words used in the narrative, את – "Et"[1] and עם – "Im."[2] את means *physical* proximity but עם indicates a *common* purpose.

_____

1. 2. With.

I would like to prove this from the following: In Genesis 12:4 is stated:

"וילך אברם כאשר דבר אליו ה' וילך אתו לוט. ואברם בן-חמש שנים ושבעים
שנה בצאתו מחרן"

"אברם went as Hashem had spoken to him and Lot went with him and אברם was seventy five years of age when he left Charan"

The Commentators ask why is אברם's age mentioned in connection with Lot. The answer is that, ostensibly, Lot went with his uncle אברם to publicise Hashem as the true G-d, but his real motive was very materialistic. His uncle was very wealthy, but was also an old man who had no children. Lot calculated: "How can I let my elderly uncle go into the wide world alone? Who knows what might happen to him? What would be the "fate" of his possessions?" That is why the תורה uses the words וילך אתו לוט – Lot went with him only outwardly – not with the same purpose in mind!

On the other hand: When עשו[1] was going to meet יעקב with four hundred soldiers, the angel reported to יעקב:

(Gen. 32:7) "הלך לקראתך וארבע מאות איש עמו"
"He (Esau) is coming to meet you and four hundred men (עמו) with him."
(wholeheartedly)

Now we have the answer: Hashem told Bilam "Do not go "עמהם" – do not join in their evil enterprise (Num. 22:12), but later Hashem told Bilam, if you just want to journey with them "אתם" לך – go with them as long as you do not take part in their designs. However, Bilam went עם שרי מאב – with the princes of Moab, not just as a fellow traveller but as an accomplice! That is why G-d became irate (Num. 22:22) and sent an angel to stop him, because Bilam wanted to fulfill their request to curse Israel. Now we can understand an episode described at the end of the sixth chapter of פרקי אבות.[2] Rabbi Jose ben Kisma was asked to live in a certain town. He would receive thousands upon thousands of golden dinars and precious stones and pearls from the townspeople. However, he declined the offer saying: "Even if you were to give me all the silver, gold and precious stones in the world, I would not live anywhere but in a place of תורה." The Maharal of Prague asks: "Why did he refuse such a fantastic offer? Surely with all that

---

1. Esau.
2. Ethics of our Fathers.

money he could establish many תורה institutions?" He answers it as follows: "Because they said עמנו במקומנו – with us in our town." The words "in our town" would have sufficed. However, they wanted the Rabbi to live with them not only "in our town" but עמנו – with us in unison with the town's set of values. They wanted the Rabbi to fit in totally with their mode of living. That was not in accordance with the ideals of the great Rabbi, and he had to decline the offer.

Finally, a person may reach a very high standard – which Bilam certainly did – to the extent that he was called a Prophet, yet he may later drop down to a very low position. When Bilam realised that he could not curse us, he caused us great harm by attacking our strong point which he himself described in his blessing – מה טובו – "How goodly" – our family values, by sending Midianite girls and disguising them as Moabites (*Alshich*) to corrupt our youth. That caused twenty four thousand deaths in a plague! (Num. 25:1 and 6-9). *He could sting!*

To sum up!

Bilam had neither the power to curse us nor to bless us. He did not have the goods! His blessings were conveyed to him by Hashem and that is why he could not bless Moab. Although he did not have the endowment and the capacity to curse, Hashem had to prevent him from doing verbal harm to us, because it would have lifted the morale of our enemies, who were his followers during the forthcoming conquest of Israel and would also have been used by us to blame any misfortune – G-d forbid – in our future history. His intentions to accompany the officers of Moab were to identify himself with their evil plans עמם – not merely to accompany them out of courtesy.

Therefore, Hashem created the episode of the talking ass to drag his name into the dust. He wanted to rule a nation by his word, but was impotent against his animal. He wanted to be arrogant towards lords and princes, but became a laughing stock before his own attendants.

This story contains an important lesson. A person must never "rest on his laurels" and imagine that he has reached such a high standard that it is impossible to drop from it. Bilam the Prophet eventually became the instigator of the permissive society and all its evils.

In contemporary times, there are many disciples of Bilam who try to bring profanity and denunciation on the Jewish people and our תורה. There are many who try to break up our stronghold – the family. We must beware not to go עמם –

but rather to go אתם, to try to bring them to a level that will bring them back to our תורה way of life and its blessings. In this way we must work together to bring our people back to the ideal of:

"מה טובו אהליך יעקב משכנתיך ישראל"

"How wonderful are your tents O Jacob and your dwelling places O Israel!"

THE GREAT ACHIEVEMENT
OF PINCHAS

פינחס

"וידבר ה' אל משה לאמר: פינחס בן אלעזר בן אהרן הכהן השיב את
חמתי מעל בני ישראל בקנאו את קנאתי בתוכם ולא כליתי את בני
ישראל בתוכם בקנאתי: לכן אמר הנני נתן לו את בריתי שלום"

"Hashem spoke to Moses saying: Pinchas the son of Elazar, the son
of Aharon the Cohen turned back My wrath from the Children of
Israel when he zealously avenged Me among them, therefore I did
not consume the Children of Israel in My vengeance. Therefore say:
Behold I have given him my Covenant of Peace."   *(Num. 25:10-12)*

Bilam gave the advice to entice Jewish men to become idol worshippers by
means of an orgy of immorality with Midianite girls dressed as Moabites
(*Alshich Hakadosh*). This caused the deaths of twenty four thousand men (see
the end of the *Sidra* Balak – Num. 25:9). When פינחס witnessed an open act of
intimacy between a Jewish prince from the tribe of Shimon and a Midianite
princess, he killed them both and stopped the devastating plague. However,
instead of applauding him, the people criticised him by saying: "How dare the
grandson of an idol worshipper (Yitro) kill a Jewish prince!" Hashem, however,
called him a descendant of אהרן (Rashi), his other grandfather who was
distinguished for his "love and pursuit of peace" (Avot 1:12) and awarded him a
"Covenant of Peace" (Rashi, Num. 25:11).

To introduce this subject let me share with you the following anecdote:
During a long and boring address in the House of Commons delivered by a
member of the Opposition, Churchill slumped forward and closed his eyes.
"***Must*** you fall asleep whilst I am talking?" demanded the speaker. Churchill
replied with his eyes still closed: "No, I do this purely ***voluntarily***!"

During this episode the Jewish public fell asleep, so to speak, when the terrible attack upon them to pervert their youth by means of the Midianite girls reached its peak with an attempted intermarriage and they did not act.

פנחס, however, took the law into his own hands with great מסירות נפש[1] and averted an even greater tragedy than the golden calf: There we lost three thousand men and here we lost twenty four thousand! For his courageous action he received a special accolade from Hashem.

There are two kinds of people: sleepers and talkers on the one hand, and doers on the other – members of committees and executives. When all is said and nothing done at the committee meeting, the meeting is over – back to the armchair and to slumber. Pinchas would have no dealings with such people. He was even more than an executive. He was an executor. Better still, he was an executioner! A true קנאי.[2] He had to break the peace in order to achieve peace at that decisive time. That is why the Vav in the word שלו*ם, peace, is split.

To try and shed a little more light on this baffling story, a number of questions need to be answered:

1. פנחס was dealing with the law: כל הבועל ארמית קנאין פוגעין בו (Sanhedrin 81b).
   If someone is intimate with a non-Jew, one may kill him. But if this is the law, why does one not teach it to the public – הלכה ואין מורין כן? (Sanhedrin 82a).
2. Why did משה רבינו not execute these two people himself?
3. Since the achievement of פנחס was so great, why did he have to suffer so much criticism from the general public?

To answer these questions:

The תורה states:

"בקנאו את קנאתי" – He zealously avenged Me (Num. 25:11). Rashi says, "He avenged the anger which I should have avenged" תחת אשר קנא לאלקיו – because he took vengeance for his G-d (Num. 25:13). In this matter Hashem leaves the action for us. Just like מילה;[3] G-d could have created boys who do not need מילה, but He leaves it to us to have this Mitzvah. He could have given sustenance to

---

1. Risk to his own life.
2. A zealous person for Hashem.
3. Circumcision.

the poor, but He leaves it to us – as Rabbi Akiva says in Baba Batra 10a in answer to a question by Turnusrufus: "Why does Hashem not give food and shelter to the poor?" "This is to give us the merit to be saved from Gehinnom (hell) by doing this Mitzvah. "We see that קנאין פוגעין בו – zealous people should execute him – is really a matter to be done *by Hashem*. However, here, He wishes *us* to do this for Him as long as one important condition is fulfilled: It must be done *purely* לשם שמים[1] – and not for any ulterior reasons, since one is being zealous for Hashem! That is why one does not teach this law in public. Only a person who feels like פנחס, that action has to be taken for the sake of Heaven, can fulfill this law.

This solves the first problem. However, the second question remains: Why did משה רבינו *himself* not execute Zimri, the prince of the tribe of Shimon? Surely משה רבינו could be relied on to fulfill a law purely for the sake of Heaven?

The answer given by our Great Sages is very convincing: משה רבינו had to flee to Midian to escape from Egypt after he killed the Egyptian who had ill-treated a Jew. There he was welcomed at Yitro's house. His sense of **gratitude** prevented him from executing a Midianite princess. We remember that he also did not hit the water to produce the plague of blood for the same reason – הכרת הטוב.[2] The waters of the River Nile were instrumental in saving his life when he was a baby. פנחס, however, did step into the breach and stopped the plague successfully. Not only did he receive a Covenant of Eternal Priesthood for himself and his offspring (many High Priests came from his line [Ibn Ezra], but all future כהנים would receive the following parts from any slaughtered animal: זרע לחיים והקבה – the foreleg, the jaw and the stomach (Deut.18:3).

> The Foreleg – פנחס took the spear in his *hand* (Num. 25:7)
> The Jaw – פנחס *prayed* (Psa. 106:30)
> The Stomach – He thrust the spear into her *stomach* (Num. 25:8)
> (Gemara Chullin 134b).

This explains why these gifts for the כהנים are not mentioned previously in the *Sidra* of Korach, which enumerates most of the twenty-four gifts given to the כהנים (Num. 18:8-20), but they are mentioned in the later portion of Shoftim (Deut. 18:3). Furthermore, no-one else received such a great honour from

---

1. For the sake of Heaven.
2. Gratitude.

Hashem, not even משה רבינו, although he often suppressed G-d's anger; for example, at the episodes of the golden calf and the spies, or אהרן when he stopped the plague with the incense after the revolt of קרח. We might ask, "What is the reason for this strange differentiation?" The answer given by our great commentators is as follows: Neither משה רבינו nor אהרן could **completely** eradicate the sins of the Jewish people. At the golden calf it says:

" וביום פקדי ופקדתי עלהם חטאתם"

"On the day that I make My account, I shall bring their sin to account against them" (Exod. 32:34).

That means that whenever they would sin in the future, they would still suffer some of the punishment they should have received in retribution for the sin of the Golden Calf (Rashi quoting Gemara Sanhedrin 102a).

Similarly, at the sin of the spies, משה רבינו's pleas did not fully succeed. They still had to die in the desert. Also אהרן's great deed of stopping the plague with his spices, obviously combined with prayers did not succeed completely. Their grumbling about אהרן's elevation to the High priesthood continued until they were shown that אהרן's staff blossomed and produced fruit whilst the others did not.

פנחס, however, _**totally**_ eradicated the evil plan of Bilam which was to destroy the purity of our nation, the blessing of מה טובו אהליך – how goodly are your tents (families) (Num. 24:5) by sending non-Jewish girls into our camp.

This Hashem himself testifies:

"שבטי קה עדות לישראל"

"The tribes of Hashem are a testimony to the purity of Israel" (Psa. 122:4).

הראובני, for example, a letter 'H' at the beginning and a letter 'Y' at the end of all the names. These letters form one of the names of Hashem to signify that Hashem testifies that they are the sons of their fathers (Rashi on Num. 26:5). After the courageous action of פנחס the moral status of our people was impeccable! That is why פנחס received this wonderful accolade!

פנחס was not a man of compromise. It has been well said that compromise makes a good umbrella but a poor roof. Remember what happened to Chamberlain clutching an umbrella at Munich when he said "Peace in our time" just before

World War Two! Remember what happens to the children and grandchildren of all those who "water down" our תורה! Resolute action can be painful and risky, but if it is absolutely necessary, it has to be taken, as פנחס has shown us.

However, now the third problem is even more pressing. If פנחס had done such a great deed, why did the others deride him? Did they not realise his magnificent achievement? He had actually saved the Jewish People! The Lubavitcher Rebbe ז"ל gave the following answer:

The people had three complaints:

a) How did such an insignificant man, who was not even a כהן at that time, take it upon himself to execute a Prince? Surely, this goes against the honour of Israel and משה רבינו?

b) פנחס's ancestry was not without a blemish. Perhaps he inherited the cruel streak of his grandfather who slaughtered calves for his idols.

c) Perhaps he was just a limelight seeker.

This reminds me of the election of a new Rabbi at a certain congregation. Reb Sishell, the tailor, was the only one who voiced his objection by voting against him. When the Rabbi asked him after the appointment for his reason, Reb Sishell replied: "I wanted to be noticed!..." Here everyone realized the great attainment of פנחס but they accused him of doing it שלא לשמה – not for the sake of Heaven. Hashem, however, eliminated all three complaints.

(i) He is also the grandson of אהרן and therefore had a good יחוס.[1]

(ii) He had no evil streak. He was like אהרן who was an אוהב שלום – a lover of peace – ורודף שלום, a pursuer of peace. (פרקי אבות – Ethics of The Fathers 1:12).

(iii) פנחס, like his grandfather אהרן, was no publicity seeker. ואהרן מה הוא כי תלונו עליו – Who is אהרן that you (Korach) revolt against him (Num. 16:11)?

Finally, it is interesting to compare the strong action of פנחס with the inaction of Rabbi Zecharia ben Avkulus at the famous story of Kamtza and Bar Kamtza (Gittin 55b). Bar Kamtza, who was expelled from a party, took bitter revenge by informing the Roman Emperor of an alleged Jewish rebellion. He was, therefore, a *Mosser*, a traitor who deserved to die. Rabbi Zecharia decided against executing

---

1. Ancestry.

him and caused the destruction of the second Temple in Jerusalem, according to the Gemara.

From this episode of פנחס we can derive a multitude of important guidelines for our times.

When the future of Judaism is threatened, as it is today, when disciples of Bilam are so numerous and intermarriage is increasing disastrously, one must **_act_** and make no **_compromises_** or **_excuses_** like, "Why should we mix in Hashem's 'business'?" We also should not say "Let other people do it!"

It is essential to act with zeal and enthusiasm, especially in these spiritually cold surroundings in which we find ourselves, and not "fall asleep." How should one act? Obviously, not by throwing spears at people but by educating our youth, by sending them to Jewish schools, yeshivot and seminaries and by giving them an example of מה טובו אהליך – how wonderful our family life is.

Finally, when one sees a person trying to do something for the good of the congregation, one must not jump to conclusions that he is a publicity seeker and does not act לשם שמים.[1]

The tribes were wrong about the motives of פינחס! Even if someone does not act לשם שמים, our Rabbis say "מתוך שלא לשמה בא לשמה" (Gemara Pessachim 50b).

"From something which was **_not_** for the sake of heaven something will emerge that **_is_** for the sake of heaven."

One should never dissuade or discourage anyone, even if that person has no claim to leadership or distinction, if he is מקנא לאלקיו – takes vengeance for his G-d and he does not stand for compromise! Rather, one should join him with enthusiasm and zeal so that like פינחס one will receive

בריתי שלום – My Covenant of Peace!

---

1. For the sake of Heaven.

LEADERSHIP

מטות –
מסעי

These two פרשיות contain the laws of vows, war against the Midianites, and the spoils from this victorious war to be divided among the soldiers, the High Priest, the לוים and the rest of the people. The tribes of גד and ראובן asked to remain on the East bank of the Jordan River, later joined by half the tribe of מנשה. Description of the forty year route and the borders of Israel are outlined. Cities of refuge were established for people who killed unintentionally.

The following anecdote shall serve as the introduction to these subjects. A person once gave his *Tallit* to a reputable firm of dyers and cleaners to be cleaned in time for Yom Tov. The bill for this work was as follows:

For cleaning:	£10
For undoing the knots:	£ 5

These two Sidrot have a large number of knotty problems which have to be unravelled. In the ציצית there are twenty double knots, but I intend to deal with only six single ones....

They all come under one heading: **The Qualities Of A Jewish Leader**

1. Why were "ראשי המטות" – "Heads of the Tribes" – given the laws of vows to the exclusion of other laws (Num. 30:2)?
2. Why does the תורה call leaders "ראשי המטות" – "Heads of Tribes" – here, but "עיני הקהל" – "the Eyes of the Congregation" – in connection with a wrong decision given by the Sanhedrin – the Highest Court (Lev. 4:13)?
3. What can we learn from the leadership of משה רבינו in the war against Midian and the story of the two and a half tribes?
4. What is the importance of the distribution of the spoils of the war against Midian that it occupies twenty verses in the תורה?
5. Why were those guilty of manslaughter sent to the cities of the לוים?

6. Why were these people only released after the death of the High
    Priest?

The great חתם סופר answers the first question in the following manner:

Political leaders are wont to make lots of promises and they obligate
themselves to improve things. They pledge to bring "heaven on earth" to any
would-be supporters. However, this is **_before_** they are elected. But **_after_** the
election, many of their promises fall by the wayside. Therefore, the תורה
addresses this law to the elected heads of the congregation to keep their vows
and declarations even **_after_** they have been elected!

This leads to the solution of the second problem posed:

In which way do "Heads of the Tribes" differ from "Eyes of the
Congregation"?

There are different kinds of leaders: "Eyes of the Congregation" are leaders
who only _see_ what is happening amongst the flock but are forced to turn a blind
eye and do not act to improve matters. This is often the fault of people who do
not give them enough respect and authority. That is the reason why the
Congregation has to bring a sin offering and not the Sanhedrin (Lev. 4:21).

In our _Sidra_ we deal with ראשי המטות – **Heads** of the Tribes who are
strong-minded leaders. However, they must not use their strength to lead the
people like dictators but should work **_with_** the Congregation, and above all, keep
to their election promises and vows.

This steers us on to the third point raised: The example of leadership par
excellence, namely that of משה רבינו! To introduce this subject I would like to
share the following anecdote with you:

A poor woman used to bring two Challot every Friday to the great Shaagas
Arye who lived in the Eighteenth Century. He blessed her that someday she
would attain wealth and would earn merit by building two synagogues, one in
Minsk where she lived and one in ארץ ישראל. She did indeed become wealthy and
built a synagogue in Minsk which was known as Chavele's Shul. When she
became older she decided to go to ירושלים to build the second one. When she
went to Rabbi Chaim of Volozhin to say goodbye, he asked her why she was
going to Eretz Israel. She told him that the Shaagas Arye had assured her she
would live to see two synagogues built in her name – one in Minsk and one in
ירושלים. Now, as she was getting on in years, she wanted to see the second part of

her blessing being fulfilled speedily. Rabbi Chaim told her: "If you have had the blessing of such a great Rabbi that you will live to see it built – *__why the rush?__*...."

(From *The Maggid Speaks* by Rabbi Krohn)

משה רבינו was commanded by Hashem to do battle against the Midianites (whose girls had corrupted our youth), and then he would have to die. He **was** in a rush to fulfill Hashem's command *__immediately__* and joyfully despite the knowledge that this would be his last מצוה before his death (Rashi, Num. 31:3). That is how a leader of high class calibre conducts his affairs. A command from Hashem must never be delayed. It overrides one's own interest even if it affects one's life-span.

The question arises, however: If that is so, why did he not *__personally__* lead the battle against the Midianites but appointed פנחס to be the Commander-in-Chief?

The answer is convincing. משה רבינו was known for his exemplary gratitude. He was given shelter by Midian when he had to flee from Egypt. How could he now engage Midian in battle? Just like he could not kill the Jewish prince who wanted to marry a Midianite princess. He left that to פנחס, too (Num. 25:6-8).

Now let us move on to learn more from the great **diplomatic** skill and leadership of משה רבינו.

He displayed this skill during the episode of the two and a half tribes who wanted to remain in Trans-Jordan and not join the others. It appears, according to some commentators, that at first these tribes – גד and ראובן – did not intend to take part in the battle to conquer Israel at all. They said: "The conquest of Trans-Jordan was achieved by Hashem," namely:

"הארץ אשר הכה ה'"
"The land which the Lord smote" (Num. 32:4).

They claimed that their help was not required to conquer Israel proper either. However, משה רבינו countered their contention by saying:

"האחיכם יבאו למלחמה ואתם תשבו פה"
"Should your brothers go into battle and you settle here" (Num. 32:6)?
"Where is your sense of fair play?"

"ויגשו אליו" – "And they approached him" (Num. 32:16) after deliberating amongst themselves and agreed to take part in the forthcoming battle after building "pens for our livestock and cities for our children." "We **shall** arm ourselves and join the others." We see now that justice to the others demands this. "Before the Children of Israel" (Num. 32:17). However, משה רבינו had to correct them in two points: "Your priorities are wrong!" "**_First_** you must build cities for your children and **_then_** make pens for your flock!" (Num. 32:24). The physical and spiritual welfare of children comes **_before_** looking after your material possessions! Furthermore: It is not sufficient to deal correctly "Before the Children of Israel" alone but you must be vindicated before **_Hashem and Israel_** (Num. 32:22). You not only have a physical duty to your people but also a spiritual one towards Hashem by fulfilling the מצוה of the conquest of Israel! They agreed to both these points, too: "The children of Gad and the children of Reuben said to Moses, saying: Your servants shall do as my Lord commands. Our small children, our wives, our livestock and all our animals shall be in the cities of Gilead. And your servants should cross over – and every armed person of the legion – before **Hashem** to do battle as my Lord speaks" (Num. 32: 25-27).

Now we see that משה רבינו won them over on every point by his great negotiating skill. He instructed them that והייתם נקים מה' ומישראל – You shall be vindicated from Hashem and from Israel – (Num. 32:22) and that their children are their priority, not their wealth.

Let us now move on to try and solve the fourth problem which is connected to the first three. Why does the תורה devote such a lot of space to the details of the distribution of the spoils of war?

It has been suggested that the תורה wants to convey to us a very important lesson: Victory is achieved not only by the soldiers but also by the rest of the people, who support the army physically, as well by the students and teachers of the תורה, the כהנים and לוים. Some share goes to Elazar the High Priest (Num. 31:29) and some to the לוים, "The guardians of the Charge of Hashem's Tabernacle" (Num. 31:30). They are the **spiritual** warriors and **leaders** of Israel. Without them the Jewish people could not survive! Therefore, they are entitled to a share of the booty.

The חפץ חיים illustrates this fact by the following parable:

Once a prince travelled on a luxury cruise ship. He admired the beautiful appointments and fittings. But he was horrified when he inspected the engine room and saw that it was covered with grease and oil. He was also perturbed by the dirty clothing of the sailors in that compartment. Therefore, he ordered a thorough cleaning of the engine room and a change of clothes for the sailors. Eventually the ship came to a halt!....

The חפץ חיים said: "Our Yeshivah students may not wear kosher-made Saville Row suits, but they are the spiritual engineers who make the ship of the people of Israel move...They are our potential spiritual leaders!"

This also resolves the final questions: Why do people who killed inadvertently have to live in the cities of the כהנים and לויים and why are they only released at the death of the High Priest?

Qualities of sincere spiritual leadership should filter through to the general public. כהנים and לוים were the leaders. I quote:

If you have any difficult queries "you shall come to the כהנים and לוים and to the Judges who will be in those days. You shall inquire and they will tell you the word of Judgment" (Deut. 17:9).

Rabbi Aaron Kotler ל"ז said: The Jewish people are one big soul. Part of each one's soul is in the others. So, each is influenced by the others. All Jews are responsible for one another (Gemara Shevuot 39a). They *are* one great unit. The spiritual leaders, the כהנים and לוים, must teach the people the supreme importance of the life of every individual. Every person is a whole world (Sanhedrin 37a). Therefore, in the Temple, the כהנים atone for sins which were committed inadvertently in connection with sacrifices. Also, in the Cities of Refuge the כהנים had to atone for and influence those who killed through carelessness, and to teach them to be more careful with human life. And since the High Priest is partly responsible for the manslaughters committed because his prayers and his influence were not strong enough (Gemara Makot 11a), therefore, only his death completes the atonement. Then the unfortunate person is released from exile in the Cities of Refuge.

We now see, after unlying the knots that these two פרשיות give us a wealth of important messages:

Any person who is a ירא השם,[1] or a בן תורה,[2] has a great responsibility towards the general public. Such a person can surely be counted amongst the "Heads of the Congregation." In a sense, many of us belong to this elite. Whether elected

1. A G-d fearing person.
2. A Torah scholar.

or not, we must act as leaders and not desecrate our word or our promises. We must act as "Heads of the Congregation," not just as the "Eyes of the Congregation" who suffer wrongdoing without taking any appropriate action. משה רבינו showed us how to do this task in the correct manner.

First of all: The importance he rated a מצוה even if it was extremely difficult for him to perform. The benefit of the people is paramount, for example, in the war against Midian just before his death. We can also learn from his quality of הכרת טוב[1] by not fighting his former hosts, the Midianites, himself.

We can also learn from his diplomatic skills, namely, how he dealt with the two and a half tribes with great success to bring them to דעת תורה – the right attitude of the תורה. From the distribution of the spoils of war we learn that we should give our utmost support to the students of the Yeshivot, who are the spiritual engineers of the ship of the Jewish people and our future leaders. They not only keep the ship afloat, but propel it forward on its journey through history. They are our future captains.

Finally, as leaders, we must always be concerned with the physical and spiritual welfare of others and try to prevent any misfortunes from occurring. All Jewish people are one big soul, and we are all responsible for one another.

May Hashem help us in this noble endeavour!

---

1. Gratitude.

DEVARIM

THE THREE TEMPLES

דברים

"איכה אשא לבדי טרחכם ומשאכם וריבכם"

"How can I (משה רבינו) carry your contentiousness, your burdens
and your quarrels on my own?"
(Deut. 1:12)

The fifth book of the תורה which begins with today's *Sidra* starts with
משה רבינו's account of the wanderings of the Jewish people in the desert.
He chastised them for their failings and for their sins and urged them to realise
the enormous good that would come to them from observing the
commandments of the תורה.

This reminds me of the following anecdote:

An old man was visiting his relative in another city for יום כפור. He always
enjoyed being in the forefront of everything and somehow managed to secure a
front row seat in the Shul.

The Rabbi gave a strong מוסר[1] to his congregation in his various speeches at
כל נדרי,[2] יזכר[3] and נעילה[4] prayers, urging them to improve their ways in the new
year. However, the visitor appeared amused and he chuckled. The Rabbi was
very disconcerted by such peculiar behaviour, so he took him to task after
יום כפור. He asked the visitor: "What is the reason for your strange conduct?" The
visitor replied: "I enjoyed the way you gave it to these people – it was a real hell
and brimstone talk. However, as I am not a member of this congregation, I just
sat back and had a good time...."

All of us are members of כלל ישראל[5] and should take serious note of every

---

1. Reproof.
2. Kol Nidrei.
3. Yizkor.
4. Neilah.
5. The Jewish people.

word of מוסר[1] contained in משה רבינו's last speech before his death and in particular, his complaints of ריבכם – your strife and disunity! With the use of this particular expression he put his finger on our greatest weakness, as we shall see.

We find ourselves now in the three weeks of mourning for the destruction of our first Temple in Jerusalem by the Babylonians, and the second one by the Romans, and the exiles following them. Let us devote our talk today to discover:

a)   Why did the first exile last for seventy years whilst the second one is still continuing, nearly two thousand years later?

b)   What is the deeper significance of this difference?

Before trying to solve the problem with the help of our great Sages, I would like to share the following stories with you:

Before the terrible Holocaust, German government inspectors toured schools in order to inculcate the students with their perverted philosophy. One asked a class to recite patriotic slogans. The pupils came up with various ideas, but the inspector was most impressed with the catch-phrase of one particular student: "Our people shall live forever!"

The inspector congratulated him: "Now that is what I would call a wonderful motto. What is your name?"

"Israel Goldstein!"

Yes, the fact that we are mourning the destruction of our Temples and the subsequent exiles nearly two thousand years later is proof that עם ישראל חי[2] and will live forever!

No other nation could survive the loss of its country for thousands of years. That is what Napoleon realised when he passed by a Shul on the 9th of Av and saw Jewish worshippers sitting on the floor and wailing. He asked, "Why are they lamenting?" When he was told that they were weeping over the devastated Temples of nearly two thousand years ago, he remarked: "That proves that the Jews will actually have it back again!"

The Bobover Rebbe explained so aptly:

---

1. Ethical criticism.
2. The Jewish people are alive.

Why did יעקב – Jacob refuse to be comforted when his son יוסף[1] went missing (Gen. 37:35)? The reason is because יוסף was *alive*. We refuse to accept the חורבן[2] as final. Mourning after the death of a relative is for twelve months, but the mourning for ציון[3] carries on until the building of the Third Temple (may it be soon in our days). So we are looking forward to the arrival of משיח and the building of the Third Temple. However, in the meantime, it is beneficial to look back at the two former Temples and their sad fate by answering the questions posed.

It is most remarkable that the length of גלות בבל[4] is already clearly stated in the תורה, as well as the difference between the first and second exiles. The famous commentator, Nachmanides, claims that the first תוכחה[5] in the *Sidra* Bechukotai (Lev. 26:14-46) is a complete prediction of the destruction of the First Temple and the exile to Babylon following it, whilst the second תוכחה in the *Sidra* of Ki Tavo (Deut. 28:15-69) is a clear prophecy of the destruction of the Second Temple and the subsequent exile. We shall discuss the proofs for this assertion in our talk on the *Sidra* of Ki Tavo.

Now to answer our questions:

Why is the second exile not confined to a limited number of years like the first one and what is the difference between these two?

The Gemara (Yuma 9b) provides the answer!

"ראשנים שנתגלו עונם נתגלו קצם אחרונים שלא נתגלו עונם לא נתגלו קצם"

The first ones whose sins were revealed to them (idol worship, murder and immorality), the end of their exile was revealed (by the prophet Jeremiah 25:11-12 and 29:10), but the latter ones whose sin was not revealed, the end of their exile was also not revealed. Their sin was שנאת חנם.[6] The people did realise that to transgress the cardinal sins is wrong and they repented, but שנאת חנם was not wrongly regarded as sinful. For example, one sometimes hears: "He is a wicked person and it is a מצוה to hate him!" Therefore, they did not repent.

---

1. Joseph.
2. The destruction of the Temple.
3. Zion.
4. The exile to Babylon.
5. Rebuke.
6. Hatred without cause.

The Alshich Hakadosh on the *Sidra* Vayetze gives a remarkable insight into this phenomenon.

The first בית המקדש[1] was built in the merit of אברהם. However, it was destroyed by the descendants of his bad son, ישמעאל, namely the Babylonians.

The second בית המקדש was built in the merit of יצחק. However, he also had a bad son, namely עשו, whose descendants, the Romans under Titus, destroyed it. The Gemara (Gittin 56b) describes Titus as being a descendant of עשו.

The third בית המקדש will be built (soon we hope) by the merit of יעקב. All his sons were great and they became heads of the twelve tribes (except for Joseph whose sons became heads) – it is true that there was a quarrel between יוסף and his brothers for some time but it was resolved in the end.

This analysis goes even deeper:

אברהם was the pillar of kindness to others – he invited strangers and provided great hospitality. His son ישמעאל pushed this quality too far. He was מצחק – making fun and mocking (Gen. 21:9). Rashi explains that he practised immorality and the other two cardinal sins of murder and idol worship which are the consequences of this kind of behaviour. As the Talmud Sanhedrin (63a) says: The real motive of these three sins is immorality. In order to practise it, one becomes an idol worshipper to give it a "seal of Kashrut," and if anyone opposes him, he is murdered. ישמעאל used a ***wrong type of kindness***. He used it to commit indecency. We find in the תורה (Lev. 20:17), "If a man takes his sister – חסד הוא – he has done a kindness (but the wrong type of kindness). ישמעאל's descendants destroyed the first בית המקדש.

יצחק's greatness was גבורה.[2] He was ready to lay down his life for the service of Hashem. His bad son עשו stretched it too far. "Live by the sword!" (Gen. 27:40). Halacha has it that עשו hates יעקב and, therefore, his descendants laid waste the second בית המקדש. Rabbi S. R. Hirsch puts it so succinctly! The people of the first בית המקדש were ***pleasure***-seeking but those of the Second Temple were ***self***-seeking.

However, יעקב was the pillar of תורה which he taught to his children. He was studying at Yeshivat Shem and Ever (Rashi, Gen. 28:11). The תורה gives the

1. Temple.
2. Strength of character.

borderlines on how far kindness and strength should go. Therefore, the Third Temple, which will be built in his merit will never be destroyed!

The Maharal of Prague penetrates even deeper into this subject. History has a pattern set by Hashem.

The period of the first בית המקדש had an advantage and a disadvantage. It had prophecy, miracles and revelation of the Divine Presence but no unity. The kingdom of the Jewish people was split. The second בית המקדש period _did_ have unity but had no more overt revelation of the Divine Presence, no prophecy and no more overt miracles. Neither did it have the Holy Ark with the Ten Commandments. Satan knows how to attack the important, strong points. During the period of the first בית המקדש where one could witness the open revelation of Hashem, a period of purity, Satan introduced the opposite – impurity, immorality, the hallmark of ישמעאל. During the time of the second בית המקדש when there was unity, the Satan introduced the opposite, too – שנאת חנם – unfounded hatred. "עשו hates יעקב."

Lust – the main trouble during the existence of the first בית המקדש – has limits. Therefore the exile was limited, too. But conceit and hatred have no limits. Therefore the exile lasts so long.

In our times we still suffer from the unfounded hatred of עשו during the terrible Holocaust and we continue to be exposed to the vengefulness of the descendants of ישמעאל, namely the Arabs. This, we trust, will come to an end (soon we hope) because there will be no third destruction and exile from Israel. There are "only" two תוכחות[1] in the תורה! Unfounded hatred, unfortunately, is still strong amongst _us_.

"כל המתאבל על ירושלים זוכה ורואה בשמחתה"
"Anyone who mourns for Jerusalem will merit to see its joyfulness."
(Gemara Taanit 30b).

It behooves us to take the lessons of משה רבינו in this *Sidra* ("How can I carry your quarrels") to heart, as well as those of the desolation of Jerusalem which we mourn during these weeks. It is also our duty to control our lust for pleasures of this world. It is true to say that these are limited, but they still require strong restraints according to the guidelines of our תורה. Above all, it is

---

1. Rebukes.

essential to overcome the disunity which is still prevalent amongst us and proves to be unlimited.

Let us transform שנאת חנם[1] into אהבת חנם[2] and so contribute our share in the rebuilding of the third בית המקדש speedily in our days.

---

1. Unfounded hatred.
2. Unconditional love.

ADDITIONS OR
SUBTRACTIONS OF MITZVOT

"לא תספו על הדבר אשר אנכי מצוה אתכם ולא תגרעו ממנו לשמר את
מצות ה' אלקיכם אשר אנכי מצוה אתכם"

"You shall not add to the word that I commanded you nor should
you subtract from it, to observe the commandments of Hashem
your G-d that I command you."   *(Deut.4:2)*

In the course of the last speech of משה רבינו he commands the Jewish people,
in the name of Hashem, not to add, such as five chapters instead of four in
the תפלין and five ציציות instead of four (Rashi), or to deduct any detail from
them.

Before delving into this fascinating subject I would like to share the following
charming anecdote with you:

The Rabbi of a Shul was very concerned about an elderly gentleman in his
congregation who always fell asleep during his sermons. He noticed that a little
boy – the grandson of the congregant – was sitting next to his grandfather, so the
Rabbi called the little lad and promised him £1 per week for jogging his
grandfather during the speech. It worked for a number of weeks but one שבת the
grandfather went back to his bad old ways. When the Rabbi asked the youngster
for an explanation, the boy replied: "Please Rabbi, but 'Zeide' promised me £2
per week for ___not___ disturbing him...."

Our great Sages say:

"כל המוסיף גורע"
"Anyone who adds, diminishes" (Sanhedrin 21a).

By adding £1 the "Zeide" missed the Rabbi's "derasha."[1]

---
1. Sermon.

Let us deal with the following questions:

1. Why is the law of "No adding and no taking away from מצות" only mentioned here for the first time?

2. The Gemara Rosh Hashana (28b) states that a כהן when blessing the congregation must not add to the threefold blessing of the תורה (Num. 6:24-26) which are:

   (I) "May G-d bless you and guard you"
   (ii) "May G-d illuminate His countenance for you and be gracious to you"
   (iii) "May G-d lift His countenance for you and give you peace."

   A חקירה[1] into this law leads us to the following:
   If a Cohen **does** add, does he fulfill the מצוה of blessing the congregation but sins by adding, or is his **whole** blessing null and void and he has to repeat it?

3. How could our great Rabbis add a number of laws to the תורה and even institute new Festivals such as Chanukah and Purim?

It is interesting to note that the very first sin was caused by transgression of this law. G-d commanded אדם and חוה not to eat from the Tree of Knowledge of Good and Bad (Gen. 2:17), but חוה **did** eat from its fruit and gave some to her husband (Gen. 3:6). This caused their expulsion from the Garden of Eden. The Midrash says that אדם told her in the **name of Hashem** not even to touch the tree. So the Tempter, the serpent, pushed her against the tree and told her: "You did not die just by touching the tree and you will not die from eating from its fruit either...." (Bereshit Rabba 19:3). The trouble was that אדם added to Hashem's command which was only **_not to eat from it_**. That is why the Gemara Sanhedrin (29a) asks: "How does one know that when one adds, one diminishes?" Because it says: (אדם said) "that G-d commanded us not to eat and not to touch it."

To answer the first question:

The reason why the law of בל תוסיף[2] is mentioned here for the first time is very clear. The Jewish people found themselves in an entirely new situation prior to their entry into Israel. Therefore, they might say: "New circumstances

---

1. An investigation.
2. Not adding or diminishing.

require new laws." However the תורה, which is Divine, never changes, as we say in the Yigdal prayer:

"This law G-d will never alter and not change for any other at any time."

That is why it was essential to command here not to change any מצוה by addition or subtraction.

Concerning the second problem: What is the nature of this לא תעשה?[1] Does the addition destroy the whole מצוה or not?

Here we have the "Kle Chemda" who claims that Rashi and Ramban differ in this very חקירה. Rashi quotes examples of five chapters inside תפלין instead of four, or five kinds at the מצוה of לולב or five strands of ציצית (Deut. 4:2) whilst Ramban quotes the example of a כהן adding a blessing to the three blessings of the תורה. According to Rashi, only in the case of לולב, תפלין and ציצית the מצוה **objects** have become unfit by the addition, but in the case of the blessing of the כהנים, their three-fold blessing is valid but the addition is a sin. Ramban, however, holds that the "official" blessing is also invalid.

The Rogotchever Gaon proves from a verse in the תורה that if one adds to a מצוה one destroys it completely.

"ארבעים יכנו לא יוסיף פן יוסיף להכותו על אלה מכה רבה"

"Up to forty lashes shall he strike him – he shall not add lest he strike him a **severe beating**" (Deut. 25:3).

This refers to the punishment for transgressing a תורה law. We see clearly from this that if one adds then *all* the lashes become beatings rather than corrective strikes. Then they *all* become sins rather than מצות....

The Gemara Shabbat (104a) says:

Why do the letters of שקר[2] stand on one leg (in the ספר תורה the letter shin is written on a pointed base) but in the word אמת[3] all its letters stand on two legs? Truth stands firm but lies do not. A lie is bound to fall sooner or later. Consequently, if one adds a leg it can only prop up the lie and if one takes a leg away from the אמת, it causes its downfall.

---

1. Negative commandment.
2. Falsehood.
3. Truth.

The rationale behind this commandment is very clear. By adding to a מצוה one sets oneself up as a critic of the Divine Lawgiver, חס ושלום.[1] It implies that what Hashem commanded is only four fifths of the desired effect, for example. It needs to be completed by human reasoning. Such a philosophy destroys the whole מצוה. This applies even if one intends to observe the command (Deut. 4:2) by "beautifying" the davening in shul by playing an organ, for example. That is why the Gemara states in Sanhedrin (29a), יתר כנטול – By adding, one diminishes!

Furthermore, in the Gemara (Chullin 58b) it is decided that a calf which is born with five legs is regarded as one with only three legs and is טריפה – unfit for food.

This can best be illustrated by the following parable:

A customer of a big department store had a grudge against the management. One day he hid in the store and changed all the price tags. When the manager opened the store next morning he was confronted with an array of very confusing prices. A toy had been priced at £1000, a mink coat at £10 and a diamond ring at £1. He had to close the department store temporarily.

Hashem has defined the exact details on each מצוה and no human being may tamper with them.

"The תורה of Hashem is perfect in restoring the soul" (Psa. 19:8).

Only Hashem who "blew the soul of life into man's nostrils" (Gen. 2:7) knows the exact composition of the food for the soul, namely the מצות.

That leaves us to answer the third question: How could our Rabbis add מצות?

Our חז"ל[2] did **not** add to the תורה. They merely ***protected*** the תורה, for example by instituting מוקצה – that one may not move a candlestick or money on שבת, in order to prevent us from using them on שבת. This right has been given to them by the תורה.

"ושמרתם את משמרתי"

"And you shall guard My charge" (Lev. 18:30).

חז"ל explain:

---

1. Heaven forbid.
2. Great Sages.

"עשו משמרת למשמרתי"
"Make a fence around My charge."

Chanukah and Purim are no additions to the 613 מצות either. The events of these two festivals happened *__after__* the תורה was given, and by engaging in festivities we give thanks to Hashem for our deliverance on both these occasions. These celebrations *__certainly__* do not diminish the completeness of the תורה.

Furthermore, our חז״ל made it abundantly clear that their laws do not infringe on the תורה and are not meant to be additions to the 613 מצות. They made a rule that

"ספק דאורייתא לחומרא"
"If one is in doubt if one has fulfilled a מצוה from the תורה, one should be strict."

For example, if one is unsure whether one has said ברכת המזון[1] etc., one should be strict; but if one is doubtful about a law made by the Rabbis, for example blessings over food, etc., then one may be lenient.

In contemporary times, people cause a lot of confusion and switches of values, too. They make additions and subtractions. Many put a high price tag on the *__material__* comforts in their lives and a very low price tag on *__spiritual__* values. Everything revolves around business and pleasure and little, if anything, around the most valuable and greatest מצוה, the study of the תורה (Mishna Peah 1:1).

Similarly, in the education of one's children, everything revolves around secular levels and little or nothing around תורה levels, particularly at the most important stage of education *__after__* בר מצוה and בת מצוה. These people transgress "Do not add or diminish" at the same time.

Let us remember what King Solomon said at the end of קהלת (Eccl. 12:13):

"את מצותיו שמור כי זה כל האדם"
"Observe all His Commandments because this is the whole of man!"

Perfection of מצות is the perfection of man!

---

1. Grace After Meals.

THE PERFECT SYSTEM
OF THE TORAH

עקב

"והיה עקב תשמעון את המשפטים האלה ושמרתם ועשיתם אתם ושמר
ה' אלקיך לך את הברית ואת החסד אשר נשבע לאבתיך"

"It shall be that because you shall hearken to these ordinances and you observe and perform them then Hashem your G-d will safeguard for you the Covenant and the kindness that He swore to your forefathers."

(Deut. 7:12)

At a United Nations banquet a British Member of Parliament was seated next to a Chinese delegate. Not a word passed between them because the British M.P. could not speak a word of Chinese. However, when the soup was served the M.P. plucked up courage and said to the Chinaman: "Do you likee soupee?" The Chinese delegate nodded. When the speeches began the Chinese diplomat was asked to speak. He spoke in exquisite "Oxford" English. When he sat down, he asked the British delegate: "Do you likee speechee?"

I trust that you will like the interpretation by great Rabbis of the first verses of this *Sidra* which is part of משה רבינו's farewell speech.

Two questions present themselves:

1. Here the תורה says: "<u>If you observe the</u> מצות then you shall live...on the land that He swore to your forefathers" (Deut. 7:13). But later on (Deut. 9:5) it states:

    "Not because of YOUR RIGHTEOUSNESS and the UPRIGHTNESS OF YOUR HEART are you coming to possess their land, but because of the WICKEDNESS OF THESE NATIONS does Hashem, your G-d, drive them away from before you, and in order to establish the word that Hashem swore to your forefathers, to Abraham, to Isaac and to Jacob."

These verses seem to contradict one another.

2. What is the meaning of the word עקב?

A great rabbi gives the following answer to the first question. There are two different promises contained in these verses:

a) The oath to our forefathers that we shall ***take possession*** of ארץ ישראל, this is conditioned by the iniquities of the inhabitants, the Canaanites and Moabites, etc. This is clearly stated at the ברית בין הבתרים[1] (Gen. 15:16):

"The fourth generation will return to the Land of Israel because of the iniquity of the Amorites shall not be full until then."

b) The covenant with the Jewish people to ***keep possession*** of our precious land, this depends on us observing the תורה. This is what the תורה emphasises at the beginning of our *Sidrah*.

"And you shall perform my decrees and observe my ordinances and perform them, then you shall dwell securely in the land" (Lev. 25:18).

Also, "if you perform the מצות then you shall dwell safely in the land" (Lev. 25:18).

But if not, Heaven forfend,

"ולא תקיא הארץ אתכם בטמאכם אתה כאשר ראה את הגוי אשר לפניכם"

"The land shall not disgorge you as it disgorged the nation that was before you" (Lev. 18:28).

This leads us to the second question: What does the word עקב denote here?

Rashi explains that עקב means 'heel' and alludes to the sort of commandments that people may regard as relatively unimportant, so they tend, figuratively speaking, to tread on them with their heels. However, if they do observe even these neglected commandments, then Hashem will reward them with His love and blessings in the ***Land of Israel.***

We see how much importance the תורה attaches to the fulfillment of so-called light מצות as the Mishna (Avot 2:1) exhorts: Rabbi says:

---

1. The Covenant between the parts.

"הוה זהיר במצוה קלה כבחמורה שאין אתה יודע מתן שכרן של מצות"

"Be as careful with a light precept as with a hard one because you do not know the reward of מצות."

Nature is created by Hashem on the guidelines of the תורה. The Midrash says: "He looked into the תורה and created the world" (Midrash Bereishit Rabba 1:1).

Consequently, just like nature works on exact dimensions, so does the תורה. For example, man's body consists of 248 limbs and 365 sinews. The תורה consists of 248 positive מצות which give life to the 248 limbs, and 365 negative ones which "service" the 365 sinews. Together they add up to exactly 613 מצות. Our bodies contain chemical factories. If they produce too few or too many hormones, for example, this has serious consequences on the health and growth of the individual. Similarly in the world at large:

In תהלים it states: "The Heaven proclaims the glory of G-d and the firmament shows its handiwork" (Psa. 19:2).

Further on in the same chapter, it comments, "The teaching of the L-rd is perfect rejoicing the heart...." (Psa. 19:8). We see here clearly the connection between nature and the תורה! Some of the innumerable examples: The atmosphere contains about 21 percent oxygen. Any more and lightning would cause explosions, but any less and we would not be able to live. The earth makes one revolution every twenty four hours. Were it to take longer, the sun would burn the crops and the cold would destroy them. Similarly, if the sun were a little nearer to the earth or a little further away.... What about machines? A tiny screw out of place would bring the whole machine to a standstill. One wrongly programmed letter in a computer could cause the whole system to crash. The same applies to the תורה: The תורה is one divinely integrated perfect unit. תורת ה' תמימה – Hashem's תורה is perfect (Psa. 19:8). A 'light' מצוה is as essential to its operation as a 'hard' one! Both nature and תורה are precisely adjusted and finely tuned and should not be interfered with. Therefore, the תורה says, עקב תשמעון – if you realise the importance of every מצוה, whether light or hard, and if you observe the whole unit of the תורה, then you will be blessed and will enjoy living in ארץ ישראל, which will belong to the Jewish people forever.

The following analogy is in place to illustrate the foregoing: An old farmer, who was apparently confused in his mind, was taken to hospital. The Consultant asked him: "If you had one hundred sheep and one escapes through a little hole in the fence, how many are left?" "None!" The doctor corrected him:

"You are wrong. There are ninety-nine sheep left." However, the farmer retorted: "You know nothing about sheep. When **one** sheep goes they **all** go!" He was not so sick after all!....

Just one tiny breach in the fence of the תורה opens the floodgates. Similarly, one light מצוה draws another one in its train and one sin leads to another sin (Avot 4:2).

The famous Rebbe Moshe Lev of Sassov offers another explanation of the word עקב. He says it means '*step*'. With every step a person takes one has to consider if it is in accordance with the directions of the תורה. "If you will listen and observe the commandments of Hashem." "בכל דרכיך דעהו – in all your ways you shall acknowledge Hashem" (Prov. 3:6).

There is nothing neutral in life. Even eating and sleeping, if in order to be healthy and strong to fulfill the מצות, then they are מצות, but if not, then they are sins! (Maimonides in his eight Chapters).

When יוסף was thrown into the pit, the תורה states: "The pit was empty – there was no water in it" (Gen. 37:24).

The Gemara (Shabbat 22a) asks: "Surely if it was empty, there was no water in it?" The Gemara answers: "There was no water but there were snakes and scorpions in there." The Vilna Gaon explains that nature abhors a vacuum. In life no vacuum is possible. Either life giving water or scorpions and snakes, and either one does a מצוה or a sin! This is beautifully illustrated by the following story:

The Bobover Rebbe was once visited by the Chief of Police of his town in Poland. The officer described his many difficult duties to the Rebbe. In conclusion he remarked: "When I get home, I remove my cap – I am off-duty and I can relax." The Rebbe retorted: "I never remove my cappel (Kipah). I am always on duty...." There is never a spiritual vacuum!

That is the meaning of this verse:

If we observe every minute detail of the מצות, if we consider every step a part of our service to Hashem, **then** Hashem will bless us and preserve Israel for us permanently, and we will be able to live there in safety.

To sum up: To take *possession* of Israel is not possible unless the previous occupants, the Canaanites, do not deserve to occupy this wonderful land because of their sins, but to **keep** it depends on our observance of the תורה. This condition is only fulfilled if we regard the תורה as one Divine unit which does not tolerate differences between easy or difficult מצות. Furthermore, every step we take in our lives should be in accordance with the guidelines which our Creator has given us in the תורה.

May this come true in our days!

BLESSINGS OF TORAH LIFE

משה רבינו, in his farewell speech, says in our *Sidra*:

"ראה אנכי נתן לפניכם היום ברכה וקללה. את הברכה אשר תשמעו אל
מצות ה' אלקיכם אשר אנכי מצוה אתכם היום. והקללה אם לא תשמעו
אל מצות ה' אלקיכם וסרתם מן הדרך אשר אנכי מצוה אתכם היום ללכת
אחרי אלהים אחרים אשר לא ידעתם"

"Behold, I present before you today a blessing and a curse. The blessing that
you hearken to the commandments of the L-rd your G-d which I command
you today, and the curse, if you do not hearken to the commandments of
your L-rd and you stray from the path which I command you today to go
after idols of others that you do not know" (Deut. 11:26-28).

Before delving into these verses, let us enjoy a little story.

In a large factory, one of the main machines suddenly came to a standstill,
and the whole factory had to stop work. The Director immediately summoned
an expert engineer who used a hammer to give it three knocks, and everything
sprang back to life again. The bill amounted to £100. The Director demanded an
itemised account by protesting: "Surely three knocks cannot command such a
high fee!" The engineer presented him with the following invoice:

For knocking   £ 1.00
For applying the expertise to know ***where*** to knock £99.00

I would like to"knock" three times on these verses today to bring sparkling life
to a part of our תורת חיים[1] with the help of our Sages. After all, the commentary of
the תורה is

"כפטיש יפצץ סלע"

"like a hammer which knocks a rock and produces sparks" (Jer. 23:29).

---

1. Our Torah of life.

Also Rabbi Yochanan Ben Zakai was called "פטיש החזק" – "A strong hammer" (Gemara Berachot 28b).

The Zohar on Beshalach states:

"פשיטא חריפא בקטרו ידיע"

"A strong hammer is known by its blow."

These are three "knocks" which hopefully will produce glowing particles of תורה.

1. Why is "ראה"[1] in the singular and the rest of the verses quoted in the plural?
2. Here it says that the reward for the observance of מצות is in this world. However, the Gemara Kidushin (39b) says "There is no reward in this world."
3. Why use the expression "ראה"?[2]

There are many explanations why "ראה" is in the singular. The Eben Ezra comments that משה רבינו is talking ***to each one individually***. This can best be illustrated by the following anecdote:

A young Rabbi visited a congregation in another town. The congregation invited him to give a lecture. He accepted the invitation but consulted the local Rabbi if he could give a talk which was quite sharp and which might give offence to some people. The Rabbi assured him that there was no problem. "You can say anything you want in my congregation. They are "Yenemites." The visitor said: "I have heard of **Yemenites** but what are **Yenemites**?" The Rabbi replied: "My members always regard any מוסר[3] as something directed towards 'Yenem' – the Yiddish word for 'the other one' – and never to him or herself."

So it was! At the conclusion of his first talk, a member came up to the speaker and said: "Your lecture struck the right note! Mr. Peloni Almoni needed your מוסר very much!"

משה רבינו addressed his words to **every single individual**. Therefore, ראה is singular.

Another convincing elucidation is given by the great Chatam Sofer ז"ל. The

---

1. See.
2. See.
3. Reproaches.

Gemara Kidushin (40b) states that the world may be in a state of "half innocent and half guilty" and so may be the individual. If you observe one מצוה, you may bring yourself and the whole world to blessing, otherwise, Heavens forfend, you may cause the reverse to yourself and to the whole world. That is the enormous importance of every מצוה! That is what the verse states: "See – you individual – that I give (through your actions) blessings and curses to the **whole** nation (plural)."

This leads us to turn our attention to the second problem: How can any action lead to a reward in this world? As my great Rabbi, Rabbi Dessler ז"ל put it: There is no bank in this world which can honour a cheque earned by fulfilling a *single* מצוה, because a מצוה is a spiritual object which cannot be equalled by any amount of material wealth.

Rambam (Teshuvah 9th Chapter) answers this question by saying that the תורה does not mean that the ultimate prize for observing Hashem's ordinances is in this world. Rather, that if one conducts one's life according to the will of Hashem, one will get many more opportunities to do so in greater measure. For example, as our great Rabbis say: "Give your tithe so that you will become rich" (Gemara Shabbat 119a).

This is illustrated by the following story:

A wealthy person who gave a lot of charity became richer and richer. His friends asked him: "What is the secret?" He replied: "I shovel out and Hashem shovels in. His shovel is *far larger*!" However, the ultimate reward will be left for the world to come (Mishna Peah 1:1).

Let us now move on to answer the third 'knock.' What does the expression of "See" mean here? The Malbim gives the following solution. "*See* I give you **today, in this world** the bliss and great benefit of life under the banner of the Holy תורה. We merely need to look around to discover how elevated life is morally and spiritually in comparison with life in the permissive society surrounding us. Look at the bankruptcy of life without restraints, as the Gemara (Gittin 13a) puts it: "A slave, (to his evil inclinations) likes lawlessness!" The world at large now says: We must go back to the old moral way of life if we want to defeat the terrible plague of AIDS. That is the meaning of the verse: "The blessing if you will listen to the מצות, and the curse if you do not listen to the commandments of Hashem and turn away from the path which I command you." The reward of מצות is, accordingly, not only in the world to come, where the main bliss will be, but also in this world.

That is the meaning of the verse in Proverbs 3:17.

"דרכיה דרכי נועם וכל נתיבותיה שלום"

"Her (the תורה's) highways are ways of pleasantness
and all her paths are peaceful."

The question arises: Why does it say pleasantness in connection with highways and peace after the word paths? The answer is very convincing. A highway has an advantage and a disadvantage. One feels safer on a highway because one is not alone but it is not so pleasant. A path through fields and woods, on the other hand, may be pleasant and peaceful, but it is not as safe. If one studies and observes the תורה thoroughly, one will discover that even its 'highways' are pleasant and its 'paths' are peaceful and safe. The תורה has all the advantages. ראה – You can see – and experience all this for yourselves, היום – today!

Now we understand the well-known Midrash (Vayikra Rabba 16:2):

A pedlar called out in a street: "Who wants to buy the medicine of life?" When Rabbi Yannai asked him for it, he took out the book of Psalms and showed him the verse:

"מי האיש החפץ חיים?"..."נצור לשנך מרע"

"Who is the man who wants life?"..."Guard your tongue from evil"
(Psa. 34:13-14).

Rabbi Yannai exclaimed: "All my life I have read this verse and I did not understand it until this pedlar came and explained it!" Many people ask what new teaching did Rabbi Yannai see in this verse after the pedlar had shown it to him. However, after the aforementioned explanation of the Malbim, it becomes clear. Rabbi Yannai was of the opinion that the reward for מצות is solely in the world to come. Now, through the pedlar who sold the medicine for life in this world, he realised that מצות are a medicine for *everyday life* <u>*NOW*</u> (Rabbi Elijahu Schlesinger).

מצות give content, value, joy and bliss to the highways and byways which we traverse in our journey through life and make our lives pleasant and peaceful!

In addition, an important fact we must always keep in the front of our minds, משה רבינו exhorts us here: either blessings or curses – there is nothing in תורה life which is neutral (Sforno 11:26-28).

Even eating, drinking and sleeping is beneficial only if it is done in the service to Hashem and to other people but, if it is only to indulge, it is the reverse.

We trust that our 'knocks' have, thanks to Hashem, produced a lot of sparks in the form of teachings of the right road which we should all choose in our life's travels.

a) We should take משה רבינו's farewell speech to be directed to every one of us and not to be "Yenemites."

b) We must realise that every one of us is a small world and our actions may not only have a bearing on our own position in the Court on High but on the world in general.

c) The ultimate reward of מצות will be in the world to come but every מצוה will bring more מצות in its train and remove obstacles to their performance.

d) Even in this world, the way of life of a בן תורה[1] is on a far higher standard than that of others who are slaves to their evil inclinations, the members of the so-called "Permissive Society." We can see how their way of life leads to moral, spiritual and even to physical destruction.

e) The highways and pathways of the תורה are both pleasant and peaceful. All this – ראה – You can see!

May we always see aright!

---

1. Adherent of Torah.

STATUS OF A JEWISH WOMAN שופטים

Thi his week's *Sidra* deals with laws concerning Judges, Kings, Cohanim, superstition, false prophets, murder and manslaughter, false witnesses, wars and unwitnessed murder.

Let us concentrate on just one subject: Fairness in Judgment.

"צדק צדק תרדף"

"Pursue righteousness" (Deut. 16:20).

A human being can only **pursue** justice and often cannot reach one hundred percent righteousness. Only Hashem can achieve it.

"הצור תמים פעלו כי כל דרכיו משפט"

"The Rock – perfect in His work for all His paths – are justice" (Deut. 32:4).

However, there seems to be a contradiction in our *Sidra*. In Chapter 19:17 the verse states: The **two men** (witnesses – Rashi) shall stand before Hashem. The Gemara (Shavuot 30a) deduces "but not women." The question arises immediately: Where is the צדק?[1] Are women second class citizens who cannot be trusted?

In order to answer this question, it is advisable to establish, first of all, who the "governor" is in a Jewish marriage. Is it the man or is it the woman? This reminds me of a story of a newlywed husband who wanted to establish his superiority. He went to a fashionable book shop and asked the assistant: "Can you get me a book entitled 'Man, master of the house'?" He was directed towards the ***FICTION DEPARTMENT***!

When he and his young wife opened their wedding presents one evening, the latter unwrapped some packages containing silver cutlery, candlesticks, etc., remarking: "We shall enjoy these presents ***together***." Then they unwrapped a big

---

1. Fairness.

parcel containing a Hoover cleaner. The bride exclaimed: "Someone has sent **you** a nice present!"

What is the philosophy of our תורה? The solution to this problem can be found in the furnishing of the holy משכן which is the pattern for a Jewish home.

In the Holiest of Holies of the Tabernacle, was the ארון הקדש[1] containing the Ten Commandments. Connected with the lid of the Ark were two Cherubim – angel-like figures made out of **one piece of pure gold**. They looked like a young man and a young lady, who, being married, are one golden unit protecting the Holy תורה with their golden wings (Gemara Yuma 54a). Clearly, husband and wife are **equally important** – albeit they have different tasks – and so are men and women in general.

This fact magnifies the main problem posed. If so, why does the תורה not trust women to be witnesses in Court? The truth however is that women are trusted in the same way as men. Let us consult the Gemara (Gittin 2b). There the Gemara states:

"עד אחד נאמן באסורין"

"One witness is trusted with forbidden objects."

Tosaphot asks: "From where do we know this?" The answer is from **women** who count the seven clean days when in a state of נדה[2] (Gemara Ketubot 72a).

If a woman declares a piece of fat to be of the forbidden kind, and if a person eats it after having been duly warned and is watched by two witnesses, the sinner would receive 39 lashes! If she has seen the dead body of a husband, the widow may remarry. What about Kashrut in her home? Does she need a supervisor? Surely not! We see clearly that in matters of credibility, a woman is trusted implicitly!

If we look at the Tenach and our history, we find many women who were superior to men.

Hashem said to אברהם in connection with the very controversial wish of שרה to send הגר and ישמעאל away: "Whatever שרה tells you, heed her voice" (Gen. 21:12). Her prophecy was of a higher standard than that of אברהם (Rashi).

Through the merit of righteous women we were redeemed from Egypt

---

1. Holy Ark.
2. Impurity.

(Shemot Rabba 1:16). Our midwives did not kill our babies despite the command from Pharaoh. Women did not give any gold towards the golden calf (Pitkei Rabbi Eliezer Ch. 45). They also did not die in the forty years of wandering in the desert (Rashi, Num. 26:64).

Furthermore, what about Devorah and Queen Esther, as well as innumerable other women of valour throughout our history! The demand for a so-called "Women's Liberation Movement" is in fact hysterical but not historical, as someone put it so aptly!

The Midrash tells us the story of a pious woman who was married to a pious man. Sadly, they were divorced after ten years of childlessness. The former husband married a wicked woman and she corrupted him. The former wife married an evil man. She made him pious! (Bereshit Rabba 17:12). A woman's influence is enormous!

This goes even further.

In the *Sidra* of Tazria (Lev. 12:2-5), the תורה deals with the most sublime phenomenon in the universe: The creation of human life. There it is stated that after the birth of a boy the mother is טמאה[1] for seven days, but after the birth of a girl, she is impure for two weeks! The question arises: "Why is that so?"

One answer given by a great Rabbi is as follows: There is a principle in the תורה that the greater the holiness of a place or of an object, the greater the impurity if the holiness is taken away.

The holiness of a girl is, in one respect, greater than that of a boy. A girl, when she is an adult, can bring human life into the world, which a boy cannot do. Therefore, the impurity which the mother suffers when her daughter is born is double that of a son! A woman is, in a way, more of a partner to Hashem in creation than a man! In the account of the creation, woman was created after man, maybe for this reason. She is the very summit of creation in this respect. The Gemara tells us to honour one's wife more than oneself (Yevamot 62b). So we have far more "women's liberation" already for over three thousand years.

However, the question arises: Why does the Mishna (Kiddushin 1:1) couch the way to get married in the following terms:

The woman is **_acquired_** in three ways, with money (a wedding ring nowadays) etc. Is she a chattel which one acquires with money?

The fact is, however, that she is a person in her **_own right_** in many respects.

---

1. Impure.

For example, she has possession of the property which she brought into the marriage, called "Nichsei Melug." The husband can make use of it and keep the profits such as rent, but the wife is the owner and is entitled to have it returned to her at his death or in the case of a divorce. If so, what does the husband acquire? "Ishut" – the rights of married life.

After all the foregoing, the question still persists: "Why can women not be witnesses?"

A major trait in a woman's personality is צניעות.[1] This is a fundamental part of Judaism in general: What does G-d demand? "To do justice and kindness and walk humbly with your G-d" (Michah 6:8). A woman is not meant to be on public display, for example, to be Queen in her own right, a leader or a Rabbi. Rambam (Laws of Kings 1:5):

"כל כבודה בת מלך פנימה"
"The honour of a daughter of a King is in the innermost" (Psa. 45:14).

This leads us to the answers. Witnesses do not only give credibility to someone's allegation or accusation, for example, but more than that, witnesses are essential to convict a criminal. The Gemara (Shevuot 34a) tells the story of Rabbi Shimon, the son of Shetach, who saw one person, sword in hand, running after another one into a ruin. Rabbi Shimon ran after him and saw him leaving that ruin with the sword dripping with blood and the other person lying dead. Rabbi Shimon said to him "Who killed the victim, you or I? But what can I do? The תורה says there must be two witnesses seeing the actual murder. But **Hashem** will punish you." Not long after that, the murderer was bitten by a snake and died....

The best circumstantial evidence is not sufficient to convict a criminal! There are a number of more technical requirements needed to validate a testimony. For example, if the witnesses did not see one another, one from this window, the other from another window (Gemara Makot 6b), or if one of the witnesses was disqualified by gambling, for example, or by charging interest, etc., then even one hundred witnesses are unfit to testify if the disqualified one is part of that group (Gemara Sanhedrin 9a). We see that certain knowledge of the crime is not enough. The disqualification of women is a **technical** rule, not due to their lack of credibility. Even Moshe and Aaron cannot testify together,

---

1. Modesty.

and they are surely trustworthy! However, technically brothers cannot be witnesses (Tossaphot Gemara Zavachim 103a). It may also well be that women are exempt from the מצוה which requires a person to testify, just as they are exempt from all מצות which are bound to time, i.e., תפלין, ציצית, שופר, לולב etc.

There is more to this. Since the glory of a "daughter of the King" – and all our women are "daughters of the King" – is innermost, therefore, we do not subject her to public cross-examinations and interrogations. That would be counter to her privacy, although she has **_full credibility._** A Jewish King could not be called to testify either, for a similar reason – it would be below his dignity (Ramban – Law of Kings 3:7) (Moshe Meiselman).

Now we also understand why women do not need to observe מצות bound by time.

Far from being a demotion, this is to be regarded as a **compliment.** Men who are involved in public life need more מצות to remind them constantly of their status as soldiers of Hashem, for example, ציצית and תפלין. Women do not need them. They are busy looking after their husbands, their children and their homes, which, after all, is the centre and main pillar of Jewish life (Rabbi S.R. Hirsch ז"ל).

Rabbi Yosi Haglili says: "He who is busy with one מצוה is free from another" (Gemara Sukkah 26a).

The following charming anecdote will illustrate the above:

A Jewish judge in London once celebrated the elevation of his wife to the title of J.P.C. Justice of the Peace – magistrate. He remarked then: "Now we have reached the ideal state in our marriage **she honours me and I worship her**.... (Judges in England are addressed to as "Your Honour" and magistrates as "Your Worship.")

We do care for and cherish our women-folk very much indeed. The Jewish woman who patterns her life according to the תורה laws enjoys the most elevated status amongst civilized people. Despite all accusations and insinuations to the contrary, deeper study of our תורה reveals the truth of the verse

"צדק צדק תרדף"

"Pursue righteousness" coupled with the verse

"כי כל דרכיו משפט"

"All His paths are justice!"

ONE MITZVAH DRAWS
ANOTHER IN ITS WAKE

כי תצא

Our *Sidra* today contains a wealth of material, in fact, seventy-two מצות out of six hundred and thirteen.

However, we have to confine ourselves to two problems only:

1. What is the connection of this portion, כי תצא, with the previous *Sidra* of שפטים?[1]
2. At first glance, the seventy-two מצות, in particular the first ones, seem to be completely unconnected. What, for example, has the law of the "אשת יפת תאר" – "The beautiful captive woman" got to do with the law of "שלח הקן" – "Sending away the mother bird before taking the eggs or the young," and the law of ציצית?

Let us introduce the solution to these problems with the following anecdote: A very wealthy miser once had a life-threatening fever. His doctor prescribed tablets and told him: "If you will perspire then you will be on the road to recovery, but if you do not, then may Hashem help you!"

The chairman of the charity funds of his congregation came to visit him with some of the members of the Committee to raise funds for their charities. They quoted the famous verse:

"צדקה תציל ממות"
"Charity saves from death" (Prov. 10:2).

Then they asked for funds for the Yeshivah. He replied: "Put down £1000, plus £500 for the Shul Building Fund, and £250 for the poor of the town." Suddenly the "donor" exclaimed: "**I am perspiring. Cross it all off!**"

Rabbi Samson Raphael Hirsch ז"ל answers the first point by saying that שפטים

---

1. Judges.

was dealing with affairs of **national** importance, matters which needed to be arranged now that בני ישראל were about to enter Israel and settle there, judges and their functions, the special laws concerning Kings, cities of refuge for those who killed unintentionally, wars, etc. Our *Sidra*, however, deals primarily with *private* relationships, family and social life.

It starts with the law not to abuse the beautiful woman prisoner in war-time, returning lost articles, building a fence on a flat roof, rape of a betrothed woman, hygiene, relationships between employer and employee, divorce, creditors and debtors, looking after the poor, and many more subjects.

חז"ל[1] connect the seemingly unrelated מצות at the beginning brilliantly by working with the principle:

"מצוה גוררת מצוה ועבירה גוררת עבירה"
"One מצוה brings another מצוה, but one sin causes another sin"
(Avot 4:2) (Rashi Deut. 21:11 and 22:8).

This can be illustrated with the following story:

When Kashrut was forbidden in a certain community, a Jewish restaurant owner procured kosher meat and other kosher food for his Jewish customers and served them secretly. One customer ordered meat but was shocked when the bill was presented. It was for pork, which, incidentally, was much cheaper. When he quietly remonstrated, he was told: I did not see you wash your hands for נטילת ידים before the meal and therefore did not know that you were Jewish!.... One sin comes after another!

The תורה deals with the uncontrollable desire of a Jewish soldier in wartime, warning that this will have grave consequences – **one sin produces another!**

- a) He will hate her eventually;
- b) They will have a rebellious son who will be executed, followed by other sins which have a common denominator.

But then, from the מצוה of שלוח הקן[2] if you want to take the little ones, one מצוה causes other מצות. You will acquire a home, and you must make it safe by putting a fence around the flat roof, etc., and you will have a vineyard where you must not plant other plants and a field where you must not plough with a mixture of

---

1. Our great Sages.
2. To send away the mother bird.

different animals, such as an ox and a donkey. You will have garments which must not contain שעטנז[1] in its manufacture, followed by the מצוה of ציצית which is as great as all six hundred and thirteen מצות put together (ציצית has a numerical value of six hundred to which are added five knots and eight cords), מצוה comes from the word צוותא – union – with Hashem. It can be compared to a seed, when, combined with earth, produces many more, so מצות make that union and with help from Hashem cause many more.

However, the following question arises: Why does Rashi, quoting Midrash (Tanchuma כי תצא Chapter 1) start with the first מצוה, which brings others in its train, of "Sending away the mother bird" (Deut. 22:6) and not from the מצוה of "returning a lost animal or article" at the beginning of Chapter 22?

The famous Dubno Maggid gives the following striking answer: The sudden fire generated by the beauty of the captive woman is really only a deception. Our חז"ל[2] in Gemara (Kiddushin 21b) say that "the תורה speaks here against the יצר הרע." The Satan who represents the יצר הרע is a master deceiver. The soldier overcome by that fire thinks "וחשקת בה" – "that he desires her," that he has some spiritual affinity with her, but in the end, after undergoing all the prescribed actions of the תורה such as cutting off her hair, changing her fashionable dress into a simple one, etc., he realised that "לא חפצת בה" – he discovers that it was a deception – "he did not like her" – and sent her away....

The word איש[3] has a Yud in the middle whilst אשה has a Hay at the end. Our חז"ל say:

"איש ואשה שכינה שרויה ביניהם"

If man and wife live under the banner of G-dliness, "Yud and Hay", then the Divine Presence will be with them. However, if one takes these two letters away, then only the two letters אש[4] remain" (Talmud Sotah 17a).

We find similar expressions in the episode of the kidnapping and violation of Dinah, the only daughter of יעקב, by the Prince of Shechem, the Hivite. Chamor, the father of Shechem said: "My son Shechem

---

1. Wool and linen.
2. Sages.
3. Man.
4. Fire.

"חשקה נפשו בבתכם"

"Longs deeply (has a spiritual affinity) for your daughter" (Gen. 34:8),

but later on it says:

"כי חפץ בבת יעקב"

"He desired the daughter of Yaacov" (Gen. 34:19).

It was a mere animal lust!

Therefore, this whole chapter of deception by the יצר הרע[1] continues with "If you find the ox of your brother, or his lamb which had run away, and you <u>hide yourself from them</u>, you shall surely return them to your brother" (Deut. 22:1). We see that this is another example of deception. This is followed by "Do not hide yourself from helping someone whose ox or donkey had fallen on the road" (Deut. 22:4) and "A woman must not wear a male garb and a man may not wear a feminine garment, for anyone who does so, is an abomination to Hashem" (Deut. 22:5).

We must keep society orderly and not practice deception (Heaven forbid). This solves the question, Why does Rashi not start the positive part from the Mishna of "Returning a lost article"? The answer is that it also comes under the heading of the sin of deception, the **negative**, sinful part.

However, why is the first מצוה "Sending away the mother bird?" Why just this example?

There are various reasons given by our Commentators:

1) This מצוה is the exact opposite of the sin of the "beautiful woman." She came into the soldier's dominion through war. There the תורה warns the soldier:

"לא תתעמר בה"

"Do not enslave her." "Do not exploit this fact."

Rabbi Chaim Sonnenfeld ז״ל, the late Chief Rabbi of Jerusalem, points out: "How could one possibly catch the mother bird?" By taking advantage of its maternal instincts to protect its young.

Therefore it says:

---

1. The evil inclination.

"לא תקח האם על הבנים"

"Do not take the mother with the children" (Deut. 22:6).

Then:

"שלח תשלח את האם ואת הבנים תקח לך"

"Send away the mother bird and **then** you can take the young for yourself"
(Deut. 22:7).

2) This מצוה is called an easy מצוה. "Why is that so?" You might answer:
    "Because there is no expense connected to it."

However, there are many מצות which cost nothing, for example, visiting the sick
and accompanying the dead, etc. If so, why is just שלוח הקן singled out?

The Gerer Rebbe ז"ל answers this question by pointing out: Here is no
preparation required.

"כי יקרא" – "You just happen to come across a bird's nest." Other מצות require
preparation. That is why the תורה starts this subject of consequences of fulfilling
מצות with this easy מצוה. Because, as explained in the *Sidra* עקב,[1] מצות which
seem to be insignificant (which one treads on with one's heels) matter very
much indeed. They are an integral part of the system of all the six hundred and
thirteen מצות which form one divine unit. Even such a "light" מצוה causes more
מצות on your home and fields which Hashem will give you.

3) In contrast to the negative sins of the first part which are all based on
    pretence and deception, this מצוה is a **genuine** one. No one was
    looking – "כי יקרא" – "if the bird's nest happens to be before you on
    the road." Yet one fulfills the מצוה: No display of pious deeds before
    others. All this leads to the מצוה of ציצית.

"וראיתם אותו"

"And you shall see it" (Num. 15:39).

Then you will see the real vision of life, not through the coloured glasses of
bribery – of the יצר הרע. Not to be deceived – "לא תתורו אחרי עיניכם" – "do not be
deceived by your eyes" (Num. 15:39).

As the Baal Haturim so aptly remarks: "The eight cords symbolise the eight
organs of enticement, namely, the eyes, mouth, ears, nose, private parts, heart,

---

1. Ekev.

hands, and legs. They are knotted and controlled by the five knots – the five books of the תורה – wherever one may turn, on all four corners. The ציצית are the uniform of the soldiers of the צבא ה'.[1] They bear the acknowledgment of Hashem by the symbol of the binding cords: One binds seven, eight, eleven, and thirteen times which, together, equals the numerical value of "ה' אחד"[2] as stated in the Shema, namely thirty-nine. Incidentally, we refrain from thirty nine kinds of work on שבת to acknowledge that "ה' אחד" and a sinner sometimes received thirty nine lashes for transgressing against "ה' אחד"!

This goes further still: In the Gemara (Bava Metziah 61b) it states: Hashem said: "I have made a difference between first-born and not first-born in Egypt (when the first-born were being killed). I shall punish a person who puts vegetable dye on his clothing (ציצית) and says that this is the תכלת – the authentic blue colour."

There are some people who shun piety in public. They show _false_ colours. They are deceiving others in the reverse way. That kind of failing is all too common. Someone who wears the correct blue ציצית but proclaims that it is a mere copy. Hashem not only despises the hypocrite who passes off the artificial as genuine but also the moral coward who disguises the authentic with "Ersatz."

This may sound strange but it is a fact, nonetheless. For example: Some people decline an invitation from business associates on Friday night by saying: "It is my 'family night.'" He is ashamed to admit that it is שבת. Or what about people who claim that they support Israel because it is the "only democracy in the Middle East." Again they are wrong. "If there were other democracies in the Middle East would they not support Israel?" Why do they not come out with the real "תכלת" and say it is because it is our Holy Land which has been given to us by Hashem at the Covenant between the Parts (Gen. 15:18) and promised to us in many places in the תורה. Why disguise the truth?

This, consequently, is the message of this Sidra: We should conduct our personal lives under the banner of our _true_ colours! Under the banner of the right outlook of תכלת and not under any Ersatz colour. We must never be ashamed and disguise our Yiddishkeit but, on the contrary, be proud that we are trying to obey the מצות of Hashem, whether they are light or difficult. One must

---

1. The Heavenly army.
2. Hashem is one.

not be influenced by the simulated outward beauty of the יפת תאר[1] – or by the bright lights and excitements of modern "civilization." One must not be deceived by the "Master Deceiver", the יצר הרע, but see Hashem in everything and observe His מצות even when no one is looking. **<u>We are bidden to fulfill our vows even when perspiring!</u>** We must not allow the evil inclination to overpower us but be true to ourselves.

Then our Divine צוותא – Partner – will grant us opportunities to fulfill even more מצות to be observed with gratitude and joy!

---

1. Beautiful woman.

FULFILLMENT OF TORAH PROPHECIES

This portion of the תורה deals with the laws of בכורים[1] and the blessings and curses on Mount Gerizim and Mount Eval.

The main part, however, promises untold blessings which accrue to the Jewish nation for fulfilling the commandments of the תורה, followed by the תוכחה[2] if we do not observe the מצות (Heaven forbid).

This talk will concentrate on the two תוכחות[3] that is in the *Sidra* בחקתי (Lev. Chapter 26) and the one in this week's *Sidra*. Both predict terrible disasters, amongst them that the Jewish nation will have to leave Israel and go into Exile after military defeat. Eventually our people will come home to our land from all over the world, after returning to Hashem and His תורה.

"גל עיני ואביטה נפלאות מתורתך"

"Open my eyes and I shall see wonders in Your תורה" (Psa. 119:18).

We shall discover in these Sidrot, and in other texts of the Torah, revelations and exact fulfillment of prophecies made nearly over 3,300 years ago concerning our nation's fate. Obviously, such predictions can only have been made by the Master of History, Hashem – never by "human inspiration," a term which so called "moderns" bandy about so much nowadays.

However, before going into this subject in depth, I wish to share the following anecdote with you, which I heard from Chief Rabbi Lau שליט"א. He spoke about a famous symposium between the British historian, Professor Toynbee and the late Rabbi Jacob Herzog ז"ל, the Israeli ambassador to Canada, on Canadian radio. Professor Toynbee said that we the Jewish people do not deserve a land of our own but are merely a sect whose task it is to propagate

---

1. First fruits which are given to the Priests.
2. Admonition and reproof.
3. Rebukes.

monotheism all over the world. Dr. Herzog ז״ל replied that our תורה speaks about a Jewish nation, about redemption and about Israel, our country.

The debate centred about the following:

a)   Are we a nation?
b)   If so, what makes us a nation?

Chief Rabbi Lau שליט״א gives the solution by means of the following striking parable:

Let us imagine that an Olympic aircraft lands at Athens airport. An old man leaves the aircraft, makes his way down the stairs, while an airport worker goes up to help him with the luggage. The old man asks him: "What is your name?" However, the porter does not understand classical Greek, so an interpreter has to be engaged. It was SOCRATES who landed in his own homeland. He asked: "Where is the temple of Zeus?" "There is no Temple, but the Greek Orthodox Church rules the religious life of this country." "Where is the Senate?" "There is none." "The King?" "There is no King." "The power of Greece as ruler up to India?" "No more – we are part of NATO under the aegis of the United States of America, and not an important part." "Art?" "Nothing special." "Sports?" "Just some basketball."

The Greece of Aristotle – culture, power, mentality – nothing remains, and yet they are a Greek nation....

Now let us imagine an Al Italia aircraft landing in Fiumicino near Rome. An old man appears at the door. A worker goes up. The old man exclaims: "Veni, Vidi, Vici" (I came, I saw, I conquered). Nobody at the airport understands him. They think he is crazy. An interpreter discovers that the old man was JULIUS CAESAR. "Where is the Temple of Jupiter?" "No more! But we have Vatican City in the heart of Rome. The Pope, John Paul II, was born in Vadowice near Cracow in Poland. He is our spiritual leader." "Senate?" "No Senate." "Where is the Emperor?" "We have no Emperor!" "Colonies – Angola, Libya, Ethiopia, etc.?" "No more – the Rome of Fellini is not the Rome of Caesar!" "Power?" "We are just a part of NATO under the aegis of the United States of America, and not an important part. Yet they are a nation....

Now let us imagine an El Al plane landing at Ben Gurion Airport. An old man comes down. He was never in Israel before, was not born there and has never touched the ground. The old man says "שלום עליכם"[1] to the worker who comes to help him. "עליכם שלום"[2] is the prompt reply.

"Who are you?" asks the Porter. "משה – and you?" "Moshika from Georgia, Russia. I work here and I can now speak Ivrit." They could converse without an interpreter after 3,300 years interval!

MOSHE RABBEINU said to the worker: "I am only here on a visit. I forgot my טלית and תפלין" (My prayer book and Tefilin).

"No problem – I will lend you mine." "You have a טלית and תפלין?" "Of course I have and I use them every day. I can take you to one of the airport synagogues on the ground floor or the second floor for שחרית'[3] prayers."

There משה רבינו heard his very own words:

"אז ישיר משה"

"Then Moshe Sang" (Exod. 15:1).

"מי כמכה באלם ה'"

"Who is like You among the mighty ones, Hashem?" (Exod. 15:11) and much more.

The same טלית and תפלין. No change! And משה רבינו was not born here. He lives on! Are we not entitled to be a nation? What is a nation? If we observe our מצות and live by the תורה, then we are a nation, particularly now when we have our homeland again. Jeremiah's prophecy:

"ושבו בנים לגבולם"

"The sons shall return to their borders" (Jer. 31:16) has come true.

Of course we are a nation. We celebrate Seder the same night all over the world! From Helsinki to Johannesburg, from London and New York to Moscow. The same menu – Matzot – to take just one example. Moshe, Moshiko, Mossika, Moise are all members of our nation, no matter where they live. Minsk or Pinsk, Kibbutz Brenner or Rio De Janeiro. THE POWER OF THE תורה, NOT JUST THE LAND, makes us into a nation.

Let us now look into the תורה to discover how so much of our history **as a nation** is already clearly mentioned in its Divine contents.

---

1. Peace be upon you.
2. Upon you be Peace.
3. Morning.

Pharaoh already recognised us as a nation.

"הנה עם בני ישראל רב ועצום ממנו"

"Behold the Jewish nation is stronger than we" (Exod. 1:9).

He was the first, followed by יתרו[1] who said:

" אשר הציל את העם "

"He (Hashem) saved the nation" (Exod. 18:10).

Later on Bilam, the non-Jewish prophet, also recognised our nationhood by exclaiming:

"הן עם לבדד ישכן ובגוים לא יתחשב"

"Behold it is a nation that will dwell in solitude and not be reckoned amongst the nations" (Num. 23:9).

We are called עם סגלה[2] (Deut. 7:6) and are under the השגחה פרטית[3] of Hashem.

Let us now quote some of the many examples of predictions concerning the fate of our nation which have all been fulfilled.

First we start with a question. Why do we have two chapters of תוכחות[4] one here and the other one in בחקתי (Lev. 26:16-41)?

The famous Ramban discovered a number of differences between the two and he explained them brilliantly, adding that it is a "מצוה to publicise his findings." He claims that the first one, in בחקתי, is a complete and exact prophecy of the destruction of the ***first*** great בית המקדש in Jerusalem and the subsequent exile by Nevuchadnezzar, the Babylonian King. Our *Sidra*, however, predicts the destruction of the ***second*** בית המקדש by the Romans and the exile following, the one in which we the Jewish people find ourselves at the present time. Therefore, in בחקתי the destruction of idols is foretold (Lev. 26:30), but not in our portion, because there was no more idol-worship during the period of the second בית המקדש.

What is even more amazing is that the end of the first exile is clearly predicted (Lev. 26:34):

---

1. Jethro.
2. A treasured people.
3. Special supervision.
4. Rebukes.

> "The land (of Israel) will be appeased for its sabbaticals during
> all the years of desolation while you are in the land of your foes."

Rashi on Lev. 26:35, comments that the Jewish people did not observe the שמטה and יובל years, every seventh and fiftieth year, in which we are forbidden to work the land. They totalled exactly seventy years during the period of the first בית המקדש! Now the land rested all those years. We know now that the first exile lasted exactly seventy years until the second בית המקדש was built! What a fantastic prophecy so many hundreds of years before it actually happened!

In our *Sidra* it is mentioned that "G-d will carry against you a nation from afar... as an **eagle will swoop**, a nation whose language you do not understand (Deut. 28:49). Ramban points out that the emblem of the Romans was an eagle and the Jews did not know Latin. However, we did understand the language of the Babylonians because they were our neighbours. The monstrous cruelties of the Holocaust are clearly hinted at in our *Sidra*, too, as well as other terrible events during our long years of גלות.[1]

In Deut., Chapter 30, verses 1-10, the end of the גלות is prophesied.

"When all these things come upon you – the blessing and the curse that I have presented before you – then you will take it to your heart amongst all the nations where Hashem had dispersed you, and you will return unto Hashem and listen to His voice.

Then Hashem will bring you back from your captivity and will gather you from all the peoples to which Hashem has scattered you.

If any of you dispersed will be at the <u>end of the Heavens</u>, from there Hashem will gather you.

And Hashem will <u>bring you to the land that your forefathers possessed and you will possess it....</u>"

What a wealth of astonishing prophecies are contained here!

First of all, we must realise that these predictions were made when we were all together in the desert. In our *Sidra* we were told that we would be scattered all over the world.

"והפיצך ה' בכל העמים מקצה הארץ ועד קצה הארץ"
"Hashem will scatter you among all the peoples from the end of
the earth to the end of the earth" (Deut. 28:64).

---

1. Exile.

Has this not come to pass? We find Jews literally in any part of the world! What is even more amazing is the forecast that eventually we shall return to our land, which is unparalleled in the annals of any other nation and contrary to all rules of history! After nearly two thousand years of exile we have returned to Israel!

Deut. 30:4 is very mysterious indeed. What is meant by the **"ends of the Heavens** from which Hashem will gather us?"** In my opinion, it may well be a prediction of space travel!

Adventurous Jewish businessmen may go up to the moon or to Mars by space shuttle and bring back new material which they can sell at a profit down here....

Further on, in Deut. 30:5, where it says that Hashem will bring us back to our land, is the 5707th verse in the תורה. Many rabbis reckon the creation of man as year two. **If so, exactly in the year 5707** the United Nations voted to return Israel to the Jewish nation. Is this a coincidence?

No other nation in history has had events foretold as we have, thousands of years before they happened, with such accuracy!

There are many more prophecies in our תורה which we now see as having come to pass. Here are just a few more examples:

"והשמתי אני את הארץ ושממו עליה איביכם הישבים בה"

"I shall make the land desolate and your foes who dwell upon it will be desolate" (Lev. 26:32).

So it happened throughout our history. No other occupant of our land could make Israel flourish, except us. The Land "flowing with milk and honey" (Num. 14:8) became a malaria ridden uninhabitable country. A heavenly pointer to the fact that Israel is ours! (Ramban).

Furthermore, in Verse 44 of this chapter (Lev. 26):

"ואף גם זאת בהיותם בארץ איביהם לא מאסתים ולא געלתים לכלתם
להפר בריתי אתם כי אני ה' אלקיהם"

"But despite all this, while they will be in the land of their enemies
I will not have been revolted by them nor will I have rejected them
to **completely obliterate** them to cancel My covenant with them – for
I am the L-rd their G-d."

Hashem will never allow anyone to utterly destroy us. So it happened. Hitler's Final Solution did not succeed. A hidden miracle occurred. Years before his ascent to power, pogroms in Eastern Europe motivated many Jews to emigrate to England, America and Eretz Israel. So he did not have us all under his control....

Another prediction: People asked the חפץ חיים in 1930: "When will Hitler be stopped?" (He was powerful already then.)

He replied: "Look at the Prophet עובדיה[1] (1:17)

"ובהר ציון תהיה פליטה"
"On Mount Zion will be those who escape."

So it was. Rommel's army was halted just as he was about to capture Eretz Israel. That – together with the defeat of the Nazi army in Russia – was the turning point of World War II!

Furthermore:

"הנה זה עומד אחר כתלנו"
"Behold He stands behind our wall" (Song of Songs 2:9).

Our Sages explain: Hashem has sworn never to let the Western Wall be destroyed. Although Jerusalem was laid waste and rebuilt many times, the wall was not touched!

Finally, we find an **astonishing** prediction in the "Zohar" – the mystical book written nearly two thousand years ago. This has an important bearing on the situation in which we find ourselves today.

The following dialogue appears in the Zohar on *Sidra* וארא:

"The Arabs will demand Israel, since in Genesis 17: 8-12 it says that G-d has made a covenant with us (circumcision) to give us Israel. They claim that they have an equal right to Israel since their ancestor ישמעאל was circumcised when he was thirteen years of age" (Gen. 17: 25,26). [Rashi (Gen. 22:1) explains that ישמעאל even boasted to יצחק that he was circumcised at the age of thirteen whilst יצחק was only eight days old!] Hashem replied: "Yes, you are entitled to live in Israel until that merit evaporates. Then the Jews will take over. Furthermore, since your circumcision was empty (not done with all the required details) the

---

1. Obadiah.

land will be empty." Now we can see how all this has come true. The Arabs (Mohammedans) took possession of Eretz Israel in the year 636 and lived there – including the West Bank – up to 1949, the end of the War of Independence, when the Jews took over after having defeated (with the help of Hashem) the united Arab armies. For exactly **thirteen hundred and thirteen years** the Arabs were in possession of Eretz Israel. Clearly a Heavenly reward for the circumcision of ישמעאל when he was thirteen years of age. Also, the land was empty during this period and did not give of its produce. This is in accordance with the verse quoted above:

"I shall make the land desolate" (Lev. 26:32).

In the negotiations with the Arabs we should tell them: "You had your chance and now it is our turn!"

Since the establishment of the Jewish state, Israel is prospering, with Hashem's help, and has become the envy of the Arabs. Ingathering of our exiles is happening in front of our very eyes. Russian and other Jews are flocking to Israel in great numbers. We now see more and more of the wondrous deeds of Hashem unfolding. The destruction of the Communist regime in Russia and Eastern Europe, the humiliation of the modern day Haman – Saddam Hussein – on the actual day of Purim, these are truly historic and extraordinary times indeed. Above all, we are witnessing the upsurge of תורה – true Yiddishkeit, despite the Holocaust, all over the world.

No, Professor Toynbee. We are not just a sect, we are a _**nation**_, by virtue of the fact that we are the Servants of Hashem, by observing His wonderful תורה. And, unlike other nations, we continue our traditions and our way of life, even our language, since we became a nation at Mount Sinai three thousand three hundred years ago. Unlike any other nation, we remained a nation despite the loss of our land for over two thousand years. In fact, we are a nation encompassing the whole world! We observe our תורה, we eat the same menu – Kosher – we pray the same prayers and observe the same מצות. We keep together whether we live in Jerusalem, London, New York, Buenos Aires, Johannesburg, Moscow or any other town in the world. And Hashem is monitoring our progress and directing our history and looking after us wherever we may be.

If we compare these fantastic divine predictions with those of the Jewish historians after the Holocaust, who "predicted" that Judaism is no more (Heaven forbid!), we now see how utterly wrong they were!

What we need to do is to participate in the miraculous upsurge of תורה true Judaism developing all over the world at the present time and by strengthening our commitment to it. That is the way to help our beloved Israel even in the Diaspora.

Just as all the predictions mentioned above have come true, so may all the wonderful blessings in our *Sidra* be fulfilled. Furthermore, only observance of our תורה entitles us to keep Israel:

"ועשיתם את חקתי ואת משפטי תשמרו ועשיתם אתם וישבתם על הארץ לבטח"
"You shall perform My decrees and observe My Ordinances and do them
then you shall dwell securely on the land (Lev. 25:18).

Yes, Professor. It *is* our land, on the condition that we observe the מצות. Unlike all other nations, who do not have such conditions, we are a special nation – an עם סגולה.[1]

Eventually, may the following verses also come true, soon in our days:
"And many peoples shall go and say: Come and let us go up to the mountain of Hashem to the House of the G-d of Jacob and He will teach us His ways and we will walk in His Paths" (Isa. 2:3-5).

כי מציון תצא תורה ודבר ה' מירושלים
For out of Zion shall go forth the תורה and the word of
Hashem from Jerusalem.

And He shall judge between the nations and shall decide for many peoples.
And they shall beat their swords into ploughshares and their spears into pruning hooks.
Nation shall not lift up sword against nation, neither shall they learn war any more.
House of Jacob, come and let us walk in the light of the L-rd!"

---

1. A treasured nation.

תשובה – REPENTANCE

These Sidrot contain the following subjects:

נצבים: Covenant between Hashem and Israel. The option of תשובה[1] as an antidote to previous misdeeds, and the topic of free will.

וילך: The beginning of the final farewell of משה רבינו and confirmation of Joshua as leader. Ceremony of "Hakhel" – the assembly of the whole Jewish people every seven years to hear readings from the תורה by the King, and the מצוה to write a ספר תורה (the last one of the 613 מצות).

We shall confine ourselves to only one subject – תשובה. By way of introduction: A teacher asked the class: "What does one have to do in order to do תשובה?" "To sin, Sir," replied one of the pupils.

In נצבים we find the following verses (Deut. 30: 1-10). "When all these things come upon you, the blessings and the curses (the terrible admonitions in the previous *Sidra*) and you will repent...then Hashem will gather you from all the nations even from the end of the Heaven, and bring you back to Israel. And you will return and listen to the voice of Hashem, then G-d will rejoice over you for good as He rejoiced over your forefathers."

This מצוה (of תשובה) – according to Sforno and Ramban – is not far or hidden, not in heaven....but very near to you (Deut. 30:11-14).

This reminds me of the story of a Chassid who asked his Rebbe: "It says in the verse,

"כרחק מזרח ממערב הרחיק ממנו את פשעינו"
"As far as East is from West, He kept our transgressions away
from us" (Psa. 103:12).

---

1. Repentance.

Is repentance then as difficult as crossing the whole world from east to west?

"No!" said the Rebbe. "All you have to do is 'GEBBEN ZICH A DREI ARUM' – to do an about turn and face the other side towards East, towards the בית המקדש.[1] Just a change of direction with enthusiasm and sincerity is required!"

That is what the תורה says here:

"כי קרוב אליך הדבר מאד בפיך ובלבבך לעשתו"
"It is very near to you in your mouth and in your heart to do it"
(Deut. 30:14).

תשובה is a most exquisite gift that Hashem has given us. In the Talmud Yerushalmi (Makkot 2:6) it is said:

"They asked Wisdom: 'What should the punishment be for a sinner?' It answered: 'Evil should pursue sinners!' Then they asked Prophecy: 'What should the punishment be for a sinner?' It answered: 'The sinning soul should die!' Finally, they asked the same question of Hashem. He answered: 'He should do repentance and it will be forgiven to him!' We see that according to strict law תשובה does not help. After all, the sinner has sinned against His Creator. However, Hashem, in His loving kindness, stretches out His hand to receive those who do תשובה. We, therefore, must be very grateful for this wonderful Divine gift.

Our great Sages teach us: (Avot 4:22)

"Better one hour of repentance and good deeds in this world than all the life in the world to come!"

They also say: (Talmud Yoma 86a)

"תשובה is great, for it reaches the Throne of Glory...lengthens a man's life... and brings Redemption."

The Midrash (Bereshit Rabba 1:5) also teaches that תשובה was created before the natural world. So it exists outside the boundaries of natural law and can wipe the slate clean.

This leads us to the following question: What is the meaning of תשובה – literally, return? How can a person who did not observe מצות return? Or ordinary people who remain more or less consistent in fulfilling מצות? Surely returning means to go back to a place where one has been before?

---

1. The great Temple in Jerusalem.

There are three answers to this problem:

1. The Gemara (Shabbat 119b) says that the world exists in the merits of little children. They have not sinned. Accordingly, תשובה means returning to the innocence of childhood. This is proven by the fact that Jonah, after his תשובה in the belly of the great fish, came out like a newborn baby.

2. We return to the spiritual level attained at Mount Sinai when we said, "We shall do and we shall listen." As the Midrash says, "__*All Souls*__ were present at that great occasion" (Shemot Rabbah 28:4).

3. We return to the Throne of Glory where all souls come from and to which they will all eventually return. As we say in the morning davening: "My G-d, the soul which You gave me is pure!"

    תשובה returns us to that state of purity! A return to one's real personality!

In recent years we have seen that many young people, having tasted the life of permissive society with all its emptiness, vanity, falsehood and dangers, physical, spiritual and moral, are returning to their roots, to pure תורה Judaism. What is happening can be explained as follows:

A hidden miracle happened before the advent of the Nazis י״ש. In consequence of the pogroms in Eastern Europe, many of the grandparents or great-grandparents of these young people emigrated to England, to the U.S.A. and to Eretz Israel. Therefore, when Hitler י״ש came to power, he did not have ninety five per cent of all Jews left on the European continent, and although he inflicted terrible losses on those who were left, he could not complete the "Final Solution" (ח״ו – Heaven forbid) because so many had made good their escape. Hashem promised in Leviticus (26:44) never to let us be completely destroyed.

Most of the emigrants were adherents of pure תורה Judaism, but many of their children and grandchildren assimilated to the so called "free life" in the West without כשרות, שבת and other מצות. The world famous Chazon Ish ז״ל remarked on one occasion: Their parents and grandparents cried bitter tears and prayed and fasted but could not turn the tide. However, Hashem does not forget Jewish tears. He gathers them, as our Rabbis say. These tears could not help their children and grandchildren but they did help their great-grandchildren. That is why so many have returned to true Judaism in our time. We witness the emergence of a powerful בעלי תשובה[1] movement in Israel and all over the world. Special Yeshivot and centres have been established which are thriving. Also, generally, there has been a miraculous upsurge of תורה true Yiddishkeit all over the world after the terrible Holocaust, when the so called historians declared that (Heaven forbid) there was no hope of any revival after the destruction of so many communities and Yeshivot, etc.

The promise in the verses (Deut. 30:2-5) which we quoted at the beginning:

"And you will return to Hashem and Hashem will gather you from all the nations and bring you back to Israel" has been fulfilled, to some extent in our times.

This *Sidra* is read during the days of the month of אלול,[2] or the Ten Days of Repentance, when תשובה is the order of the day. Especially during these days, **everyone,** because "there is no man who does not sin," (Kings I 8:46) should join the בעלי תשובה. It is important to realise that this great מצוה is not far or hidden, not in heaven, but it is near to us. All one has to do is turn oneself around. One should also feel a great debt of gratitude to Hashem for giving us this precious gift to be able to make a new start by returning to the innocence of childhood. Furthermore, to go back to the high standard of when we said נעשה ונשמע[3] at Mount Sinai when we received the תורה, and above all, returning to the Throne of Glory where our pure souls come from, to our real personality!

Then we can look forward to a new year of good life and peace.

---

1. People who repent.
2. Elul.
3. We shall do and we shall listen.

THE JUSTICE OF HASHEM'S JUDGMENT

האזינו

"הצור תמים פעלו כי כל דרכיו משפט אל אמונה ואין עול צדיק וישר
הוא, שחת לו לא בניו מומם דור עקש ופתלתל"

"The Rock, His work is perfect because all His ways are justice; a
G-d of faithfulness and without iniquity, righteous and fair is He.
Corruption is not His. The blemish is His children's – a perverse and
twisted generation."

(Deut. 32: 4-5)

Our *Sidra* is the "song" which משה רבינו spoke about in the previous
chapter (Rashi, Deut. 31:19).

It deals with the recognition of the total harmony of creation and its mixed
past, present and future as a total reality in which there is no conflict, in which
future and past events are not only in harmony, but clarify one another. Then
everything is welded together as if it were happening at the same time (Rabbi G.
Schor).

This subject is so complicated and difficult that the following anecdote may
be of some help.

A young student went to universsty. His mother put his handkerchiefs into
his תפילין bag together with the סדור. Because she was worried that he might
forget to daven and to don his תפילין.

Some time later she received his first letter. It contained a complaint that his
mother had forgotten to pack his handkerchiefs. She wrote back: "Pray to
Hashem and you will find them...."

In order to find some answers to the question which we are going to pose,
which is an extraordinary difficult one to answer, we must surely pray to
Hashem to give us his help.

This question is an ancient one. It was already asked by משה רבינו.

"וְעַתָּה אִם נָא מָצָאתִי חֵן בְּעֵינֶיךָ הוֹדִעֵנִי נָא אֶת דְּרָכֶךָ"

"And now if I have indeed found favour in Your eyes, make your
way known to me" (Exod. 33:13).

Why is it that sometimes the wicked person is well off and sometimes the
righteous person is badly off? רשע וטוב לו צדיק ורע לו

Hashem responded (Exod. 33:19-23) There are limits to what even the
greatest of all prophets could perceive of G-d's ways. All the actions of Hashem
are "goodness" but משה רבינו can only see "My back but My face may not be
seen" (Exod 33:23). Rabbi Akiva put it as follows:

"לְעוֹלָם יְהֵי אָדָם רָגִיל לוֹמַר כָּל מַה דְּעָבִיד לוֹ רַחֲמָנָא לְטַב עָבִיד"

"A man should always accustom himself to say: Whatever Hashem
does is for the good" (Brachot 60b).

However, we only realise it is "for the good" _after_ the event. "You only see My
back!"

In the תורה there are many examples: take just one. The fact that יוסף was sold to
Egypt saved the lives of his family and that of millions of others. In the event,
conditions deteriorated in Egypt, but the misfortunes hastened our redemption
from Egypt considerably. Also, the Talmud (Brachot 60b) gives us an example of
this phenomenon.

Rabbi Akiva was once on a journey, riding on a donkey and taking with him a
cockerel to wake him in the mornings. When he reached a village late at night,
no one wanted to provide him with shelter for the night. So he went to the
nearby woods and lit his candle to study. But a wind blew it out. This happened a
number of times. Rabbi Akiva said, "All for the best!" So he lay down to sleep.
When he awoke, he discovered to his horror that his cockerel had been eaten by
a fox and his donkey had been consumed by a lion. Again he exclaimed:

"All that Hashem does is for the best!" Then he saw a number of people
rushing by. When he asked them why they were in such a hurry, they replied:
"During the night a band of armed robbers attacked our village. Join us to escape
from them!"

Had Rabbi Akiva slept in the village he might have been killed. Had the
candle been burning, the robbers might have noticed him. Had the cockerel

been noisy or the donkey been braying, he would have been found. How wonderful are the ways of Hashem!

There is a verse in תהלים

"אלהים לנו מחסה ועז עזרה בצרות נמצא מאד"

"G-d is a refuge and stronghold for us, a help in distress,
always accessible" (Psa. 46:2).

The Sfat Emet observes that the explanation for this verse is that sometimes misfortune breeds salvation.

The Prophet Jeremiah says:

"הוי כי גדול היום ההוא מאין כמהו ועת צרה היא ליעקב וממנה יושע"

"It is a time of distress for Jacob but he shall find his salvation from within it" (Jer. 30:7).

From distress itself, salvation is born.

The following true incident confirms this fact, too. Someone was involved in a car accident and was examined by brain scan in the course of his treatment in hospital. The scan revealed a growth in his brain which had to be removed **_immediately._** The accident saved his life!

I can relate an incident in a similar vein from personal experience:

My late father ז"ל secretly slaughtered chickens in the kosher way to enable Jewish people in Koenigsberg, Germany, to eat kosher meat during the Nazi י"ש regime in 1938. However, someone informed on him to the Gestapo – the Secret Police – and he was imprisoned. Things looked very bleak indeed. Eventually, however, this turned out for the good.

My mother ע"ה secured a visa for him to escape to Paraguay, thus saving his life. Later on, when concentration camps were built, such a visa would not have helped any more.

However, there are more points to be discussed. We do not really know who is a righteous person and who is not!

This reminds me of the famous story of "Simeon Kamtzan" – the stingy man – who never gave charity for any purpose. When he died the "Remo," his Rabbi, decreed that Simeon should be buried outside the Jewish cemetery. However, after his death the Jewish butchers and bakers gradually stopped supplying the many poor of their town with free Challot and meat for שבת. The "Remo" made an investigation and discovered that Simeon Kamtzan had secretly donated enormous sums of money for that purpose, without the knowledge of the townspeople. The "Remo" thereupon issued a Will requesting that he be buried next to Simeon Kamtzan outside the cemetery... and that is what happened!

Another point is that we only come into this world for a limited time and ask questions: "Why this and why that?" Just like a visitor to a Shul who asked the Gabbai: "Why do you call up the man from the back row and then the one from the front row, etc.? Why not in order, the one next to the person who was given an Aliyah (who was called up to the תורה)?" He was told: "That person received an Aliyah last שבת and the person in front had Yahrzeit (the anniversary of a family member's death) etc.! There _is_ perfect order in my distribution of Aliyot!" We cannot comprehend the wisdom of Hashem's conduct of affairs since we are like that casual visitor, busy asking questions (Chafetz Chaim).

Furthermore, supposing a wheel in a big machine possessed intelligence, it might ask: "Why must I turn round this way? I would like a change and turn round the other way!" It would, of course, bring the whole machine to a standstill! Only Hashem, who has created the _whole_ universe, can know the workings of the _whole_ huge machinery!

Another important contribution to this discussion: If Hashem would reward מצות on the spot and punish wrongdoers immediately, Shuls would be very well attended _every day!_ People would flock to them to collect the big cheques at the end of the davening which the Shammas would distribute, and no one would dare to use his car on שבת, knowing that he would immediately drive into the nearest lamppost.... One might say that this would be an ideal state of affairs! Not at all! We would lose our בחירה – our _freedom of choice_ which is the thrill of life! We would then be reduced to robots, to "puppets on a string!"

This leads us to the last point. The real reward for a מצוה will be in the world to come. It cannot be in this world since a מצוה is a spiritual matter, and therefore, all the Banks in the world could not pay for one single מצוה with all the material goods or money they possess. Wicked people, however, receive their reward for their good deeds in this world and forfeit life in the world to come. Obviously, all these points are only a tiny part of the answer to our question:

"רשע וטוב לו צדיק ורע לו"

– Sometimes a bad person is well off while a good person suffers –

We certainly cannot know all the answers. We must leave them to Hashem because

"הצור תמים פעלו"

"The Rock is perfect in His work."

What we can and should do is to heed שלמה המלך (King Solomon's) exhortation who tells us:

"סוף דבר הכל נשמע את האלהים ירא ואת מצותיו שמור כי זה כל האדם"

"In the final analysis, all things having been heard, fear G-d and keep His commandments, for this is the whole person" (Eccl. 12:13).

FEAR OF G-D IS THE FOUNDATION OF HUMAN SOCIETY

וזאת הברכה

We are coming to the end of the weekly reading of our תורה הקדושה[1] as well as to the end of the great ימים טובים[2] on this wonderful שמחת תורה celebration. Today we make the grand סיום.[3]

This reminds me of the story of a husband who, on a strict weight reducing diet, once took advantage of his wife's absence to indulge in a meal of "naughty but nice" foods. Unexpectedly, his "better half" came home, so he went to the silver cabinet and took out a silver cup and the other implements of הבדלה.[4] His wife asked him: "Why do you want to make הבדלה in the middle of the week?" He replied sorrowfully: "The יום טוב[5] is over!" For us, however, the reading of the last *Sidra* is not an occasion to make הבדלה; we follow it up immediately with "Laining"[6] the *Sidra* of בראשית[7] with great joy and enthusiasm. It truly is a continuous cycle!

Let us take one verse of this cycle as our subject at the beginning of our *Sidra*, where we find the following:

"ויאמר ה' מסיני בא וזרח משעיר למו הופיע מהר פארן ואתה מרבבת קדש מימינו אש דת למו"

"And he said: Hashem came from Sinai – having shone forth to them from Seir, having appeared from Mount Paran and then approached with some of the Holy Myriads – from His right hand He presented the fiery תורה to them"

(Deut. 33:2).

---

1. Our holy Torah.
2. Festivals.
3. Conclusion.
4. The ceremony at the conclusion of Shabbat and Festivals.
5. Festival.
6. Reading.
7. The beginning.

A number of questions present themselves:

1. What is the explanation of this mysterious verse?
2. In which way can one define the difference between the Jewish way of Service to Hashem and that of the rest of the world?
3. What can we derive from this verse for the New Year?

The Midrash Sifri quoted by Rashi explains that this verse teaches us that Hashem offered the תורה to the Edomites in Seir who asked what the תורה demands. Upon being told "You must not murder" they declined the offer saying: "Our ancestor, עשו, was blessed by יצחק to live by the sword (Gen. 27:40). Therefore, the תורה is not for us."

Then the Ishmaelites in Paran were asked if they would accept the תורה, but when they were told, "Do not steal" they rejected it, and so did the Amonites and Moabites because it prohibits adultery. When Hashem offered us the תורה by the demand of the first Commandment, to **believe** in G-d who brought us out of Egypt, we said "נעשה ונשמע"![1]

The Rabbi of Gur asked the following question on this Midrash: Surely, the nations can have a legitimate complaint. They were tested by severe demands of prohibitions on murder, theft and adultery etc., whereas we were merely told to **believe** in Hashem. They might quite rightly protest and say: Had you approached us as you did the Jewish people, we would have accepted the תורה.

He gives the following answer: "The מצות purify the person" (Midrash Tehillim 18:28). Therefore, acceptance of the תורה implies that one is willing to modify one's character traits and one's mode of life.

Each nation was asked if it was prepared to change its lifestyle for the better, and it refused. To change their **belief** was not a difficulty for them. They were so credulous that they would worship idols made out of wood and stone. Concerning us, however, killing or adultery is not on our agenda. Our weakness is our lack of faith in Hashem. After experiencing overt miracles in the exodus from Egypt and during their wanderings in the desert the Jewish people grumbled and were defiant, so that משה רבינו had to exclaim:

"ממרים הייתם עם ה' מיום דעתי אתכם"

"You have been rebels against Hashem since the day I knew you!"

(Deut. 9:24).

---

1. We shall do and we shall listen.

That is why we were told the first commandment "I am the L-rd your G-d." We did accept this challenge and were given the תורה.

The Vilna Gaon gives a different explanation which is quite remarkable. Our verse concludes:

"With His **right** hand He presented the fiery תורה to them." The emphasis is on the right hand, because we read from right to left.... So we read the first commandment first and accepted it. By doing so, we accepted all the others too. After all, they are consequences of it. The other nations who read from left to right first encounter "Do not murder," "Do not commit adultery," etc. That was too much for them....

In the final analysis, a very important principle emerges from the above. We put recognition and belief in Hashem first. From there, follows that the social order of mankind has a firm foundation and to obey the second tablet with its laws of בין אדם לחברו[1] is practical. The other nations, however, who start with the second tablet, could not avoid murder, theft and adultery. Civilization must be based on the foundation of the rule of Hashem. Without it one can always find excuses to break these laws.

Just consider what "civilized" Germany did to our people in the Holocaust!

That solves the second question.

Our fundamental principle is that the belief in Hashem must be the foundation of civilization, in contrast to other people as mentioned clearly in the תורה. אברהם did not disclose to Avimelech, the King of Gerrar, the fact that שרה was his wife, because

"ויאמר אברהם כי אמרתי רק אין יראת אלקים במקום הזה והרגוני על
דבר אשתי"
"And Abraham said: There is no fear of G-d in this place and they
will kill me because of my wife" (Gen. 20:11).

Pharaoh, the highly civilized King of Egypt, told the Jewish midwives to murder the newborn baby boys, but they did not do so because

"ותיראן המילדת את האלקים"
"And the midwives feared Hashem" (Exod. 1:17).

---

1. Person to person.

That is the lesson we can derive from this episode for the New Year!

יראת אלקים[1] must always precede relationships with our fellow men! Only then will civilization endure!

---

1. Fear of G-d.

CHAGIM

ACCOUNTABILITY FOR
OUR LIVES

"שעל כרחך אתה נוצר ועל כרחך אתה נולד ועל כרחך אתה חי ועל
כרחך אתה מת ועל כרחך אתה עתיד לתן דין וחשבון לפני מלך מלכי
המלכים הקדוש ברוך הוא"

"You were created against your will, you were born against your
will, you live against your will, and you will die against your will
and against your will in the time to come you will have to give
account and reckoning before the Supreme King of Kings, the Holy
One Blessed Be He!" *(Ethics of the Fathers 4:29)*

The fingers on the clock of time turn inexorably. Again we stand before our Supreme Judge to give account and reckoning for our deeds.

We live in truly historical times during which we experienced miracles of biblical proportions. The miraculous re-establishment of ארץ ישראל after nearly 2000 years of exile, the exodus from Russia, the humiliation of the modern Haman, Saddam Hussein on Purim, the fantastic upsurge of תורה study and practice all over the world, etc. We have a lot to thank Hashem for on this great day.

However, three problems present themselves:

1. Why should we be called to give account for our actions? We were not asked to be born. If we were non-existent we would not have sinned. If one is put on a plane to Australia without being asked, must one pay for the ticket?
2. Why is the sequence "account and reckoning?" One would expect to find reckoning first, to tot up one's credits and debits, and **then** the verdict.

3.   What can we do to win our case at the Court of דין?[1]

The Dubno Maggid gives the answer to the first question in his own inimitable manner by way of a parable.

A wealthy man had two daughters, one was ugly and the other was a nagging shrew. He had great difficulty marrying them off. However, a resourceful שדכן[2] paired the ugly one with a blind bridegroom and the shrew with a deaf man. Happiness reigned for both couples. Some years later, a famous specialist offered to cure them. He guaranteed to return the fees if they were not happy with the result. He was, it turned out, successful. However, both couples demanded the return of their fees. The consultant refused their request. After all, they could now see and hear. The case came before the בית דין.[3] They claimed that since their new found vision and hearing, their relationships had gone downhill and they suffered greatly.

One could now behold the "beauty" of his wife and the other could now regale in the constant scolding and bickering of his "better" half. The Head of the בית דין decided: "Yes, you deserve to have your money back, but only on one condition: The doctor will bring back your original ailments. Both patients exclaimed in unison: "No, this is not what we want. We want to stay cured!" "In that case," said the Chief Judge, "the physician is entitled to his fees...."

It is true that "you were born against your will." However, "against your will you will die." You want to live. Therefore, you must give account and reckoning – you must "pay the fee" and accept responsibility for your deeds in your lives.

The Vilna Gaon (who happened to be a good friend of the Dubno Maggid) supported this solution with the following Mishna (Bava Batra 1:3). If someone surrounds his neighbours field, which happens to be in the middle of his fields, with three fences from three sides, the owner of the field in the middle need not pay anything towards their cost. His field is still not fenced in, Rabbi Yossi says. If, however, the owner of the middle field puts up the fourth fence, he has to share the cost of all four fences. After all, now he derives the full benefit of all the fences. This Mishna is an exact analogy of the human condition. It is true that one was not asked when three "fences" were established – "against your will you were formed, born and live" but there is another one "against your will you will

---

1. Judgment.
2. Marriage broker.
3. The Jewish Court.

die." Everyone wants to live. Everyone treasures the most wonderful gift of life given to us by Hashem very much indeed. So we accept the other three conditions and, therefore, have to meet our obligations to "pay" for them by observing His מצות. They make our life meaningful and joyful.

The Mishna says in פרקי אבות (4:17):

"יפה שעה אחת בתשובה ומעשים טובים בעולם הזה מכל חיי העולם הבא"
"One hour of repentance and good deeds in this world is better than all
the life in the world to come" (Ethics of our Fathers 4:22).

It is true that עולם הבא[1] is the realm of incomparable bliss, but this world of ours is the domain of incomparable achievement. Our "payments" will make us grow in stature, which is only possible in this world.

After having seen that accountability for life is justified, the second question remains. Why is this done in this order? Surely the חשבון[2] should come first and then the דין?[3]

There are various answers:

1. Rabbi Bunem ז"ל says that דין does not refer to the **_verdict_** but the reckoning whether the person's actions go according to the דין – the **_law_** – or not.

2. There is another explanation: חשבון[4] refers to the person's **_character_**. That means a stingy man does not give charity in a proper measure and does not fulfill the various positive and negative מצות as he should. However, one could say in his defence, that happens to be his nature. He does not even open his hand to spend on himself. However, if it is established that he is extravagant for himself, i.e., he takes many holidays at five star plus hotels yet when it comes to giving real amounts of money for charity or building a סכה, etc., he economises and counts every penny. That is the meaning of "law and reckoning." Even if he does fulfill the minimum דין of the מצוה, but according to his חשבון – his own private reckoning – he could and should have fulfilled the מצוה in a far more generous way. That is the

---

1. The world to come.
2. Reckoning.
3. Verdict.
4. Reckoning.

explanation of that part in the מוסף prayer on Rosh Hashana. מעשה איש ופקודתו – The work of man, his background, special assignment and task.

A third answer is given by the great Vilna Gaon ז"ל:

He claims that the דין does mean **verdict** but חשבן is <u>**additional**</u> to the verdict. He is judged on what he could have done positively during the time he used to commit the sin....

This leads us to solving the final problem. What can we do to win our case at the Court on High? Obviously, we must brief the best barristers. The Mishna advises us who the best ones are.

Rabbi Eliezer ben Yaakov says:

"העושה מצוה אחת קונה לו פרקליט אחד והעובר עברה אחת קונה לו
קטיגור אחד"

"He who fulfills a מצוה acquires a defender but he who commits a sin
acquires an accuser" (Ethics 4:13).

The defending Queens' Counsellors (Q.C.'s) are the finest ones! We can have very many of them. Every word of תורה study is a מצוה and we say one hundred blessings every day, etc.

However, it is logical to assume that the defenders and, chas veshalom (Heaven forbid), the accusers will not be simply good or bad. They correspond exactly to the quality of our deeds. Sometimes one is a little deaf at a Shiur[1] so the angels produced by that Shiur will be partially deaf. Sometimes one might be dragging one's feet to go to shul or to do another מצוה, then that angel will be wobbly on both legs, etc.

On the other hand, when an opportunity presents itself to listen to evil talk, one hears it very well, or if one goes to a questionable place of amusement – all systems go! The accuser will then be strong and healthy!

Our task, in order to be successful, is to reverse this situation. To be deaf to evil talk and to go enthusiastically to do a מצוה. In this way our זדונות נעשת כזכיות – the sins will convert into merits and our Q.C.'s will not only win our case but add many credits to our accounts at the בית דין on High.

Yes, we are born against our will, but we want to enjoy the wonderful gift of life

---

1. A lecture.

and are very happy to pay the "price" to our Creator who gave it to us. We are pleased to pay the fees. We are grateful to share the cost of all four "fences" because they are to our advantage. We do want to use this great gift by fashioning our actions according to the דין. We will try to match our charity and מצוה spending to that for our personal needs. We shall also resolve to use the time given to us in this world positively and not, Heaven forbid, negatively.

Then our barristers will be of the highest rank and will help us to put the successful verdict into the Book of Life.

"למענך אלקים חיים"
"For your sake, Oh living G-d!"

CHANGING ONE'S PERSONALITY

יום כפור

"אמר רבי עקיבא אשריכם ישראל לפני מי אתם מטהרין ימי מטהר
אתכם אביכם שבשמים"

Rabbi Akiva said: "Happy are you Israel before whom do you purify yourself and who is purifying your father in Heaven!"

(Mishna Yuma 8:9)

We are now about to enter the portals of the holiest day in the Jewish year – יום כפור. We fast and pray for forgiveness for our sins and resolve to serve our Creator on a higher level during the new year. Let me say at the outset that this exalted day is not a black fast, as some call it. No! It is a festive day! We even say "good יום טוב!" After all, G-d has given us a most wonderful opportunity to do תשובה[1] and start again with a clean sheet in the book of our life. This fast is helping us to feel humble, which is a most important ingredient of תשובה.

Since יום כפור is a festival, how do we celebrate it? Surely, not with fasting? We do! On the EVE of this great day we enjoy festive meals to consecrate and honour the great day of יום כפור.

However, the resolutions which we are about to make in our prayers on יום כפור have to be sincere. They are surely meant to be **carried out** during the new year and beyond.

This reminds me of a person who wanted to open a new business. He went round town and saw a great queue in front of a shop. Over the entrance was a sign written in bold letters **Grand Opening!** So he put these words on top of the entrance to his shop. However, he wanted to attract more customers, so he went

---

1. Repentance.

round town again. Another big queue....! There it said: **Going out of Business!** So he put that on his entrance as well! Unfortunately, some people who do not really understand what יום כפור is about and are not sincere in their prayers and resolutions, make the same mistake. They flock to the synagogues for יום כפור and make a **Grand Opening**, but they "go out of business" straight after. It should be a **Grand Opening** full stop!

Let us, therefore, examine briefly some of the points concerning this wonderful, supreme festive day. To help us understand what יום כפור really means, let us take just three points:

1) We start tonight's service with כל נדרי, i.e., a declaration to cancel any vows we may have made and regretfully not kept. Does that imply that any promises to people can just be declared null and void at the כל נדרי service?

2) Why do we start this great day with the cancellation of vows and not with recitation of our sins?

3) We petition to Hashem in many of our prayers for cancellation of any unfavourable decree which He may have ordained against us. Surely, Hashem is not a human being who changes His mind and whose will can be bent to conform with ours?

To answer the first question: כל נדרי cancels only vows which we make to HASHEM. For example, we promised ourselves to attend synagogue or a shiur[1] of תורה study and we did not fulfill our pledge for some reason. We pray that such promises may be cancelled by Hashem. But any commitment, to **people** are not annulled. They have to be made good or renegotiated with that person to whom we have made them.

And that applies to any sins, too. On יום כפור G-d forgives sins we have committed against **Him**, but sins against **people** can only be put right by personal apology or refund, etc., to that person!

To solve the second problem: כל נדרי is a declaration of sincerity of our prayers and of our resolutions. After all, we are going to use our gift of speech to the fullest advantage by davening the whole day. Therefore, it is absolutely essential to purify this heavenly gift by removing any traces of impurity which may have soiled this wonderful present. We may have made verbal vows and

---

1. Lecture.

promises which we may have not carried out; therefore, we start the day with
כל נדרי and cancel any unfulfilled promises.

This leads us to the third question, which I would like to introduce with the
following anecdote:

Rabbi Saadia Gaon, a famous Rabbi of the early Middle Ages, was seen by his
students weeping whilst reciting the ודוי[1] on יום כפור. The students asked him:
"Rabbi! You surely have nothing to confess since you spend all your time
teaching תורה and praying?" He answered with the following story:

Once, a world famous Rabbi was staying at an inn where he received very
good service. However, a number of delegations came to see him and the
innkeeper discovered his identity. When they left, the inkeeper came up to his
room trembling and in tears: "Please Rabbi, forgive me for not having served
you properly!" "But you did treat me very well! Why do you apologise?' 'I
treated you just like any other guest. Had I known who you are, I would have
served you as befits a person of your stature."

The nearer we come to the presence of G-d on ראש השנה and יום כפור, the
more we realise that we should have led a life of higher spirituality and more
commitment to our תורה הקדושה.[2] "That is why I wept at my prayers. I feel that I
had not done enough in my service to Hashem!"

That, of course, applies to all of us, too. It has been well said that the greatest
room in the world is the room for improvement!

We all come nearer to our Creator on this great day. That makes us realise
how much **more** we have to do in the future.

That answers our last question: How can we expect G-d to change his mind?
Surely, that can only apply to a human being? The word התפלל[3] means to judge
oneself: Namely, how much one is dependent on Hashem's bounty and help, life
itself and everything else connected with it. The more prayers we say, the nearer
we come to G-d. Once one realises this fact and acts upon it one's personality
changes.

The decrees issued on the fate of the previous Mr. Cohen, say, do not apply
any more to his new personality. Therefore, by prayers, it is not **G-D'S WILL**
that has changed, but **WE** have changed!

---

1. The confession of sins.
2. Our holy Torah.
3. To pray.

This is so clearly illustrated with the story of the prophet Jonah which is read on יום כפור at the afternoon service. Jonah was instructed by Hashem to go to the town of Nineveh and to tell the inhabitants that it will be destroyed because of their sins. He did not obey this commandment and tried to flee by boat to Tarshish. However, a storm arose, and since he was the cause of that storm he was thrown into the sea and swallowed by a huge fish. He prayed and repented inside the fish. Eventually, he was put on the beach by the fish and his life was spared. He did go to Nineveh and made the inhabitants repent. They were also saved. Here we see the power of true repentance. Jonah's prayers made him like a newborn baby coming out of the belly of the fish. Symbolically that happens if a person davens (prays) with great devotion and repents. He becomes a new personality! No! One cannot change the mind of Hashem – one can only change **oneself**! Rabbi Saadia Gaon became a different person the nearer he came to G-d. He did not try to change G-d's will, but his own, by **sincere** repentance and prayers.

Accordingly, our task now on יום כפור is to make use of this wonderful opportunity to affect a change, a real change in our way of life. Let us make a **GRAND OPENING**! Then we can pray that

חתמינו בספר חיים טובים
Seal us in the book of good life!

PREPARATIONS FOR THE NEW YEAR

"דרך המלך נלך לא נטה ימין ושמאול"

"We shall go on the Highway of the King, we shall not turn right or
left."   *(Num. 20:17)*

At this sublime moment of נעילה,[1] when the gates of this great day are being
closed, we beseech Hashem not only to accept all our prayers which are
being offered up to Him, but also to help us throughout our further journeys
through life.

How apt is the beautiful parable of the Dubno Magid in this connection:

A princess married a villager and had to do ordinary farm work. One day the
king announced a visit. Before his arrival everything was cleaned and decorated,
and the king was pleased. However, when the day arrived for the king to depart,
his daughter burst into tears. "How can you leave me? What you saw was only a
show for your benefit. After you leave, I shall have to return to ordinary
farm work, milking the cows, etc." On hearing this, the king confronted the
husband: "How can you do this to my daughter? After all, she is a princess!"
"Yes, I know, your Majesty" was the reply, "but when I married your daughter I
had hoped you would help to keep her in the manner to which she was
accustomed."

Hashem wanted to give the תורה to אדם, but he was a glutton, and to נח, but
he was a drunkard, so He gave it to us.

However, during the whole year we do not give enough honour and respect
to our תורה as the Mishnah states:

---

1. Final prayer of Yom Kippur.

"בכל יום ויום בת קול יוצאת מהר חורב ומכרזת ואומרת אוי להם לבריות מעלבונה של תורה"
"Every day a heavenly voice goes forth from Mount Chorev (Sinai)
proclaiming these words: Woe to mankind for its contempt of the תורה"
(Ethics 6:2).

In the month of Elul we prepare for the arrival of the King of Kings. On
ראש השנה[1] the retinue of Hashem arrived and was pleased with us. On יום כפור,
the King of Kings Himself appeared and saw us dressed in white and conducting
ourselves with great dignity towards His תורה. However, after נעילה the נשמה[2]
cries out: "Why do you forsake me? Soon you will make me go back to mundane
things and take off the ornaments of Fear of G-d and cleaving to Him. Please, our
Father, who possesses הארץ ומלואה[3] grant us Your help during the ___ordinary___ days
which are coming!"

Rabbi Nachman of Braslav ז״ל puts this point so convincingly:
    "Reminding oneself too much about old mistakes and sins and about one's
past can be sinful in itself. One should be able to put past events ___behind___ oneself.
Too much occupation with sin can be destructive, since it can depress and drain
one's energies. To allow this to happen is the greatest sin of all. One must have
faith in Hashem's forgiveness and to move ___forward___ with vigour and joy to fulfill
one's mission in life!"

The great Chatam Sofer ז״ל once remarked:
    "Why do we sing at the prayer of אשמנו – We have sinned – and the rest of the
confession of sins?"
    He answered: "It (the confession of sins) is a מצוה and one must fulfill it with
joy!" One must not sink into a deep depression. Just as Hashem forgives the
person, the person must be able to forgive him or herself. The main thing is
never to ___go back___, but to ___go forward___ with all the spiritual wealth which we
hopefully have acquired on this יום הקדש,[4] בדרך המלך – on the highway of the
King.

In conclusion, I would like to illustrate this thought with the following analogy:

---

1. The New Year.
2. The soul.
3. The world and all that is in it.
4. Holy day.

Let us imagine that we are astronauts in a spiritual spaceship. In the month of Elul, before ראש השנה,[1] we have **countdown**, on ראש השנה we have **blast off**, and on יום כפור we have reached our maximum height above earthliness, no eating or drinking just prayer and repentance. But now comes the crucial test of our skill to pilot our spacecraft correctly – the **re-entry** into the earthly atmosphere.

Many plunge down too fast after יום כפור and are burned out by the earthly environment and climate.

A good spiritual astronaut makes the descent *gradually.* What is more, we should never make an earthly landing at all but keep orbiting *above* the earthly atmosphere to enjoy the fabulously joyful festivals of סכות and שמחת תורה[2] and continue piloting our craft above earthliness during *the whole year* and *throughout our whole life*.

During the journey through life on the (air) ways of the King, we must *always* keep in contact with mission control – Mount Sinai – our תורה הקדשה[3] and not deviate to the right or left. Our task is to obey its signals. That will enable us to enjoy a divine, happy, and safe תורה journey.

Let us keep orbiting into a year of blessing and success – a good and sweet year, with the help of Hashem!

---

1. The New Year.
2. Rejoicing with the Torah.
3. Holy Torah.

REPENTANCE OUT OF LOVE סכות

"ושמחת בחגך אתה ובנך ובתך ועבדך ואמתך והלוי והגר והיתום
והאלמנה אשר בשעריך"

"And you shall rejoice in your festival – you, your son, your
daughter, your servant, your maidservant, the Levite, the proselyte,
the orphan and the widow who are in your cities." *(Deut. 16:14)*

Three questions need to be answered on the subject of the joyful festival of
סכות:[1]

1. Why is the commandment to celebrate סכות with שמחה[2] mentioned
    three times (Lev. 23:40, Deut. 16:14-15), whilst it is not touched
    upon at all at פסח[3] and only once at שבעות[4] (Deut. 16:11)?
2. All this שמחה is underpinned by many מצות on סכות combined with
    prayers and תשובה.[5]

    "בחג נדונים על המים" – on סכות we are judged about water –
    (Mishna Rosh Hashana 1:2) culminating at הושענא רבה,[6] which is a
    day of repentance again. Why is תשובה required again so soon after
    יום כפור?[7]
3. Why does the תורה put such an emphasis on

    "למען ידעו דרתיכם כי בסכות הושבתי את בני ישראל... אני ה' אלקיכם"
    "In order that your generations should know that I caused the

---

1. Tabernacles.
2. Joy.
3. Passover.
4. Shavuot. Festival of weeks.
5. Repentance.
6. The seventh day of Succot.
7. The Day of Atonement.

Children of Israel to dwell in booths (when I took them out of the land of Egypt) – I am the L-rd your G-d" (Lev. 23:43).

We rarely find a similar reminder – "in order that you shall know" – mentioned elsewhere.

4. Why do we say in the evening service at *Hashkivenu*:

"ופרוש עלינו סכת שלמך" – "Spread over us the סכה[1] (the protection) of your peace." Surely a סכה is only a *temporary* building. Do we pray just for a *temporary* peace?

Before trying to solve all these problems with one answer, I would like to share the following anecdote with you.

A lady celebrated her fortieth birthday. Amongst the presents displayed was an expensive wrinkle removing cream. Her friends asked her: "Who gave you this gift?" "My teen-aged daughter!" "What did she give you last year?" "**THE WRINKLES!**"

יום כפור gave us the wonderful chance to remove our spiritual wrinkles – our עבירות.[2] Hopefully, our complexion has become smooth again. However, more is required to regain our natural youthful appearance.

The Gemara (Moed Katan 16b) says that King David raised the standard of תשובה quoting Samuel II-23:1.

"The saying of David the son of Yishai raised on high, the anointed of the G-d of Jacob and the sweet singer of Israel."

The Vilna Gaon explains: Whilst Adam could not re-enter the Garden of Eden, nor cancel the decree of death despite his repentance, and King Saul could not regain his lost kingship, King David not only retained his kingship but succeeded in returning to the same relationship with Hashem that he enjoyed before his "sin" with Batsheva. His repentance not only eradicated the "wrinkles" but restored his youthful spiritual complexion. How did he succeed where the others had failed? By being "the sweet singer of Israel," by *repentance out of love* with *songs of joy*! Adam and Saul only repented out of fear.

That is what the Maharal so strikingly points out in his work Gevurat Hashem (5:26). He compares the three festivals as follows:

---

1. The hut.
2. Sins.

On פסח we became Servants of Hashem after having been slaves of Pharaoh. It was the festival of spring to our people. On שבעות we were elevated to be a "Chosen People" by the acceptance of the תורה. The Torah calls it יום הבכורים[1] (Num. 28:26). These were the "first fruits" of our taste of becoming servants of Hashem on פסח. On סכות after having failed through the golden calf and after having received atonement on יום כפור, we returned again to our Master in perfect communion. How? **By repentance out of love!**

Therefore, we find the word שמחה – joy – used three times in the תורה on סכות. That is why we have such a great number of joyful ceremonies during סכות. For example, the שמחת בית השואבה, the rejoicing at the water drawing ceremony.

Our Sages say: "Whoever has not seen this event has never seen a rejoicing in his life" (Mishna Sukkah 5:1).

The שמחה of סכות culminates on the last day, הושענא רבה, with prayers of repentance, the summit of תשובה באהבה – **repentance out of love!**

The Sfat Emet comments on the seven circuits which we make in the synagogue on this day by saying that they are symbols of returning to the purity of the creation of man. As we say at the beginning of the morning prayer:

"O, my G-d, the soul which you gave me is pure" The Midrash Rabba (14:8) says that the water libation took place at the very site of man's creation. So symbolically the perfect original relationship with our Creator has been restored. There can be no greater cause for joy.

Now we are able to answer the third question as to why the תורה commands שמחה three times on סכות, unlike on the other Festivals. Rejoicing with Hashem's תורה is the main ingredient of **repentance out of love**, following יום כפור's **repentance out of fear!**

Whilst repentance out of fear converts willful sins into inadvertent ones, repentance out of love converts all sins into merits (Gemara Yuma 86b).

Now the third problem is also solved, namely, the תורה only emphasises here at the Festival of סכות,

"In order that your generation shall know...."

The מצוה of סכה should make us realise that Hashem took us back under His "wings" – so to speak – under the clouds of glory, because we returned to Him with **repentance out of love**! That is why סכות is called חג האסיף – the Festival of

---

1. The day of the first fruits.

the Ingathering (Exod. 23:16) – not only referring to the physical ingathering of the harvest but also the spiritual one.

Looking at many of the מצות of סכות, we will discover that all of them point to שמחה – love of Hashem and love of His people. The temporary סכה[1] points to the fact that our sojourn in this world is only temporary and, therefore, we must make the most of it by joyful observance of the תורה, our Divine guide on how to do it.

This reminds me of the story of a wealthy American Jew who paid a visit to the great Chafetz Chaim in Poland before the Second World War.

He was very surprised to see that the world-famous sage lived in a humble home with lots of sefarim[2] but very little furniture. So he asked him: "Rabbi, where is your furniture?" The Chafetz Chaim replied: "Where is yours?" "Mine is at home in Brooklyn!" "Why did you not bring it with you?" "I am only here for a short time!" "So am I!" said the great Rabbi. "This world is a temporary abode. Hashem gives us the wonderful opportunity to study and observe the תורה, and we should joyfully seize this gift with both hands!"

There are many more teachings סכות conveys to us:

We are not protected by our roof but by Hashem. In our times, in the atomic age, we realise this fact far more than in previous generations. סכות also generates a sense of gratitude to Hashem for the comfortable home which we enjoy during the rest of the year. Furthermore, a סכה only requires two walls and part of a third so that it is open to others.

"And you shall rejoice...your man-servant, your maidservant, and the stranger in your gates."

It has well been said: "Everything becomes smaller by division except if one shares with others. The more sharing, the more joy!"

The four kinds of plants over which we say our blessings during סכות are also providers of our שמחה.[3] We joyfully serve Hashem with all these four species, namely:

אתרוג – the fruit of a citron tree
לולב – the branch of a date tree

---

1. Hut.
2. Books.
3. Joy.

הדסים – the myrtle branches

ערבות – willow tree branches (Lev. 23:40)

Our Sages explain that they symbolically represent our limbs. The אתרוג is the heart, the לולב is the spine, the הדסים are the eyes and the ערבות are the lips. We utilise all our faculties to serve Hashem. Another symbolisation is that they typify four different kinds of Jews and emphasise that **ALL** are needed to be soldiers in the army of Hashem.

The אתרוג Jew has all the qualities of leadership. A good taste (learning) and fragrance (transferring his knowledge and goodness to others).

The לולב Jew – the date on the palm tree – has taste but no aroma which symbolises a scholar who is deficient in good deeds.

The הדס Jew has fragrance but no learning and the ערבות Jew has neither (Midrash Vayikra Rabba 30:11).

Everyone is part of our people and everyone's contribution is needed. Without the ערבות we would not be able to make the ברכה[1] over the four species! This symbol of unity creates שמחה.

I would add that the ערבות Jews can be classified into four groups, too.

1. **The Cardiac Jews:** Those who say "I have a good Jewish heart!" They do not observe מצות but put everything on the "poor" heart.
2. **The Gastronomic Jews:** They like chopped liver, kneidlach, schmaltz herring and lokshen soup – that is what their Judaism consists of.
3. **Orange Juice (Jews):** One has to squeeze them very hard to get any charity out of them.
4. **Revolving Jews:** Those who visit a shul during the High Holidays and go through the revolving door until the following year. We hope and pray that these Jews will eventually rise to the higher standard of the הדס and לולב Jews until they will reach the summit of becoming אתרוג Jews.

This אחדות[2] was started on יום כפור when we began the כל נדרי service by stating that we are permitted to daven with the transgressors. However, this unity was

---

1. Blessing.
2. Unity.

through **FEAR**, but now on סכות it has progressed to **LOVE**, culminating in dancing together with all kinds of Jews on שמחת תורה. תשובה מיראה[1] has been replaced by תשובה מאהבה.[2]

In this vein we can now answer our final problem: When we pray "Spread over us the סכה of Peace" do we pray for temporary peace (like a סכה)?" Of course we daven for real permanent peace!

However, there are two kinds of peace:

    a.   Balance of power. This kind of peace is only a cease-fire. It requires constant vigilance and a continually increasing stock of armaments and nuclear shelters. This is peace מיראה.[3]

    b.   Warmth and real friendship. When one feels secure even in flimsy dwellings such as סכות, this is peace מאהבה.[4]

May Hashem grant us the kind of peace מאהבה, and may we enjoy the wonderful שמחה of this Festival with all its מצות and, after shedding all our spiritual wrinkles on יום כפור, regain our youthful appearance and the pure spirituality of our creation.

---

1. Repentance out of fear.
2. Repentance out of love.
3. From fear.
4. Out of love.

JOYFUL DAYS

"ביום השמיני עצרת תהיה לכם"

"The Eighth day shall be a day of Solemn Assembly for you."

(Num. 29:35)

Rashi says: After having sacrificed seventy bullocks for the seventy nations of the world during סכות, we offer only one bullock on the last day. Hashem says to us:

"קשה עלי פרידתכם"

"Your leaving is hard for Me" (Num. 29:36).

Stay another day to enjoy your intimate company with an exclusive banquet.

"והיית אך שמח"

"And you shall be completely joyful" (Deut. 16:15).

Our Sages combined this festivity of pure joy with שמחת תורה, the completion and new beginning of the Torah reading, the summit of the joyful days.

We have reached the pinnacle of all the great days of the month of Tishrei which began with ראש השנה – the head of the year. The Karliner Rabbi said that the Days of Awe were a preparation for these joyful days. As a matter of fact, the latter were three times more numerous than the Solemn ones, which is a clear indication that:

"עבדו את ה' בשמחה"

"One should serve Hashem with joy" (Psa. 100:2).

However, the following questions come to mind: What happened to the "overflow services" which were so much in evidence during the **Solemn Days**? Why has the attendance dropped so drastically during the **joyful celebrations**?

This reminds me of the following story. Once a grandfather ordered from a mail order catalogue a doll for his granddaughter's birthday. When it eventually arrived it came minus its head! The little birthday child shed many tears over the headless doll. What did the grandfather do? He looked at the invoice which contained the following note: ___ALL ORDERS WILL BE PROMPTLY EXECUTED!___

That is exactly what many worshippers of the overflow services have done. They executed the head of the year – ראש השנה!

However, the following questions present themselves:

1. Why is there an interval of seven weeks from פסח to שבועות (the עצרת – the final festival of פסח) whilst שמיני עצרת (the final festival of סכות) follows **immediately** after סכות?

2. Is שמחת תורה a superimposition of שמיני עצרת? Surely this contradicts the precept of אין מערבין שמחה בשמחה[1] (Gemara Moed Katan 8b)? (In Israel, both festivals are celebrated on the same day.)

3. Should not parting company (on שמיני עצרת) have been sad rather than an occasion for rejoicing?

To answer these problems:

At פסח time we achieved a standard of יראת אלקים – _**Fear of Hashem**_ – after having witnessed all the wonderful miracles of the Exodus from Egypt. There, it took us seven weeks to rise in our מדרגה[2] until we could say נעשה ונשמע[3] and be worthy to receive the תורה on שבועות, the final festival of פסח. Then we could transform חרות הגוף[4] (of the Jewish nation) – to חרות הנפש[5] as well.

However, at סכות a different situation prevailed. After having achieved תשובה מיראה[6] – _on the Days of Awe, we graduated to_ תשובה מאהבה[7] – on סכות.

We have a dictum by our Sages as follows:

---

1. Not mixing one joyous occasion with another.
2. Spiritual standard.
3. We shall do and we shall listen.
4. Freedom of the body.
5. Freedom of the soul.
6. Repentance out of fear.
7. Repentance out of love.

"אהבה מקלקלת את השורה"
"Love destroys normal routine" (Bereshit Rabba 55:8).

Therefore, love for Hashem, which was generated on סכות by all the joyful מצות, led to **immediate** and spontaneous singing and dancing, namely the עצרת – the final festival of סכות, followed by שמחת תורה (in the diaspora).

To penetrate a little more deeply into the sequence of the great Festivals in the month of Tishrei: There is a statement by our Sages in the Gemara (Avoda Zara 3a):

"אין הקב"ה בא בטרוניא על בריותיו"
"Hashem does not impose impossible tasks on His creatures."

If so, how can Hashem expect our spiritual warm soul, which is part of Hashem above, to survive in this cold climate of עולם הזה[1] which is permeated with materialism? Let us imagine an inhabitant of deepest Africa, who is wearing tropical garb, being dropped by parachute on the North Pole without any protective warm clothing. How long could he survive?

Therefore, Hashem gave us some help:

קדושת הזמן – <u>The Holiness of Time</u> – during the solemn Days of Awe – בהיותו קרוב – when He was near to us (Isa. 55:6).

This was followed by קדושת המקום – the Holiness of the Place – קדושת בית המקדש – the Holiness of the Temple and of the סכה. However, both of these are restricted to time and place. Eventually, He gave us the greatest help of all, למוד תורה[2] and we are told

"והגית בו יומם ולילה"
"And you shall study it by day and by night" (Joshua 1:8),

when the שכינה שרויה – the Divine Presence abides among us (Ethics 3:7).

Accordingly, שמיני עצרת and שמחת תורה are the greatest and most joyful festivals of all (Rabbi Sorotzkin ז"ל).

This leads us to answer the second and the third questions.

---

1. This world.
2. Study of the Torah.

שמחת תורה is not a superimposition of שמיני עצרת. Rather, it is a reply to the great compliment which Hashem gives us by saying: "It is hard to say 'farewell' to you." We say: "**We shall not leave you**, but we will stay with you always." We start בראשית[1] again. **No parting at all!**

That is the greatest שמחה![2] That leads us into spontaneous singing and dancing....

May we be privileged to make good use of all the various means of Heavenly help in our lives. The קדושת הזמן[3] which occurs every seventh day on שבת and on less frequent intervals at festivals, the קדושת המקום,[4] the Bet Hamedrash and Bet Haknesset[5] and the summit of all, the study of תורה by day and by night. Then we can keep up the wonderful warmth of our Divine soul in this spiritually cold climate in which we find ourselves.

---

1. Genesis.
2. Joy.
3. The Holiness of Time.
4. The Holiness of the Place.
5. The synagogue.

MIRACLE AND NATURE   חנוכה

T here is a custom to eat latkas (potato pancakes) on חנוכה[1] because they are fried in oil, which was the ingredient of the miracle.

Once. a hostess at a חנוכה party said to one of her guests: "Please take another latka." He replied: "Thank you very much, your latkas are so delicious, I've already had three." The hostess said: "Three? You've already had ten, but who's counting?"

I have to count the precious pearls of תורה in the limited space allocated....

There are three questions asked concerning חנוכה:

1. Why do we pay so much attention to the miracle of the oil which lasted eight nights instead of one? Surely, a similar miracle occurred for many years in the Temple in ירושלים? The Gemara Shabbat (22b) asks: "Why did Hashem need the light in the משכן?[2] Surely, **He** guided us in the desert with a Pillar of Fire at night!" The Gemara answers that it is a testimony for the Jewish people that the Divine Presence rests in Israel. The Western Light, (towards the קדש קדשים[3]) was given the same amount of oil as the other six lights. Whilst the others went out in the morning, the Western Light went on burning until the evening, from which time the others were lit. Therefore, the lights kept on burning without the need to ignite them. Incidentally, that is why we have the נר תמיד[4] in the synagogue. So we see that this miracle occurred in an even greater measure than the חנוכה lights because it lasted for many years.

2. What insights can we derive from the dispute between בית שמאי,[5]

---

1. Festival of lights.
2. The Tabernacle.
3. The Holiest of Holies.
4. The everlasting light.
5. House of Shammai.

which holds that we should light eight candles on the first night of חנוכה and go downwards, and בית הלל[1] which says that we should start with one candle and increase every evening (Gemara Shabbat 21b)?

3.   What can we learn from all this for our own times?

Let me introduce the answers with the following משל[2] from the "חפץ חיים":[3]

An employer had to go on a business trip. He left written instructions to his manager explaining how to conduct the business affairs during his absence, and he told him to read the instructions many times. On his return the employer discovered that nothing had been done. When he confronted his employee he was told, "I **_did_** read your instructions many times...." What really matters is to **_carry out_** the directions.

The "חפץ חיים" says that we pray in the עמידה:[4]

"חננו מאתך דעה בינה והשכל"

"Grant me knowledge, understanding and intelligence,"

but some people do not take time to sit down and study. We also say in the davening:

"ואהבת את ה' אלקיך בכל לבבך ובכל נפשך"

"And you shall love the L-rd your G-d with all your heart and all your soul"
(Deut. 6:5),

but some Jews do not act on it.

The חשמנאים[5] **_did act_** with great sacrifice – with **_all_** their souls. Although few in number, they saved the Jewish people. The words of Winston Churchill, "Never in the history of mankind was so much owed by so many to so few...." can aptly be applied to them.

The first question is answered by the Ponevitzer Rav ז"ל. "Yes, they did have a similar miracle for a long time before, in the Temple, but it **ceased** under the Syrian rule. The Syrians tried to assimilate us by making the oil in the Temple

---

1. House of Hillel.
2. Parable.
3. Chofetz Chaim.
4. The Amida.
5. The Hasmoneans.

impure – **NOT** by destroying it! They wanted to drag us down to their kind of unclean standards, both morally and spiritually. Unfortunately, many Jews joined them and became Hellenists. The חשמנאים tried very hard to reverse this sorry state of affairs by searching for, and finding pure oil, and G-d brought back His Divine Presence, as is *evident* from the חנוכה miracle.

That was the cause of great rejoicing. The very fact that they looked for *pure* oil to fulfill the מצוה,[1] בהדור – with beauty, although strictly speaking it was not necessary because impurity was permitted if the whole congregation was impure (Gemara Sanhedrin 12b), revealed their determination to counter the impurity of Hellenism. That is why the expression מהדרין מן המהדרין – those who do the מצוה with special beauty (Gemara Shabbat 21b), used in connection with the miracle of חנוכה. Since the חשמנאים acted beyond the minimum duty required, Hashem gave them His גושפנקא "approval" with the miracle of the oil. According to the strict letter of the Law, one light each night is sufficient, but we light many and use only *pure* oil.

This leads us on to the dispute between בית שמאי and בית הלל, and whether we should go upwards or downwards. The Gemara says that בית שמאי goes by the days to come, that is, we should light eight lights on the first night and then decrease the number, to teach us that we only have a limited time in this world. Each day it diminishes and, therefore, we should use the time which is left to the best advantage.

בית הלל, however, holds that we should not worry too much about the future but

"ברוך ה' יום יום"

"Blessed be Hashem *every* day" (Gemara Beitza 16a quoting Psa. 68:20).

Use each day for a good purpose as it comes and then add it to the previous ones. הלל and שמאי go – לשטתם – according to their own opinions in the Gemara Beitza (16a). There שמאי holds that if one has a nice piece of meat, one should save it for Shabbat, but if one finds a better quality meat, one should eat the first piece and keep the better quality meat for Shabbat – in this way one eats during the week for the honour of Shabbat. But הלל holds that you should enjoy each day and not worry about the future. שמאי is the pessimist while הלל is the optimist!

---

1. The commandment.

Finally, we have another insight into their dispute. Many people make a distinction between miracle and nature. However, the truth is that this is not so. This reminds me of the story of a lecture on parachute jumping given at an RAF Station. One of the students asked the lecturer: " What would happen if the parachute failed to open?" "Then," said the lecturer, " you would jump to a conclusion...!" Many jump to the *wrong* conclusion. There is NO DIFFERENCE BETWEEN NATURE AND MIRACLE. In nature we have innumerable miracles, more and more of which are being discovered by scientists every day, but Hashem put a screen – which we call 'nature' – over them to give us בחירה[1] which is the thrill of life. If we would see the Hand of G-d clearly in everything in nature, we would have lost our freedom of choice. We would then be <u>*forced*</u> to observe the Torah and we would be like puppets on a string; therefore, G-d hides His Hand by means of this screen. However, for those who are great, G-d removes this curtain and performs for them <u>*open*</u> miracles. The Gemara in Brachot (33a) tells us a story that in the neighbourhood of Rabbi Chanina Ben Dosa, a snake bit a number of people and killed them. When the snake attacked Rabbi Chanina, the snake died. His pupils asked him: "Rabbi, how do you explain this?" The Rabbi answered: "It is not the snake that kills, but the sin that kills." The Talmud continues in a very charming manner: "Woe to a person who meets this snake and woe to the snake which meets Rabbi Chanina!"

The Gemara Taanit (25a) narrates the following story: Once the daughter of Rabbi Chanina was very upset. Her father asked her why she was so sad. She replied: "I mixed up a jug of vinegar with one of oil and used the vinegar to light the Shabbat candles." Rabbi Chanina said: "The One who said that oil should burn can also make vinegar burn." In fact, the vinegar burned very brightly until the conclusion of Shabbat.

Similarly, G-d took away that screen of nature and granted the חשמנאים <u>*open*</u> miracles.

Now the argument between הלל and שמאי becomes very clear. שמאי goes from eight candles to one candle because the longer a miracle lasts, the <u>*less*</u> it is appreciated, because people get used to it. הלל, however, is of the opinion that the miracle increases every day. In holy matters we go higher, not lower.

That answers the ancient question why we celebrate the first day of חנוכה, when

---

1. Freedom of choice.

surely there was enough oil for it. However, our Rabbis want us to realise the fact that there is **_no difference_** between miracle and nature. We are grateful to Hashem for **_all_** His innumerable miracles and celebrate **_all_** of them (even the first day of חנוכה).

What a wealth of teachings the festival of חנוכה provides us for our times! Today, cold rationalism permeates the Jewish scene. Chaos reigns in the name of "pluralism," etc. Many of our people have become modern day Hellenists. The battle continues. We few must act to try and bring back the "Divine Presence" just as in days of old, **_pure_** Judaism in all its beauty. We must remember that each day counts. We must try to be optimistic like הלל – to go higher in holy matters and never go down, מעלין בקדש ואין מורידין, to fan the sparks of holiness which every Jew possesses into a flame. We must try not to jump to wrong conclusions and remember what we say in the davening:

"נסיך שבכל יום עמנו"

"Your miracles which are with us every day."

The hidden wonders which Hashem does for us every day. We must remember that there is no difference between miracle and nature. Everything is in the Hands of G-d. Then we can look forward to open miracles.

"בימים ההם בזמן הזה"

"Like in those days, so in our times...."

and to experience the building of the Third בית המקדש speedily in our days.

SOME INSIGHTS INTO THE STORY OF PURIM

"ותאמר אסתר אם על המלך טוב יבוא המלך והמן היום אל המשתה אשר
עשיתי לו"

"And Esther said, if it pleases the King let the King and Haman
come to the banquet that I shall prepare for him." *(Megillat Esther 5:4)*

Wwhen one studies the most mysterious מגילת אסתר,[1] one is tempted to try
and make a comparison between the actions of אסתר and her adversary
המן. Questions can be asked on both:

1. Why did אסתר make banquets to which she invited המן, rather than
    plead for the revocation of the terrible decree to destroy the Jewish
    people as מרדכי[2] had asked her to do?
2. Why did המן's action to draw lots occupy such an important position
    in this story that the festival was called PURIM, which is a Persian
    word for lots?

Before arriving at a solution let us share the following anecdote:

A famous politician was once constantly interrupted by heckling from the
gallery when he was delivering a speech. Finally, a cabbage landed on the stage
near his feet. Pausing in his speech, he announced: "Ladies and Gentlemen, I see
that one of my adversaries has lost his head."

המן did eventually lose his head – his life to be more precise –in a most
remarkable manner after having reached the pinnacle of power and having made
an iron-clad plan to destroy the Jewish people. However, the gigantic jigsaw
puzzle fate was turned against him through the mysterious hidden intervention

---

1. Scroll of Esther.
2. Mordechai.

of Hashem, the Guardian of Israel. All the pieces of this puzzle were turned –
ונהפוך הוא (Esther 9:1) – the other way around by Hashem in the most wonderful
way after they did תשובה[1] and declared 'קימו וקבל היהודים' that they were
accepting the Torah again in its entirety with great joy (Megillat Esther 9:27).
Explains the Gemara Shabbat 88a: They resolved to fulfill what they already
accepted before (at Mount Sinai), namely, the Torah. That was their repentance
for joining the great party of King Achasuerosh in order to assimilate to a foreign
culture.

To answer the questions posed at the beginning, I shall quote two seemingly
mysterious statements of our חז"ל.[2] The Gemara Chullin (139b) says:

"אסתר מן התורה מנין"
"Where do we know Esther from the Torah?"

"ואנכי הסתר אסתיר פני" (Deut. 31:18)
"And I shall surely hide My countenance."

אסתר and אסתיר are similar words. Then the Gemara asks:

"המן מן התורה מנין"
"Where do we know המן from the Torah?"

"המן העץ אשר צויתיך לבלתי אכל ממנו אכלת"
"Have you eaten from the tree from which I commanded you not to eat"
(Gen. 3:11)?

Haman and Hamin are similar words. Very strange indeed at first glance. What
do the similarities denote?

However, there is a deep thought contained in these observations. Let us try to
unravel the puzzle of the pronouncement concerning אסתר first.

I will attempt this by way of sharing with you a story of very recent times:
    A Jewish Russian soldier, who was not observant, was sent to Afghanistan to
fight the rebels. He was a lover of nature. His battalion was stationed on a
strategic high road area overlooking miles of flat land. Snakes fascinated him
very much. He fed them and almost befriended them. One day the order was

---

1. Repentance.
2. The great Sages.

given to move on. Before leaving, however, he returned to his "friends" to feed them and to say goodbye. Suddenly, a large cobra uncoiled and stood erect, hissing out of its hood. He knew that one single move could be his last, so he waited. He heard his battalion leaving, but he could not do anything for three hours! He stood motionless praying to Hashem to save him. Eventually the cobra recoiled and slid away. The soldier then ran to join his battalion. When he had reached them he saw that they were all dead, killed in an ambush on a mountain road. He exclaimed: "Now I know that there is a G-d! My life has been spared by a cobra! How the concealed Hand of Hashem has saved me." This soldier now became a G-d-fearing person.

That is the explanation of, "I (Hashem) am hidden" – אסתר – אנכי הסתר אסתיר אסתר and אסתיר are very similar words. המן "that poisonous snake," who wanted to destroy us first spiritually at that great party by assimilation and then physically, eventually became the heavenly tool of bringing us back to Torah life from the brink of the abyss, just as the cobra saved the Jewish soldier both physically and spiritually.

The Gemara Megillah (14a) says:

"The ring that the King Achasuerosh gave to המן to authorise him to destroy our people was more effective in bringing us back to repentance than 48 prophets and 7 prophetesses. **They** did not succeed, but that ring did."

There is a great difference between the miracle of Purim and that of Pesach. On Pesach we experienced open miracles, but on Purim the **ordinary** turn of events turned out to be **extraordinary**. Purim bids us to look behind masks and disguises and discover that Hashem has not disappeared or abandoned us, G-d forbid. He is behind the mask, if one may say so; He is concealed but present at all times. Incidentally, this seems to be one of the reasons behind the custom for children to dress up and wear Purim masks.

How all the seemingly unimportant pieces of the gigantic jigsaw puzzle suddenly fitted together to **thwart** the elaborate plans of that venomous cobra, המן, how all his plans and schemes ונהפך – turned the other way around (Esther 9:1). They all moved in our favour and המן got a *suspended sentence*, together with his ten sons, on the very high gallows which he had prepared for מרדכי, our leader. It emerged that it was made to measure for him and his ten sons dangling down below him! There are many more examples, but they are too numerous to elaborate on in the course of this article.

That is why Purim will never be abolished (Gemara Megillah 7a) as the Rabbis comment on the verse:

"וזכרם לא יסוף מזרעם"
"Their remembrance shall never perish from their descendants"
(Esther 9:28).

Similar hidden miracles happen very often throughout history. Some we know about and some we don't. Only a few years ago, Saddam Hussein, the modern המן, was utterly humiliated on the **very day of Purim**. Israeli children could then exchange their gas masks for Purim masks. This cannot possibly be a coincidence – it is the Hand of Hashem.

This goes further. אסתר emulated the example of Hashem and also acted in a concealed and restrained manner. The Vilna Gaon quotes the verse:

"ובהגיע תר נערה ונערה לבוא אל המלך"
"And when the turn came for every maiden to come before the King"
(Esther 2:12)

On *"every maiden"* the chant contains קדמא ואזלא – meaning quickly. But when אסתר's turn came, the chant is מונח מונח – restrained (Esther 2:15). She did not push herself forward but **had** to go – when she did go, she went with **restraint.** This quality of being cautious and calculated was evident in her way of dealing with her "husband" the King. When the verdict of המן to destroy the Jewish people became known, מרדכי, her relation, urged her to go and see the King to plead for our survival. However, she did not do that but acted in her own way. When the King saw her, he asked her, "What is your desire?" She replied, "Can we have a party with המן?" This request was granted. At the end of that party the King asked her again, "What would you like?" To the King's great surprise she asked for another feast with המן. That is the reason why the King could not sleep the following night. He was afraid that אסתר wanted to elope with המן and that המן was after his crown (Gemara Megillah 15b). Therefore, he asked himself, "Why does no one tell me of this plot? What about the MI 5 Intelligence Service?" So he had the Book of Chronicles read to him. There it was reported that someone (מרדכי) had saved his life from an assassination attempt. He demanded to know what reward מרדכי had received for it. The reply was: "Nothing!" So he decided there and then to reward מרדכי in public so that people should come forward to inform him in case of a plot. Just at that very moment המן came to ask permission to hang מרדכי on a huge gallows that he had prepared. But before המן could say anything, the King asked him: "What should be done to a person whom the King wishes to honour?" המן, in his conceit, thinking that obviously it must refer to him, replied: "He should wear the King's clothing and the King's crown and ride through the streets of Shushan." This was exactly what the King feared. Therefore, he commanded: "Do this to מרדכי!"

This was the turning point, and from now on *everything* rebounded against המן's scheme. אסתר's plan to **_make the King jealous_** succeeded with the help of Hashem! Her strategy not to plead with the King during the first visit, as מרדכי had desired, but to ask for a party and then for another party triumphed! That may be the reason why the scroll of the story of Purim is called מגילת אסתר[1] and **not** מגילת מרדכי[2]!

What a contrast to the conduct of המן. Haman is compared to Hamin – "did you eat (the fruit) of the tree that I commanded you not to eat from?" However, what has one to do with the other?

The answer is that Adam and Eve were guilty of the opposite – *lack of restraint*. They were only commanded a few hours before Shabbat not to eat from the Tree of Knowledge up to Shabbat, but they could not wait (Beer Mayim Chayim 9-16). This is in contrast to the Jewish people, who can wait for three years until they are allowed to eat from the fruits of the new tree – orla (Lev. 19:23).

The conduct of Amalek was similar to that of Adam's (Midrash Breshit Rabba 21:9):

זכר את אשר עשה לך עמלק בצאתכם ממצרים אשר קרך בדרך ויזנב בך כל"
"הנחשלים אחריך ואתה עיף ויגע ולא ירא אלקים

"Remember what Amalek did to you on your way from Egypt, how he **met**
you on the way and smote the weak ones at your rear and you were tired
and weary and he (Amalek) did not fear Hashem" (Deut. 25:17-18).

Since he was not G-d-fearing he held that there is noone to restrain him;

---

1. Scroll of Esther.
2. Scroll of Mordechai.

therefore, he took the **chance** to attack the helpless people at the back who were not protected by the Pillar of Cloud because of their sins.

המן, their descendant, followed in their footsteps. At that time, he was the lowest ranking of the King's counsellors, but he "jumped in first" as the Gemara puts it (Megilla 12b). He took the chance of entering the limelight. He counselled that Vashti should be hanged because she did not obey the King's command to attend the big party. When the King objected by saying: "This should be decided by the courts," המן, replied: "A King does not need courts." This turned against him when המן was in trouble later and asked for a court hearing. The King, however, reminded him that a King does not need Courts, and he was hanged immediately. If his case had been dealt with by a judge, it would have taken a long time and the King's anger might have subsided. His impulsiveness to see the King early to request authorisation to hang מרדכי turned against him, too. So all his actions and plans boomeranged in the end. That is the meaning of the Gemara by connecting המן with Hamin.

Adam and Eve suffered from similar impetuousness.

We see that the hallmark of המן's and Amalek's attitude was that there is no higher power directing the world. It is all coincidence. It is *Purim* – **Lots** – everything happens by chance. Life is a lottery! There is nobody on high who could restrain one's deeds. That is why we call this festive day by the Persian word, *Purim* – **Lots.**

אסתר, however, knew the truth and so do we. Hashem is the Master of history though He may be concealed. He gave us the Torah to suppress one's impetuousness and to control one's haste in one's actions. The Torah guides us on the divine path of life.

"שויתי ה' לנגדי תמיד"

"Hashem is always in front of me" (Psa. 16:8).

"קימו וקבל היהודים"

"The Jews in these days fulfilled and accepted the Torah" (Esther 9:27).

Hashem helped them in such a wonderful concealed way בימים ההם[1] so may we emulate their example and that of אסתר and מרדכי, so that Hashem can help us just like in those days – בזמן הזה – at this time!

---

1. In those days.

THE WISE AND THE
WICKED SON

הגדה
של פסח[1]

"כנגד ארבעה בנים דברה תורה... ואחד חכם ואחד רשע אחד תם ואחד
שאינו יודע לשאול"

"The Torah speaks about four sons...one wise son, one wicked son,
one simple son and one who does not know how to ask."

(Pesach Haggadah)

פסח is called חג החינוך[2] when the father takes over the role of educator and teacher at the Seder nights. At the anniversary of the **_birth_** of the Jewish nation, we celebrate with our youth who are the guarantors of the **_survival_** of the Jewish nation. Before I begin my words of תורה, from the Haggadah, I would like to share with you the story of Israeli prisoners who complained to the Rabbi who was looking after them that they were not allowed to celebrate the Seder. The Rabbi was surprised to be told this because he had arranged that the prisoners should be given מצות,[3] wine and all other items for the Seder. They said that when it came to the part of the proceedings where one has to open the doors at שפך חמתך – "pour forth Your wrath upon the heathens who have not known you" – to denote our trust in Hashem on this "ליל שמורים"[4] the warders would not permit it. "Is this a Seder?" they asked....

In my talk on the Wise and the Wicked son I want to try to open the gates of understanding to their respective philosophies. Both seem to ask legitimate questions, yet the wise son receives a polite reply, whilst the wicked son is

---

1. Haggada of Passover.
2. The festival of education.
3. Matzot.
4. Night of guarding.

treated very harshly! "הקהה את שניו" – set his teeth on edge (provoke him) – and say to him:

"בעבור זה עשה ה' לַי בצאתי ממצרים לי ולא לַו אלו היה שם לא היה נגאל"

"Because of this, Hashem has done to **me** when I went out of Egypt. To me and not to **him**. Had he been there he would not have been redeemed"....

(Pesach Haggadah).

It is important to realise that both the wise and the wicked sons are very intelligent people. They are not called צדיק – righteous, and רשע – wicked, but חכם – *wise* and רשע – wicked: Both have attained a high standard of wisdom and mental power; however the trouble with the רשע is that he is very conceited and self assured, just like so many, so called "moderns" in our times.

It is interesting to note that of the four sons, which are all mentioned in the תורה (three in the *Sidra* בא and the wise one in the *Sidra* ואתחנן), only the רשע – the **wicked one** – is in the plural.

"If your sons will tell you..." (Exod. 12:26). The other three are in the singular. "You shall tell your son" (Exod. 13:8) – the son who cannot ask; "If your son will ask you at some future time what is this?" (Ex. 13:14) – the **simpleton**; "If your son asks you tomorrow saying 'what are the testimonies and the decrees and the ordinances that Hashem your G-d commanded you.'" (Deut. 6:20) – the **wise son**.

Throughout a great part of our history the secular Jews were in the majority. Only one-fifth of our people went out of Egypt – four-fifths were killed during the plague of darkness (Rashi on Exod. 13:18).

However sad this fact may be, it is not decisive. We know where the truth is to be found. אברהם our father was called עברי – meaning the whole world on one side and he on the other. They were idol worshippers, but he was the *only* Servant of Hashem! What we need to do is to pull the so called sophisticated "modern" people safely down to earth from their imaginary heights (even if they may lose some teeth in the process).

This reminds me of the story of an elderly lady who took her first airplane flight. Timidly she asked the pilot:

"You *will* bring me down safely, won't you?" The pilot replied: "I have never left anyone up there!"

Our task is not to leave the wicked sons up there.... Let us see how the great Rabbis, the editors of the Haggadah did this.

If we look at the questions a little more carefully, we discover that there are three important differences clearly apparent:

1. The Wise Son asks מחר.[1] First he fulfills the מצות of פסח, then he asks.
2. He enquires into the different details of our מצות. עדות[2] such as תפלין and ציצית. חוקים[3] such as sacrifices, Shaatnez (the forbidden mixtures of wool and linen) and משפטים[4] – theft, murder, etc.
3. He mentions the name of Hashem.

   a. In contrast to the חכם, the רשע wants to have a reason given to him **_before_** fulfilling a מצוה. "It shall be when your children say to you, 'what is this service to you?'"
   b. He does not differentiate between מצות (precepts).
   c. He does not mention the name of Hashem.

Let us deal with these differences:

Of course one is entitled to research into the reasons for our מצות. פסח is a festival of questioning, too: the מה נשתנה. Also, the questioning of Rabbi Gamliel. Why do we have a פסח sacrifice? Why do we have מצה and מרור?

However, questions must be based on observance. נעשה – We will do – **_before_** נשמע – We will listen (and study)!

This is strikingly illustrated in the following anecdote:

Rabbi Goldwicht ז"ל, the late Rosh Hayeshivah of Yavneh, was once asked: "Why is our book of laws called the שלחן ערוך – the laid table?" He replied: "I was once invited to a very elegant and luxurious wedding in Antwerp. On the table there were eighteen pieces of cutlery laid in front of me. I asked the local Rabbi: "How can I be expected to go through all these at the wedding feast?" The Rabbi replied: "First taste the exquisite food and then ask me again!"

At the end of the party, which lasted for four hours, all the cutlery had been

---

1. Tomorrow.
2. Testimonies.
3. Statutes.
4. Judgments.

used up.... First נעשה – taste the heavenly fare of our תורה and you will see that Hashem is good, and ***then*** נשמע – enquire into the reasons.

"טעמו וראו כי טוב ה'"

"Taste and ***then*** you will see that Hashem is good" (Psa. 34:9).

That is the שלחן ערוך – the laid table. Hashem has provided us on His laid table, the spiritual food for our souls. This requires 613 "pieces of cutlery" – 613 מצות. All of them are part of the תורת ה' תמימה – the perfect תורה of Hashem. One cannot pick and choose one's menu at that שלחן ערוך. One has to observe all of them because they are relevant to each one of us (obviously, those that are applicable). It is not a table at a restaurant and one must use all the required cutlery! Once we have fulfilled the נעשה[1] then we can ask for the reasons נשמע,[2] as the חכם – the Wise Son does. This is the first point that the חכם scores over the רשע.[3]

Now we come to the second point:

Whilst the חכם legitimately wants to know the principles and reasons of various מצות ***after*** having observed them, the רשע needs to know them ***before*** fulfilling them, just like so many "sophisticated," the so-called "secular" Jews (a contradiction in terms).

The רשע says:

"מה העבדה הזאת לכם"

"What is this Service to <u>you</u> (***in contemporary times***)"
(Exod. 12:26)?

His argument is that the sacrifice of the Pascal lamb and other מצות connected with it were necessary in **ancient** days when we had to expunge the idol worship of the Egyptians who, for instance, worshipped sheep – surely we do not need it **now**? No one worships sheep in our times!

The question arises however: What is the answer which the editors of the Haggadah gave him?

---

1. Do.
2. Listen.
3. The Wicked Son.

"בעבור זה עשה ה' <u>לי</u> בצאתי ממצרים"

"Because of this Hashem has done to **_me_** when I went out of Egypt"
(Exod. 13:8).

The בית הלוי, the Brisker Rabbi, gives a convincing explanation, which also throws some light on the original question of טעמי המצות.[1] The verse does not say: Because of the historical fact of our Exodus from Egypt Hashem gave us the laws of פסח, but the very **opposite**.

As Rashi explains on this verse: Because of the מצות of פסח, מצה and מרור Hashem brought us out of Egypt to give us the opportunity and merit of observing these מצות.

The תורה and its מצות were fashioned by Hashem **_before_** the creation and

"מביט בתורה ובורא את העולם"

"Hashem looks into the תורה and creates the world" (Bereshit Rabba 1).

The תורה and its מצות are the spiritual motor that drives the physical world. **<u>They are eternal and not conditioned by any historical event</u>**. Even the laws of פסח, which give rise to so many explanations and reasons (in the Haggadah and elsewhere), are in the final analysis:

"ושמרתם את הדבר הזה לחק לך ולבניך עד עולם"

"And you shall observe this matter as an <u>ordinance</u> for you and your children forever" (Exod. 12:24).

"זאת חקת הפסח"

"This is the <u>ordinance</u> of פסח" (Exod. 12:43).

This is the answer to the רשע. No מצוה of the תורה is conditioned by any occurrence in the history of our people but they are חקים – statutes – which our limited intelligence cannot penetrate. We are able to delve into reasons up to a certain point, but no further! Lot, the nephew of אברהם, already baked מצות for the angels who came to his home. Rashi on Genesis 19:3 says that it happened to be פסח. אברהם baked מצות for his guests on פסח, too (Midrash Bereishit Rabba 48:13). These events occurred long before the exodus from Egypt. We also find in Genesis (26:5) that אברהם already observed all the various kinds of מצות long before the historic events destined to occur to our people. There it says: because

---

1. Reasons for the commandments.

Abraham obeyed my voice and observed my safeguards, my commandemnts, my decrees and my Torah.

Now we have a convincing answer to the following question. Why is the blessing

"שעשה נסים לאבותינו בימים ההם בזמן הזה"

"Who has made miracles for our fathers in those days at this time"

which is said on חנוכה before lighting the מנורה[1] and on פורים before reading מגילת אסתר,[2] not pronounced on פסח?

The reason is the following:

חנוכה and פורים were instituted by our Rabbis **following** the great miracles that happened in those days, and this blessing is the introduction and the reason for the festivals. However, פסח, מצה and מרור were given by Hashem **before** the miracle of the Exodus from Egypt – even before the creation of the world.

Unlike חנוכה and פורים, it was not the miracle that caused the fashioning of the פסח laws.

They are חקים – ordinances – which are *__beyond our understanding__*, just like all the 613 מצות, the 613 pieces of cutlery which adorn our Divinely Laid Table – שלחן ערוך – which provides the spiritual food for our Divine souls.

In conclusion, we know that there is a strong connection between the spiritual and the natural world. The physical universe was built according to the blueprint of the תורה. For example, modern science has discovered that the many millions of cells in our bodies contain DNA – a tiny computer which programs all the characteristics of that person in such detail that it is estimated that it would require a 1000 volume encyclopaedia to print them all! That is just what is known to us now but what about all the information which is not known yet? It is in fact a most complex computer code which needs various agents to transform it into the protein of that particular person. This code is beyond our understanding.

Similarly, the תורה and its מצות are the חק – the heavenly code of the universe. It needs decoding through oral laws, which are also Divine and were given on

---

1. Candelabra.
2. The Scroll of Esther.

Mount Sinai to משה רבינו. But the underlying code is a חק.[1] However, there are reasons for many מצות in the תורה and the oral law as clearly explained by great Rabbis throughout the generations. These are going down different levels in the "sea of the תורה", but no human being is capable of understanding the profoundest depths of the מצות just as no one can understand the workings of the DNA and other innumerable systems in the vast universe. In this light, the whole basis of the criticism of the "intelligent" Wicked Son falls away! מצות are not limited by any period of history, they are eternal for all time!

May Hashem grant us, through diligent study, even more understanding of the wonderful great profoundities of the תורה, just as He gives humanity in general increased knowledge of the wonderful miracles of nature.

We hope that these words have opened gates of comprehension and help to bring the Wicked Son to see the error of his ways, and bring him down to earth from his height of conceit, and teach him to subordinate his very limited intelligence to the infinite wisdom of His Creator. Who knows if he won't occupy the place of the Wise Son at the next Seder?

---

1. A statute.

FESTIVAL OF WEEKS　　　　שבועות

We are celebrating today the greatest event in human history: מתן תורה – the giving of the תורה to the Jewish people. It is the **summit** of the שלש רגלים – the three "foot festivals."

A summit is the smallest part of the mountain, so this is the ultimate experience of the divine revelation. It is a festival of only two days compared to eight or nine days of the other festivals.

The following anecdote may serve as an introduction to the better understanding of this wonderful celebration.

At a well established congregation a new Rabbi was appointed. To his great sorrow he soon discovered that his new congregation was a nest of מחלקת.[1] Every שבת the service was interrupted by members shouting at one another before the prayer of Shema. Some said: "It should be said standing because, after all, many martyrs gave up their lives על קדוש השם[2] with the Shema on their lips."

The other half quoted the Shulchan Aruch (Orach Hachaim 63:2) that if one is seated, one should remain so. Those who stood yelled at those seated: "Stand up!" whilst the others shouted: "Sit down!" This was destroying the whole decorum of the synagogue and driving the Rabbi crazy.

Some time later it was brought to the Rabbi's attention that at an old age home there was a very old man who happened to be one of the founding members of the synagogue. So the Rabbi organised a delegation consisting of one "Sitter" and one "Stander" and himself. They went to visit the elderly worshipper.

The "Stander" asked him: "What was the custom at the beginning? They stood of course!" "No!"

The "Sitter" said "Surely they sat?" "No!" The Rabbi could not contain

---

1. Quarrels.
2. For the sanctification of the Holy Name.

himself any longer. "Just tell me one or the other – now our members yell at one another every שבת." "THAT WAS THE TRADITION!" said the old man.

At מתן תורה,[1] the whole Jewish people was **united** and that was the essential factor at the receiving of the תורה. Harmony and fellowship are fundamental ingredients of a nation, as well as the Torah.

At this great event on Mount Sinai we witnessed the revelation of the Divine Presence in all its glory and splendour. This surely was the ultimate experience. Yet, our Rabbis tell us that this does not seem to have been so. The Talmud (Shabbat 88a) narrates that Hashem inverted the mountain over the Jewish people like a cask and told them: "If you will accept the תורה, all is well, but if not, then this will be your grave." However, later they accepted the תורה voluntarily in the days of Achasuerosh (at Purim) as it states in the Scroll of Esther (9:27): "The Jews confirmed and undertook...." The Gemara comments that they undertook to observe the תורה which they had already accepted before (at Sinai).

The following questions present themselves:

1.   Does this mean that we accepted the תורה only by coercion?
2.   Should the occasion of celebrating our acceptance of the תורה not have been Purim, since we received it **voluntarily**, which is obviously far greater than שבעות, when we were forced to do so?
3.   Since we are commanded to celebrate שבעות, why are there no special מצות given **by the Torah** to commemorate it as for פסח and סכות?

The answers can best be illustrated by the anecdote of a שליח[2] who was sent by a famous Rabbi to outlying communities to strengthen Judaism. On his return he reported to the Rabbi that one of the estranged Jews had asked him to explain his mission. "I answered: In olden times Rabbis would travel from town to town filling in letters that have been rubbed out from the Jewish souls. That is what I am trying to do, too."

The Rabbi shook his head. חס ושלום[3] that a letter of a Jewish נשמה[4] should

---

1. The giving of the Torah.
2. Emissary.
3. Heaven forbid.
4. Soul.

become erased. It is rather like an engraving that becomes filled with dust (of earthliness)....

The statement of the Gemara that Hashem "overturned the mountain and confronted them with the choice of either accepting the תורה or dying" obviously must not be taken literally. The meaning is, since they witnessed overt miracles such as the ten plagues, the splitting of the sea, etc., it was not possible to refuse the offer by Hashem of the תורה. On the other hand, the miracles at the period of Purim were all hidden. Had one lived at that time, one could have explained everything. For example, Haman did not have a very good intelligence service. If he had had a first class one, it would have discovered the collusion between Esther and Mordechai. Yet, the people felt a hunger, a void in their lives which they decided to fill with תורה.

We have now answered the first question by explaining that the Jewish people were not actually forced to accept the תורה at Sinai, but the second question remains. Since at the Purim period we voluntarily and **willingly** consented to return to the תורה, should this not have made Purim more important than שבעות?

However, if we delve a little more deeply into this subject we will discover that מתן תורה at Sinai was a far greater event. At Sinai we laid the very foundation, **the basis** of our right to the precious, divine תורה by **uniting** like "one man with one heart," as Rashi comments on the verse

"ויחן שם"
"And they encamped there" (Exod. 19:2).

in the singular.

We were united as one, with love, respect and honour for one another; then all the people responded **together**:

"ויענו כל העם יחדו ויאמרו כל אשר דבר ה' נעשה"
"And the people answered and said together: All that Hashem has spoken we will do" (Exod. 19:8).

By this wonderful unity all our 600,000 men fashioned themselves into a **huge** ספר תורה consisting of 600,000 letters. Each one had a letter of the תורה **engraved** in his heart – not only those who were present, but even all those who would be born in the future – __all__ souls were present at Mount Sinai (Midrash Rabba Shemot 28:4).

Now we understand the meaning of the well known Midrash that every Jewish baby is taught the תורה in the mother's womb, but an angel makes it forget after birth. תורה is engraved on every Jewish soul. One only needs to refresh it during one's lifetime. At the end of the morning prayers and after being called up to the תורה we say:

"וחיי עולם נטע בתוכינו"

"The everlasting life is planted __within__ us."

Also, at the Amidah Prayer "Bring us __back__, our Father, to our תורה." The תורה is already part of our personality. Just help us to return to it.

That is why שבעות is of far greater importance than Purim with regard to the acceptance of the תורה. At Mount Sinai we __established__ the means by which letters of the great ספר תורה[1] would be __engraved__ into our souls by our display of complete unity and love for one another. This was not coerced by the miracles. On Purim, however, we merely blew away the dust of earthliness which had accumulated in the grooves of those letters. This solves the second problem. However, the third question still remains: Since שבעות is so important why does it not have specific מצות like פסח and סכות?

Rabbi Aharon Kotler ז״ל, who lived in the United States, gives the following convincing answer: פסח and שבעות were one-off events of the past. They need constant reminders and symbols.

"למען תזכר את יום צאתך מארץ מצרים כל ימי חייך"

"In order that you remember the day of your exodus from Egypt
all your lives" (Deut. 16:3);

but the revelation of the Divine Will at מתן תורה only __began__ at Sinai and is an __ongoing__ process.

By studying תורה and observing all its precepts we discover new revelations _every day_. We actually receive the תורה _every day_.

"קול גדול ולא יסף"

"A great voice which does not end" (since Sinai) (Deut. 5: 19).

---

1. Torah scroll.

(Gemara Sanhedrin 17a) There is a lot to be revealed...even מצות which were instituted by the Rabbis are incorporated in the תורה (Vilna Gaon ז"ל). Therefore, there is no need for any symbols, memorials or reminders on שבועות. That is also the reason why no date is given in the תורה for מתן תורה. It is topical in all ages and can never be dated. In this vein the third problem is answered, too.

To sum up: We have seen that there was no force used to make us accept the תורה. We have also discovered that שבועות is the foundation of our engraving the divine letters of תורה into our hearts and that מתן תורה is an ongoing occurrence which requires constant study and observance.

May this greatest Festival of all rekindle in our hearts that unique experience of love and respect for one another and unity with our brothers and sisters, to blow the dust away from our holy letters by more תורה study and observance of מצות, thus helping us to reactivate and complete the ספר תורה[1] of the whole Jewish people.

---

1. Scroll of the Torah.

FI-P17